TEAMING UP FOR THE 90s

A GUIDE TO
INTERNATIONAL JOINT VENTURES
AND STRATEGIC ALLIANCES

TEAMING UP FOR THE 90s

A GUIDE TO
INTERNATIONAL JOINT VENTURES
AND STRATEGIC ALLIANCES

Timothy M. Collins
Thomas L. Doorley III

BUSINESS ONE IRWIN
Homewood, Illinois 60430

© Deloitte & Touche, 1991

Project editor: *Karen J. Murphy*
Production manager: *Bette K. Ittersagen*
Cover designer: *Renée Klyczak-Nordstrom*
Compositor: *Precision Typographers*
Typeface: *11/13 Times Roman*
Printer: *The Book Press, Inc.*

Library of Congress Cataloging-in-Publication Data

Collins, Timothy M.
    Teaming up for the 90s: a guide to international joint ventures and strategic alliances / Timothy M. Collins, Thomas L. Doorley III.
      p.   cm.
    Includes index.
    ISBN 1-55623-430-9
    ISBN 1-55623-481-3 (Special Edition)
    1. Joint ventures. 2. Strategic planning. 3. International business enterprises. I. Doorley, Thomas L. II. Title. III. Title: Teaming up for the 90s.
HD62.47.C67 1991
658′.044—dc20   90–3654

Printed in the United States of America
1 2 3 4 5 6 7 8 9 0 BP 7 6 5 4 3 2 1 0

FOREWORD

One of the most important developments we've observed in the way our multinational clients do business—and one of the most interesting—is their dramatic increase in the use of strategic partnerships, ranging from fairly small investments to full mergers of large divisions.

It is clear to us that these clients, and hundreds of other large companies that all of us read about and hear about every day, are taking advantage of the opportunities that are created by man-made and natural changes in the competitive environment. The most dramatic of these are the political forces that are literally reshaping the world's economies. Probably the most visible, at least today, are the changes that are under way in Europe—the move toward virtually unfettered trade in the European Community by 1992 and the astonishing developments in Eastern Europe that are, at least theoretically, opening an entirely new and large corner of the world to participation in Western-style enterprise.

But those are hardly the only developments, or even necessarily the most important ones, in the phenomenon of globalization. The U.S.-Canada Free Trade Agreement will reconfigure the largest bilateral trading relationship in the world. And the opening up of Japan, at least to an extent, to outside investment and distribution will result in yet another major shift in the way we do business.

Whatever their objectives may be, the growth of strategic partnerships is leading to business realignments that create a challenge to managers all over the world.

For Deloitte & Touche, strategic partnerships offer the same challenge—and an opportunity as well. Through our global professional team, we serve many of the companies that have pioneered and refined many of the variations on the partnership theme. Like those companies,

EXHIBIT
The Strategic Partnership Continuum

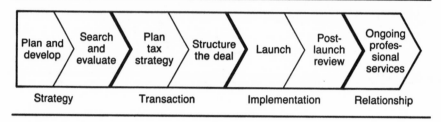

| Plan and develop | Search and evaluate | Plan tax strategy | Structure the deal | Launch | Post-launch review | Ongoing professional services |

| Strategy | Transaction | Implementation | Relationship |

our aim is world leadership in our field—accounting, tax, and consulting services.

The services we provide are those that the successful multinational needs to compete in a globalizing economy—and that is why we undertook the research that led to this book. *Teaming Up* does not pretend to offer radical new techniques; we and our clients have been doing most of these things for most of the modern economic era. As the leading mergers-and-acquisition firm in the accounting profession, for instance, Deloitte & Touche has been at the forefront of the diversification of American business into worldwide markets for years.

The contribution of *Teaming Up*, in our view, is the bringing together of concepts and notions that until now had not been captured in a coherent framework—because until lately, there was no need for them to be.

While the focus of this book is on companies engaged in manufacturing and distribution, its principles apply equally to the service sector. Our own profession (and our own firm) provide ample evidence of that fact; the Big Eight are now the Big Six. Although the merger that created Deloitte & Touche was a complete union of two firms and thus not entirely analogous to the joint ventures and partial mergers so thoroughly analyzed in *Teaming Up*, we were motivated by the worldwide economic forces it examines, notably the opportunity to achieve a competitive advantage by exponentially increasing the scale and coverage of our global client service network.

Teaming Up has the names of our two Strategic Partnership Directors on its cover, Tim Collins, the leader of our firm's comprehensive services to Dow Chemical, and Tom Doorley, a founder of our strategy-consulting division, Braxton Associates. But it is really the product of dozens of Deloitte & Touche men and women around the world. On be-half of the 55,000 people in our worldwide organization, we thank each of them for the contributions to the firm and to our clients reflected in this book and in their day-to-day service.

J. Michael Cook
Chairman and Chief Executive Officer
Deloitte & Touche
Edward A. Kangas
Chairman and Chief Executive Officer
DRT International

ACKNOWLEDGMENTS

This book is the product of thousands of hours of research and analysis led primarily by our former colleague in the United Kingdom, David Connell, the overall Project Director. David subsequently organized his findings into a report of almost 500 pages (with nearly 60 exhibits)—out of which emerged a summary booklet that received wide distribution chiefly in Europe. In turn, the success of that booklet encouraged us and BUSINESS ONE IRWIN to develop the research findings not only into this book but also into the set of services we at Deloitte & Touche call our "strategic partnership" package.

David has continued to be indispensable in bringing the manuscript to publication by updating the research data and making sure we kept our editorial focus exactly where it should be. We are grateful to him for his energy, intellect, and good nature.

Patrick J. Waide Jr., who was Vice Chairman of our predecessor firm Deloitte Haskins & Sells and head of Multinational Client Services during the period the research was being conducted and analyzed, also deserves our gratitude. From the outset, Pat was the project's keenest champion, and except for his constant support, there would be no book today.

Finally, in developing the research and organizing its findings, David and Pat drew on a steering group led by James E. Copeland Jr. of Deloitte & Touche in Atlanta. Later, as we approached publication, we relied on an informal advisory committee, led by James H. Quigley of Deloitte & Touche's Office of the Chairman, whose members included Eli H. Fink, our firm's head of International Tax Services; Alan L. Goldberg of our Special Acquisitions Group; Charles H. Noski, now Vice President and Controller of Hughes Aircraft; and J. Thomas Presby, leader of our Europe 1992 program. Robert S. Keefe was our general editor and provided liaison with our publisher. And contributing to the logical integrity and readability of our manuscript were R. C. Broadstone, Thomas J. LoPinto, and Elsie Maio. To all of them too we extend our thanks.

Timothy M. Collins
Thomas L. Doorley III

CONTENTS

United States of Europe? Political Imperatives and Commercial Strategy. Unit-by-Unit Strategies. Exploiting Collaborative R&D Programs. Barriers to Acquisition in Europe. Opportunities in Eastern Europe. Making It Work This Time. The U.S. Dimension: *Decline in Economic Leadership. The Narrowing Window of Competitive Advantage. Coming to Terms with Being Equal.*

ORGANIZATIONS INTERVIEWED

North America

Allelix
General Motors
GMF Robotics
Microelectronics and Computer Industry Corporation (MCC)
Monsanto
National Semiconductor
New United Motor Manufacturing Inc. (NUMMI)
Siecor
Stratus

Europe

Ab Weibulls
Alcatel
ATT & Philips Telecommunications B.V.
British Telecom
BT&D
European Computer Industry Research Centre (ECRC)
European Silicon Structures (ES2)
Fokker
Groupe Bull
International Computers Limited
IVECO

IVECO-Ford
Olivetti
Philips BV
Rhone Poulenc
Siemens AG
Thomson
Thorn EMI
Welding Institute (UK)

Japan

Barclays de Zoete Wedd—Tokyo
Canon
Fanuc
Fujitsu
Isuzu
Jaffco (Investment Bank)
Japanese Research and Development Corporation
JVC
Keidanren
MITI
Mitsubishi Electric
Showa Denko
Yamatake Honeywell

South Korea

Goldstar
Samsung
Sunkyong

INTRODUCTION

The term *strategic partnership* covers a wide variety of business relationships:

- The merger of substantial components of a company's business—e.g., Marion Merrell Dow.
- Making strategic investments in business partners—like General Motors' stake in Isuzu and Northern Telecom's stake in STC of the U.K.
- The creation of equity joint ventures to build new business, such as BT&D, a joint venture between duPont and British Telecom to manufacture opto-electronic components.
- Joint development projects, like Siemens and Philips' "Mega project" in semiconductors.
- Investment in small companies to acquire new technological competencies, like Monsanto's investments in such companies as Collagen, Genex, and Genentech.
- The use of a strategic trading relationship to build global distribution networks—like Matsushita/JVC's supply of video recorders for resale under their own brands by Thorn–EMI, Thomson, and Blaupunkt.

The purpose of this book is to provide practical guidance to top management on the deployment and management of different forms of strategic partnership in the global arena.

Our international organization is also a global business. Member firms around the world serve many of the multinationals most closely affected by the strategic-partnership phenomenon. Like them, we aim to achieve a position of global leadership in the services we provide—accounting, tax, business strategy, and management consulting.

The growth of international strategic partnerships affects each of these service areas. To put in place the financial and business advisory services that our clients will need in the 1990s, we must analyze the major trends of today and anticipate those of tomorrow. The strategic-partnership phenomenon is one of the most important of those trends. Indeed, our own contribution to the spate of mergers that has changed the venerable "Big Eight" structure gives us first-hand experience of the value of partnership and demonstrates our commitment to the principles underlying this book.

When we looked at the research that had been carried out on the subject, we found that much of it, though excellent in its own right, was aimed at an essentially academic audience. Relatively little had been written on the practical aspects of managing strategic alliances. Attempts to provide an overall framework for strategic partnerships and to assess their impact on the management of multinational companies as a whole were at an early embryonic stage.

Then, when we started speaking to line managers in industry, we found that many of them were greatly concerned about how to tackle this new situation. Some had already been involved in alliances. Along with tales of success, there were others of misjudgment, mismanagement, and misadventure. Perhaps more worrying, executives of some companies were focused almost entirely inward—on their own R&D programs and on increasingly narrow and competitive markets. Most worrying of all were the companies that were effectively blackballed by potential partners and thus missing valuable business opportunities. "We would never do a joint venture with them; we know they couldn't handle it."

The overall picture was disconcerting. The whole pattern of international business was changing, and managers around the world were embarking on strategic alliances for the first time with little or no practical guidance. For this reason we decided to mount a major research study of the strategic-partnership phenomenon and to publish the results. We hope to provide a better understanding of the new management challenges facing our clients and others and to enable Deloitte & Touche to provide better multinational client services.

We were fortunate in already having within our firm a wealth of experience with strategic partnerships. Over the years we have been involved in almost every aspect, from strategy advice and partner selection to financial structuring and organization and management consulting. Our network of offices around the world gives us an intimate knowledge of local legal and tax environments, as well as of less easily defined national business practices. However, we decided that to do the job properly we needed to conduct an extensive interview program with executives who had been involved in a wide variety of strategic partnerships. Our interviews had to include companies in the United States, Europe, and the Far East.

We focused on technology-based businesses in the advanced industrial nations. Partnerships between companies in these countries have the potential for a major strategic impact on each of the multinational companies involved—companies that are in many cases natural competitors. But we also wanted to look at partnerships involving the new industrial competitors that are emerging in low-wage countries. Many of these newly industrialized countries (NICs) are in Asia. We chose to focus on one of the most powerful, South Korea, a nation with a population of 42 million and an annual economic growth rate of 10 percent over the last five years. Like the other NICs, Korea offers multinational companies a low-cost manufacturing base in exchange for the technology and know-how that it needs to scramble up the economic ladder.

To get the best value from our research program, we obviously had to do a lot of homework. We studied seven industries in detail, concentrating on sectors in which strategic partnership was common. Our object was to understand the economic forces that were encouraging partnerships and the kinds of alliances being formed in different circumstances. The industries studied in detail are:

- Commercial aerospace.
- Motor vehicles.
- Computers.
- Telecommunications.
- Semiconductors.
- Consumer electronics.
- Biotechnology.

Our sample of companies was drawn predominantly from these seven sectors, and we tried to select examples that were evenly spread across different geographic regions, types of partnership, objectives and market maturity. To do this, we had to prepare extensive lists of strategic partnerships and compile basic information about them from press reports and other published sources. We then eliminated collaborations more appropriately classified as tactical rather than strategic and those either too old or too new to yield useful data. This process eventually produced a list of some 50 major collaborative ventures that were suitable for study. From this we selected a sample of 20 for detailed investigation.

We chose to concentrate on successful ventures. Our plan was to interview all of the major parties involved—the senior executives in the parent companies and the management of any collaborative entity. The majority of the companies we approached were enormously helpful and very open in their discussions with us.

International business research is extremely complex and very expensive. It means gaining the cooperation of companies operating in many different business cultures. While only an organization with the kind of resources and international network available to Deloitte & Touche could hope to succeed in this endeavor, the most important contribution came from the executives and directors of the companies we interviewed. We owe an immense debt of thanks to all those who helped.

OUTLINE OF THIS BOOK

Our air throughout is to give practical guidance on the commercial and management issues involved in different kinds of alliances, rather than to produce numerous examples and statistics. In many cases we have constructed new analytical frameworks as management tools to help executives involved in alliances understand their own particular situations and plan their negotiating and management approaches.

Chapter 2 provides a strategic framework for the various forms of partnerships we have studied. Chapter 3 then examines the relevance of different types of partnerships to seven important generic strategic business objectives. It compares these new approaches with the more traditional methods of business development.

Chapter 4 looks at the kinds of collaboration that have been used in five industries. Chapters 5 and 6 present the general conclusions that we have drawn from our study, examining the management implications from two distinct viewpoints. In Chapter 5 we look at the key points for the structuring and management of individual alliances—the "eight golden rules," as we have called them. In Chapter 6 we discuss the implications for the strategic management of the multinational corporation as a whole.

Chapters 7 to 11 then look separately at precompetitive collaborative research, corporate venturing, new joint ventures, partial mergers, and vertical supply alliances and strategic investments. Many readers will be interested in only one of these forms of partnership at any particular time, but Chapter 9 on new joint ventures contains materials on partner selection and investigation that is recommended to all.

Chapter 12 takes a rather different perspective and examines the special dimensions of strategic partnerships in Japan, the United States, and Europe.

T.M.C.
T.L.D.

CHAPTER 1

WINNING IN A
GLOBAL ECONOMY

The world is not so large as the ordinary person might imagine it.
—Christopher Columbus
Italian navigator, 1451–1506

In 1978, Olivetti was a tired, family-owned typewriter company, hopelessly undercapitalized and on the brink of bankruptcy. By 1986, it was one of Europe's leading information-technology companies, with revenues five times higher than they were in 1978 and profits of $385 million.

The cornerstone on which this astonishing revival was constructed is one of the most extensive and imaginative programs of strategic alliances ever undertaken. Led by its entrepreneurial chairman, Carlo de Benedetti, and vice president for strategy Elserino Piol, Olivetti has negotiated a network of alliances that gives it access to products and markets all over the world. The most significant alliance was with the U.S. telecommunications giant, AT&T. In 1983, AT&T became Olivetti's largest shareholder, buying a 25-percent stake and an option to increase its holdings to 40 percent in 1988. A variety of downstream supply agreements flowed from the partnership, with AT&T supplying Olivetti with private-telephone-exchange equipment for sale in Europe, and Olivetti supplying AT&T with personal computers for the U.S. market.

By 1988, this so-called "global alliance" began to become unstuck. AT&T looked for alternative suppliers of PCs, eventually turning to California-based Intel. It also found a new Italian partner, the government-owned telecommunications equipment company Italtel, with which it agreed to set up a new venture to market telecommunications equipment in Europe. A few months later, in July 1989, AT&T liquidated its stake in Olivetti.

Though the alliance proved unequal, it gave Olivetti much-needed access to the U.S. market, twice as big as the whole of the European market for information technology, and 50 percent of the world market overall. But Olivetti has also been active in forging alliances with Japanese companies. It sold 20 percent of its Japanese operation to Toshiba and has set up joint ventures with Canon, YE Data, and, most recently, Sanyo and Mitsui. Besides this, Olivetti has made several dozen investments in young high-tech companies, predominantly in the United States. Its indirect investments through venture funds extend to many times that number. Olivetti has also formed a joint venture with two U.S. partners, Cellular Communications and Shearson Lehman, to operate car telephone networks in Western Europe.

The Olivetti story is a remarkable one, but many other companies are using alliances more and more. Rather than trying to sell directly in Europe and North America, Fujitsu (Japan's second-largest computer company, and fifth worldwide) chooses to manufacture mainframe computers for Amdahl in the United States and Siemens in West Germany and components for ICL in the United Kingdom. Even IBM, responsible for one third of the free world's commercial research and development (R&D) spending on information technology, is beginning to acquire important products from outside.

Strategic partnerships are most prevalent in the fast-moving computer industry, but companies in many other industries have adopted similar tactics. For example, General Motors, the world's largest automobile manufacturer, is in partnership with a leading Korean heavy-machinery group, Daewoo; it also has partnerships with three Japanese car manufacturers including Toyota (to manufacture cars and pickup trucks in the United States) and Isuzu (to make vans and four-wheel-drive vehicles in Great Britain). In 1989, GM announced four new European alliances, two with the car operations of the Swedish automotive and aerospace group Saab-Scania and two ambitious joint ventures in Eastern Europe, one in East Germany and the other in Hungary. All of the major new aircraft engines and commercial aircraft are now developed and manufactured by consortia, often involving companies from three continents. The success of VHS in the home-video standards war was largely the result of marketing alliances negotiated in the United States and Europe by its originators, Matsushita and its associate company, JVC.

The diversity in kinds of strategic partnerships is also increasing. Besides formal equity joint ventures, companies are getting together in less permanent ways to collaborate on R&D, teaming up to achieve major technological goals, and later splitting up to compete in specific applications. As technology becomes more complex, many companies are also finding it necessary to build relationships with suppliers that go far beyond subcontracting. And throughout the advanced nations, companies are looking at how they can use venture-capital investments in young start-up companies to gain a window on the markets and technologies of the future.

Channels of distribution are also becoming of more strategic significance. A new type of distributor—the value-added reseller—has appeared in many industries, performing an important role in customizing the manufacturer's standard products to specific end-users' requirements. This demands strong management of the supply chain, and equity investments are becoming more and more common as a means of cementing such relationships.

Technical cooperation is an important element in these alliances, because they often open up to competitors the fundamental competences on which a company's competitive advantage is based. A report to the Organization for Economic Cooperation and Development (OECD) in 1986 declared that "the spectacular growth of international interfirm technical cooperation agreements represents one of the most important novel developments in the first half of the 1980s."[1] Since then the growth in alliances has accelerated.

Quantifying such a complex and diverse phenomenon is difficult, but the growth in the number of agreements over the last 10 years has been explosive. During the first half of the 1980s, the number of international cooperative agreements signed each year by companies in the United States, Japan, and the European Community increased by more than five times (see Exhibit 1–1).

A POWERFUL, POPULAR WEAPON

Strategic partnerships differ from the more tactical affiliations that characterized the growth of U.S. multinationals between 1950 and 1975. Today's alliances actually affect the partners' overall competitive posture, and the unique complexion of today's marketing environment has fueled their explosive popularity.

For most of the postwar period, international business has been dominated by the rise of the great multinational companies, many of them American. Their corporate style was characterized by self-reliance and

EXHIBIT 1-1
Cooperative Agreements, 1978-89

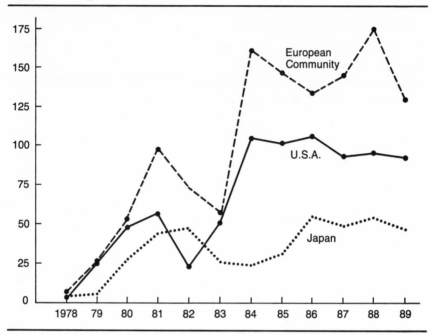

Source: INSEAD (Fontainbleu, France).

strong mechanisms of control. Growth was achieved predominantly
through internal expansion and acquisition.

Despite the emphasis on self-reliance, most international companies
had a good deal of experience with tactical joint ventures. In the 25 years
before 1975, joint ventures accounted for two of every five foreign subsidiaries formed by U.S. manufacturing companies.[2] They were often the
only way. Joint ventures were usually seen merely as a means of gaining
entry to difficult overseas markets where national laws or commercial conditions required partnership with a local firm. Necessary to establish a
presence in many less-developed markets, up to the 1970s they were virtually the only way for Western companies to invest in Japan.[3]

From the multinational partner's point of view, these tactical partnerships enable a company to achieve its sales objectives for individual, and
generally minor, export markets. But they do not affect the shape and abil-

ity to compete of the parent business as a whole. That is to say, the loss of any one of them would have a minimum impact on the parent multinational, and its long-term evolution would not be materially affected.

The 1970s brought a new phenomenon: partnerships going far beyond the objective of allowing participants to sell in minor overseas markets. These new alliances affect the elements of overall competitive strength—technology, costs, and marketing. Moreover, the way they are managed can influence the long-term trajectory of the business.

The Need for Partners

There are three fundamental reasons for the growing role of international strategic alliances: growing internationalism, technology's increasing complexity, and the speed of technological change.

Internationalization of Markets

Transportation and communication costs are steadily declining. Advances in information technology and telecommunications have removed many of the communications barriers that prevented companies from drawing on overseas technical resources. Indeed, the ability to transmit documents and even complex design drawings instantaneously from one part of the globe to another by electronic mail means that it is often more efficient to collaborate globally in product development. By using teams based in different parts of the world, it is possible to achieve an effective 24-hour working day.

Societies are becoming more and more knowledgeable about one another and more similar in patterns of consumption, enabling companies to sell similar products in different parts of the world. All of the major economies are becoming more open, and this process will continue as Japan, China, and the Soviet-block countries become more fully integrated into the world economy.

The ability to compete globally, and therefore to build larger businesses, in turn creates new cost pressures. Companies must take full advantage of international market opportunities if they are to achieve the scale economies needed to remain competitive. Just as the local and regional trading patterns of the 18th and 19th centuries were replaced by national ones in the 20th, global markets will become the norm in the 21st. Collaboration can extend the reach of strategic partners into the global marketplace. It is a key means by which the process of internationalization can be managed.

Evolving Technology

The increasing complexity of technology makes it much less likely that a single company will have all the skills and technical resources it will need for its R&D programs. It also pushes up the cost of developing new products. During the last 20 years, spending on research and development has grown three times faster than spending on capital assets.

Many companies on their own simply cannot afford to sustain the levels of R&D needed to remain competitive. Combining complementary technologies and sharing risks are powerful incentives for strategic partnerships in today's environment.

The Pace of Change

Another stimulus to the formation of alliances is the very speed of the innovation process itself. New technologies developed in one location are now rapidly picked up by companies elsewhere. Successful products are rapidly and systematically copied or emulated. And the growth of the newly industrialized countries as powerful manufacturing competitors means that companies in the advanced industrial countries must compete more and more on the basis of high-level skills—in technology, engineering, and design. Technological advantages can be expected to last for less and less time before superior or cheaper competitive offerings appear. Some of Olivetti's typewriters were produced more or less unchanged for 210 years. The product lives of the equivalent products of today are just a couple of years.[4] And the pace of product innovation is increasing all the time as the management of the innovation process itself becomes more sophisticated.

Companies must therefore gain access to and exploit new technology more efficiently. The management of innovation has now moved to center stage in the battle for markets. There is no longer enough time to rely on one's own resources to produce new products. No company has a monopoly on good ideas and, to remain successful, multinationals must be prepared to use strategic partnerships to acquire the best technology and products from outside.

As well as representing half the world's market for manufactured goods, the Triad of the United States, the European Community, and Japan are also responsible for half the free world's R&D. Four fifths of R&D

EXHIBIT 1-2
R&D Expenditure in Major OECD Countries, 1982–87

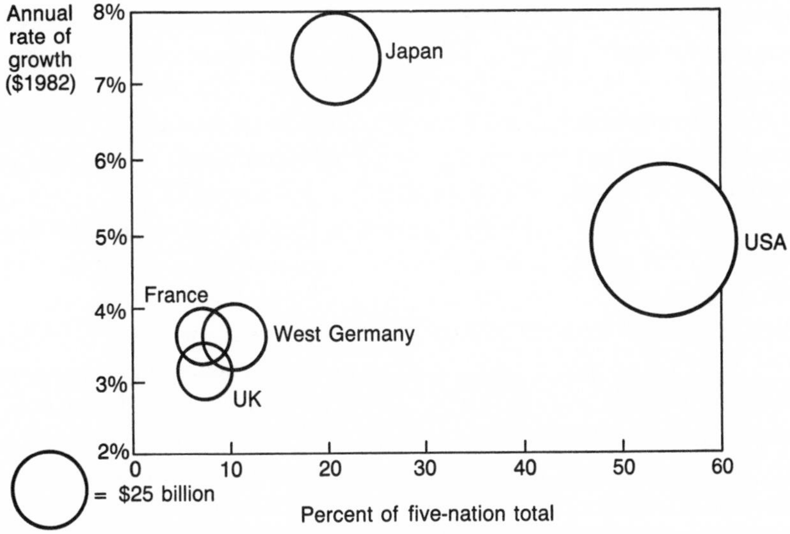

Source: OECD; Braxton Associates analysis.

expenditure in the OECD countries is accounted for by just five countries (Exhibit 1–2.). While technical and managerial strengths vary, companies based in all three parts of the Triad are able to create positions of technological and market leadership in their chosen fields.[5]

Keeping Competitive

These trends are pervasive, unremitting, and mutually reinforcing. The increasing pace and complexity of technological change mean that companies in many sectors must undertake huge and continuing investments to remain competitive in research and development. Financing this commitment to R&D demands access to a strong sales base. Companies with the largest global market share can finance the most R&D; weaker competitors must find a way of matching them if they are not to fall farther behind. Companies that do not have the necessary sales base must either internationalize their operations to achieve it or collaborate with others in product development. And underlying the whole process is the continuing erosion by competitors of each hard-won technological advantage.

Global marketing is essential if an adequate return is to be obtained and technologies and products replenished. Technological innovation becomes the means by which the ability to compete is sustained—the investment that ensures that a company will still be in business in five years' time. It is the most important fixed cost that the modern multinational must support.

Many multinationals have consequently created networks of alliances to enable them to sell their products throughout the world. Fanuc, the leading Japanese CNC and robot manufacturer, has adopted a policy of always working with a local partner to market its highly sophisticated products. The V2500 jet engine is being built by a consortium of companies from Europe, the United States, and Japan. Besides helping the partners to share costs—estimated at $1.5 billion—this arrangement provides a pedigree that will be invaluable in Fanuc's effort to capture share in the world market from its competitor, the CFM-56 engine, built by CFM International, owned by General Electric and Snecma of France.

The trend toward globalization is also having a powerful impact on industrial concentration, with more and more international mergers giving companies the economies of scale and international reach they need in order to compete.

TACKLING THE MANAGEMENT CHALLENGE

For many multinationals, strategic alliances are now a major business development tool. In 1986, General Electric, the world leader in electronics and power generation systems, started or expanded no less than 12 strategic partnerships. Jack Welch, General Electric's ambitious chairman (his goal is to make GE "the most competitive business enterprise in the world"), sees alliances as delivering a wide range of benefits. "We view them as a means to expand product lines, make the company more competitive in existing products in existing markets, and to reduce the investment and time it takes to bring good ideas to our customers," he told shareholders in 1987.[6]

Between 1987 and the beginning of 1990, the pace at which GE entered into joint ventures slowed, but the thinking behind them remained largely unchanged. An agreement late in 1988 with the West German electronics group Robert Bosch on a Tennessee-based joint venture to produce small electrical motors for the automotive industry was followed a few months later by an R&D and manufacturing partnership with Toshiba in lighting products. GE then expanded its existing partnership with Fanuc and formed four joint ventures with Britain's GEC; these are examined later in this book. In 1990, GE invited the Japanese airplane engine manufacturer Ishikawajima Harima Heavy Industries to become a partner in the production of GE's new engine, the GE-90.

Overseas business is no longer a marginal activity for manufacturing companies; it is central to their continued existence. The modern multinational must search out resources on a global scale, obtaining technology and products from the source that yields maximum competitive advantage and manufacturing in the location that provides the most favorable cost structure or best access to markets.

Indeed, recent years have seen the creation of powerful new international entities like Alcatel, the $14-billion company formed in 1986 by the merger of ITT and CGE's telecommunication interests, and STM, formed when Thomson of France and SGS of Italy merged their semiconductor interests. On a world scale, one of the most interesting new ventures of this kind was the Honeywell-Bull group of computer companies formed in 1987 and owned by Groupe Bull of France, Honeywell Inc. of the United States, and NEC of Japan—a true Triad company.

These alliances are often described as joint ventures but it would be more accurate to call them partial mergers, in which the cooperating companies pool the resources of existing product divisions. The partial-merger phenomenon is most often seen Europe, where industries are typically represented by a number of different national champions, each of insufficient scale on its own to offer world-class competition.

Alliances do not always run smoothly. A study of some 880 joint ventures and cooperative arrangements found that only 45 percent were assessed as successful by *all* sponsors. Only three out of five ventures lasted for more than four years, and only 14 percent lasted more than ten years.[7]

Some of the boldest collaborative ventures have failed. Unidata was set up by Philips, Siemens, and Bull in the 1970s to develop mainframe computers. It was designed to create a strong pan-European presence in the industry. The project failed because of the reluctance of the French government to give up independent policymaking. An ambitious alliance between JVC, Matsushita, General Electric and Thorn-EMI, which was designed to establish the new VHD video-disk technology as a world standard, failed despite the pedigrees of its participants because of technical and marketing problems. And in February 1988, Philips and GEC had to call off, at the last minute, a $2-billion proposed merger of their medical-equipment divisions because of difficulties in reaching an adequate financial arrangement. These examples illustrate some of the practical difficulties of setting up strategic partnerships. Also, alliances that start as equity joint ventures often move quite rapidly to a situation in which one party takes control.

> Finding the right balance between cooperation and competition will require every company to consider its own position and make a careful assessment of its interests on a continuous basis. I take the view that cooperation should only be entered into from a position of strength.
>
> —Dr. W. Dekker,
> President, Philips NV[8]

Apparent commercial success is not necessarily the best measure of the financial and strategic impact on the partners' businesses. There are many concealed failures in which the alliance continues, even though the objectives of both partners are not being realized. Sometimes one partner ends up achieving little or no real financial benefit but is unable to withdraw gracefully. The greatest benefits of strategic partnership often accrue to the parent businesses, outside the partnership itself, and they are never divided equally. Besides the commercial and financial benefits, a partnership can provide powerful strategic benefits to a company's core business, enabling it to acquire new competences. Many of the most apparently stable strategic partnerships are in reality trade-offs of short-term profits for a long-term erosion in competitive advantage. In addition to the game being played on the table, there may be another, going on underneath. Finally, management issues are often further complicated by the problems of working with partners many thousands of miles away who have a different language, culture, and style of business.

Against this background, negotiating and managing a major international strategic alliance can be seen as one of the most difficult challenges facing any company executive. It means balancing short- and long-term interests carefully and knowing when to draw the dividing line between collaboration and competition. It often means relinquishing a degree of control, and maybe even losing corporate identity.

If properly planned and well managed, however, a strategic-partnership program can have a powerful impact on a company's competitive power and performance. The multinational CEO of the 1990s must be aware of all the options available for developing the company, and the management team must be equipped to use those options effectively.

CHAPTER 2

THE RULES OF
ENGAGEMENT

No one today knows how to teach technology management or, indeed, even
where to start.

—Peter F. Drucker[1]

In today's environment, strategic partnership is an essential business tool
that all CEOs must be able to use effectively. One should not be misled by
the analogy, often drawn, between strategic partnerships and marriage. Unlike the modern marriage, today's strategic partnerships are not based on
some notion of mutual attraction. They are rooted in cold necessity. No
company makes a strategic alliance with another unless it has to—that is,
unless it can achieve its strategic objectives more effectively, at lower cost or
with less risk, than if it acted alone. Such a partnership is a mechanism by
which a company can achieve competitive advantage, not a strategy in its
own right. It is a weapon in the continuous battle for commercial markets.

In choosing the right form of partnership, management must understand the strategic context within which these different weapons can be developed, in order to relate them to a company's strategic goals and evaluate
them against the more familiar options. Even if a company is not the instigator of a partnership proposal, management must be able to decide on its
response in the context of a clear understanding of the relevance of the proposal to its own position and the likely objectives of its suitor. The purpose
of this chapter is to provide an overall strategic framework for the deployment of these new competitive weapons.

The means by which a company can obtain competitive advantage in a
given industry are linked closely to the degree of its market's maturity.
This in turn affects the structure of the market and the kinds of collaboration that can be deployed. An understanding of the dynamics of

EXHIBIT 2–1
Product-Market Life Cycle

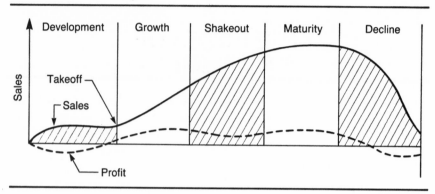

technology-driven markets is therefore essential to anyone trying to make sense of strategic partnerships and to understand their relevance to any given business situation.

THE DYNAMICS OF PRODUCT MARKETS

All of the industries that we investigated are based on technology. Each was effectively created by a technical breakthrough or a combination of breakthroughs. Each is a child of the 20th century. Over time, the technologies on which these industries are based have become better understood, cheaper to apply, and more reliable. At the same time, each industry is affected by technological developments elsewhere, with breakthroughs in "enabling" technologies periodically redefining the parameters of competition and creating new business opportunities. (An enabling technology may be described as a basic technology with wide-ranging applications. Examples include microprocessors, genetic engineering, and sensors.)

These processes have in turn fueled market growth, as improvements in price/performance ratios have led to increased penetration, stimulated new applications, and opened up new market segments. And as markets have grown and matured, so have the nature and structure of competition.

EVOLUTIONARY PHASES OF
PRODUCT MARKETS

No model can be applied with equal validity to all markets, of course any kind of conceptual framework in business is only an approximation. Nevertheless, in working with technology-driven companies, we have found that the product-market life-cycle model can provide some powerful insights into the competitive situation of different firms and the way in which their business environments are likely to change in the future. The model helps to explain how the keys to achieving competitive advantage tend to change as the company evolves from technology to market access and finally to cost leadership.

The basic principle of the model is that any product market, whether for digital watches, CAD workstations, or jet engines, is likely to pass through similar evolutionary phases.* The five major phases—development, growth, shakeout, maturity, and decline—are represented schematically in Exhibit 2-1. The characteristics of the phases are very different, as are the implications for business strategy as a market moves from one phase to the next.

Development

The first phase is a period of experimentation, before products are really accepted by the market. Research and development, with the potential to create major new markets, is continually under way in universities, government research establishments, and the corporate laboratories of large corporations. As commercial products begin to emerge, they may be taken up by the sponsoring company, or, if startup costs are low, they can provide opportunities for new entrepreneurial businesses.

Really new technologies are often difficult to apply commercially, however, and it is likely that sales will be limited to very specialized markets at this stage. There are many business failures during the development period, and industry profitability tends to be low.

---

*Note that the model applies to the market as a whole, not simply to sales of a single company's product within that market.

An example of a new industry created in this way is biotechnology, dominated initially by the R&D "boutiques" formed as spin-offs from research centers in the late 1970s and early 1980s. Another is artificial intelligence. The first AI companies were formed to exploit a series of ideas for new ways of applying computers to problem-solving. Much was expected of this field, but it has proved to be difficult to apply.

It often takes many years between a technical discovery and the establishment of real commercial applications, and companies do not necessarily gain an advantage from being directly involved in new product markets during this phase. Advantage comes from being the first to spot the beginning of the next, money-making phase and to obtain a leading commercial position.

Growth

At some point, continued technical development and experimentation lead to a major breakthrough and the establishment of important commercial applications for the technology. The takeoff point may be triggered in a number of ways: by changes in component or process technology that reduce cost, thereby making the product available to a wider range of customers; by new approaches to marketing; or by changes in customer needs—perhaps brought about by changes in technology elsewhere.

A period of rapid growth follows, as the latent demand for the new product application expands. During this phase, many new entrants are attracted to the market, some taking advantage of the potential for improving on technical performance or design, others trying to get a share of the action with me-too products. High levels of profitability are available.

Growth markets are forgiving: strategic errors and inefficiencies do not necessarily lead to inadequate profitability. Only a few companies, however, will continue to make money. The aggression with which a company builds market share during this early growth phase is the key to its ultimate position, providing the opportunity to exploit scale economies and to fight the price and R&D wars that follow. High market share in this period may also enable a company to establish de facto industry standards. The success of IBM with the PC and of Matsushita/JVC with the VHS video format are striking examples.

Shakeout

Eventually, the rapid rates of market growth must slow down. Overcapacity often begins to emerge at this time, and the competition becomes tougher, with aggressive price-cutting and falling profitability. Rapid growth is followed by an industry shakeout, with many mergers and business failures. The period from takeoff to shakeout can last just a few years.

Probably the most spectacular recent shakeout was in the personal computer sector. Entry costs were remarkably low in this market, and in the early 1980s, venture capital was readily available. The opportunities offered by rapid market growth and technical change attracted a huge influx of players from both established multinational companies and start-ups. There was no way in which all these players could continue to be successful.

Maturity

The shakeout process continues as market growth slows down and competition gets tougher. By this time, entry costs are much higher than in the development and growth phases. The accumulation of development and production expertise calls for a more sophisticated approach to engineering. There is a steady escalation in the costs of developing new products that show a performance improvement over earlier models, and the costs of establishing distribution channels are higher. Economies of scale in manufacturing are usually important.

These pressures lead progressively to a more mature market structure, and the industry is generally dominated by a handful of suppliers. A process of progressive concentration may take place over many years—a pattern most clearly illustrated in the aircraft industry.

Decline

In some markets, the mature phase lasts for many decades, with no major new developments to undermine the industry's existence. Eventually, however, all technology-driven markets must face decline. This decline often takes place rapidly, as superior technology renders existing solutions to market needs irrelevant—a mirror image of the earlier growth phase. Companies that do not make a switch are reduced to specialist applications.

Evolving Customer Profiles

The customer profile frequently changes dramatically during the early phases of the life cycle, and the way in which typical customers make their purchase decisions will also probably alter.

The first customers for any technology-based product are usually influenced primarily by the technical specifications of the product. As innovators themselves, they may be prepared to accept some shortcomings in design, documentation, or after-sale service. Research laboratories, universities, and defense establishments often provide the first customers for new industrial technologies and applications products. In the consumer field, it is the enthusiast—intent on the latest gadgets and gizmos—who buys the first of any new generation of equipment. As the market expands, more cautious purchasers join in. They make their decision much more systematically, whether they are buying industrial equipment or consumer goods. So technical excellence ceases to become the main purchase criterion, and factors such as cost, marketing, and after-sale service gain in importance.

SHIFTING PATTERNS OF
COMPETITIVE ADVANTAGE

The way in which markets mature is not smooth. It is often short-term economic or commercial problems that trigger changes in industrial structure, and it is not possible to forecast changes in it with much precision. The whole process of market evolution takes place in an environment of continuous innovation in the technologies, components, and production methods on which an industry is based. The precise shape of the curve is not important to an understanding of strategic partnerships. What is valuable is the model's ability to predict *how* the competitive environment in which companies must operate is likely to evolve.

At any given point, successful companies are building and exploiting a variety of sources of competitive advantage, but the relative importance of the three fundamental sources of competitive advantage—

EXHIBIT 2-2
Sources of Advantage Shift during Life Cycle

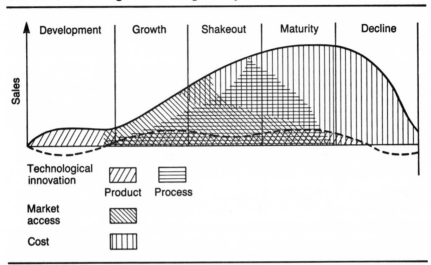

technological innovation, market access, and cost leadership—change throughout the life cycle (Exhibit 2-2). Any variations can usually be traced to political or legislative intervention.

Technological Innovation

Companies wanting to achieve competitive advantage through technological innovation must be good not only at developing new technology, but also at exploiting it commercially. And they must be prepared to borrow from others to ensure that their strategies are always based on the best technology available.

During the early part of the life cycle, the greatest impact of technological innovation tends to be on product design.* Later, the emphasis shifts to production methods, as new ways are found of improving quality and reducing costs.

Initial success goes to those companies that can recognize a new technological or market opportunity, and mobilize the R&D and mar-

---

*This is not always the case, however. Developments in new materials, chemicals, and electronic equipment depend as much or more on process innovation.

keting resources to take advantage of it. Companies whose only competitive advantage is their competence as technological innovators can sometimes be very successful during the early stages of the life cycle. Where radical innovations are involved, it is often the small, enterprising companies that can move first, particularly in the United States and other Western economies with a strong entrepreneurial culture.

It may be difficult to gain support for radical innovations within the entrenched organizational structures and R&D programs of larger companies. Small companies can often spot these embryonic opportunities and mobilize resources before the innovations appear to be significant enough to interest the management of larger companies. The entrepreneur can gain a place in the market while entry costs are still low, during the first or second phase of the curve, and take advantage of the opportunities for good profits while the market is growing rapidly and competition is relatively undemanding.

Research shows that small businesses and independent inventors have played a disproportionate role in industrial innovation during the 20th century, especially during the early stages of market development, when the technology involved is new and fluid, and provided that entry costs are low.[2] More and more large companies recognize the important role of individual champions and small teams in innovation and are trying to create an organizational environment that mimics small-firm cultures and encourages internal entrepreneurship.[3] However, the true entrepreneur will always want to go it alone. The pace of technological change ensures that there will always be opportunities for small companies to leapfrog the corporate giants.

Large companies that want to get in on the ground floor of new developments must recognize their limitations as innovators and continually scan the entrepreneurial undergrowth for the technologies and growth companies of the future. They must be prepared to enlist support through strategic partnerships to overcome their own difficulty in moving quickly when it comes to addressing new markets. And because innovation will always play some role in a product's life, these large companies must remain open to the notion throughout the cycle.

The impact of innovation may decline for some time, as products move out of the development and growth stages. As competitive position becomes more and more dependent on price, production efficiency and cost control can become the overwhelming concerns of management. But this pattern may suddenly be upset. After all, every market operates in an environment of continuous innovation. At any time, developments in technology can trigger major discontinuities or the discovery of new or improved techniques that open up new applications for existing products.

In many cases these technological discontinuities create what is, in effect, a replacement technology within an existing industry. They provide an opportunity for major changes in competitive position and even for new companies to enter the market. For example, the introduction of the first commercial jet airliner led, over the next 15 years, to a comprehensive shakeup in the commercial aircraft industry and replacement of Douglas by Boeing as the leading manufacturer.

In other cases, an entirely new market is created. Examples include the microwave oven and the fax machine. Both perform tasks that were previously impossible. They are eroding the markets for more traditional means of preparing meals and sending messages.

The impact of technological discontinuities and the speed with which companies must react to them vary by industry. The initial impact of major R&D breakthroughs is on the enabling technologies on which the rest of the industry is built—on manufacturing processes, or sensing, or measurement methods, for example. Companies in these component industries must react rapidly to technological discontinuities. Their competitive position can be overturned overnight by the appearance of superior technology. Recovery may be difficult, especially if proprietary technology is denied them.

The further up the production chain a business lies and the greater the range of technologies on which it is built, however, the less impact developments in individual enabling technologies are likely to have and the more time there is to incorporate them.

For example, major changes in competitive position in the logic-device industry (semiconductors) are quite frequent and often dramatic. A succession of product and process technology development has redefined the industry at increasingly rapid intervals. While many of the players remain the same, each new development provides scope for major changes in competitive position (see Exhibit 2–3). The likelihood of new technologies redefining competitive position is much less in the vehicle or aerospace industry, where a whole range of complex technologies contributes to the final product.

The speed at which markets pass through the life-cycle phases varies widely, depending on the impact of the discontinuity that triggers the growth of a new product market and the complexity of the product itself. However, all companies need mechanisms to identify and react to discontinuities affecting their businesses—to ensure that they are among the first to make effective commercial use of new technologies, both in existing product markets and to exploit new opportunities.

Market Access

Financing the ever higher fixed costs of innovation demands aggressive marketing on a global basis to deliver the sales volume and income required. As new markets move out of their development and early growth phases and the cost of maintaining up-to-date products and processes escalates, market access acquires increasing importance for overall competitive advantage.

The initial success of one or two companies will encourage many new entrants, including some major multinationals, with many times the resources of earlier players. As a result, competition gets much tougher, and strong engineering and marketing become progressively more important. Success in product and process development depends not just on creativity, but on continuous and systematic upgrading across all fronts.

The power of the entrenched multinational is often enormous. For example, in 1982, during the battle for leadership in the personal computer market after the late entry of IBM in 1980, IBM's total R&D budget was more than 50 times larger than Apple's.

While the key factors in competitive advantage often favor the small, entrepreneurial business at the start of the product-market life cycle, it is ultimately the ability to finance continuing high levels of R&D that is important. And while competition often takes place, initially within purely national boundaries, the battle soon shifts to the international arena, where size is critical to success.

The ultimate winners at the end of the growth phase are likely to be those companies that are able to combine good (though not necessarily the best) products with good market access, so that they can expand their market base and support and manage a continuing high level of R&D to upgrade and widen the product range.

Many small companies are simply unable to finance this growth or to manage the required organizational changes quickly enough. Even large corporations find it difficult to make the transition to global player

EXHIBIT 2–3
Shifting Dominance in Logic Devices, 1955–88

	1955 (Vacuum Tubes)	1955 (Transistor)	1960 (Semi-Conductor)	1965 (Semi-Conductor)	1970 (Semi-Conductor)	1975 (IC)	1980 (LSI)	1982 (VLSI)	1988 (VLSI)
1	RCA	Hughes	TI	TI	TI	TI	TI	Motorola	NEC
2	Sylvania	Transitron	Transitron	Fairchild	Motorola	Fairchild	Motorola	TI	Toshiba
3	GE	Philco	Philco	Motorola	Fairchild	National	National	NEC	Hitachi
4	Raytheon	Sylvania	GE	GI	RCA	Intel	Intel	Hitachi	Motorola
5	Westinghouse	TI	RCA	GE	GE	Motorola	NEC	National	TI
6	Amperex	GE	Motorola	RCA	National	Rockwell	Fairchild	Toshiba	Intel
7	National Video	RCA	Clevite	Sprague	GI	GI	Hitachi	Intel	Matsushita
8	Rowland	Westinghouse	Fairchild	Philco/Ford	Corning	RCA	Signetics	Philips	Fujitsu
9	Elmac	Motorola	Hughes	Transitron	Westinghouse	Philips	Mostek	Fujitsu	Philips/Signetics
10	Lansdale Tube	Clevite	Sylvania	Raytheon	American Micro	American Micro	Toshiba	Fairchild	Mitsubishi

if they do not already have strong international marketing networks for other products or business units in place. Building these networks is critical to continued success. Without them, it will be virtually impossible to match competitors' R&D. Strategic alliances may offer the only practical solution.

Cost Leadership

For companies that have been successful in rapidly building up international market share and have not been squeezed out in the R&D wars by larger competitors, manufacturing cost now becomes increasingly important.

As a competitive weapon, cost leadership comes into its own during periods of overcapacity. And it is most potent when the potential to develop defenses based on product differentiation and specialization is limited.

Overcapacity frequently emerges during the shakeout phase of the product-market life-cycle, and it is often coupled with increasing standardization of product offerings, as optimum designs emerge and it becomes more and more difficult to differentiate one product from another.

By this point, price dominates purchase decisions. Achievement of cost leadership can enable a company to undercut competitors' prices until they withdraw from the market. The survivors are those with the best cost structures—with market shares sufficiently large to give economies of scale, and with a manufacturing strategy that delivers the lowest unit costs possible.

The pressure on costs can continue for years, as production becomes progressively more concentrated at national, regional, and international levels. In some industries, this leads to adoption of financial controls that are so tight that innovation is seriously inhibited. Such companies become the dinosaurs of industry, successful in financial terms for at least a few years, but so locked into a particular market that they are unable to respond to changes in technology.

The Innovation Treadmill

The shift in the balance of competitive advantage from technology to price is apparent across a range of consumer product markets.

Ultimately, a product that started by being technically sophisticated can acquire some of the characteristics of a commodity—until some new technological breakthrough occurs.

The early history of the pocket calculator provides an extreme example of the rapid shift to cost competition. The early 1970s saw a proliferation of companies active in the pocket-calculator market, including U.S. companies such as Texas Instruments, Bowmar, and Commodore; Japanese manufacturers including Canon and Casio; and an entrepreneurial British company, Sinclair Radionics. The Sinclair Executive, considered when it was launched in 1972 as a triumph of miniaturization and exhibited in New York's Museum of Modern Art, originally retailed for about $185. The next three or four years saw companies fighting to introduce more powerful semiconductors and improve designs. It was not long before design norms had become established, and the potential for using product innovation to differentiate products had disappeared—at least in non-specialty markets. Prices fell dramatically. After five years, the price of a machine equivalent to the Sinclair Executive was about $10 (Exhibit 2-4). The pocket calculator has become a commodity.

There were many casualties of this price war. Bowmar, the second largest U.S. producer, filed for bankruptcy in 1975, and Canon, Texas Instruments, and Sinclair suffered heavy losses.

One of the main winners was Casio, a small Japanese family-owned company founded in 1957. Total Japanese production of electronic calculators increased from 4 million in 1972 to more than 40 million in 1978. During this period of rapid growth, Casio invested heavily in production capacity, tripling its market share to about one-third and achieving scale and learning-curve economies much greater than those of most of its competitors. Competition now revolves much more around price, production volume, and marketing, and is dominated by Japanese manufacturing companies with a global approach to marketing.

The pocket-calculator industry provides a classic illustration of the life-cycle curve at work, but the pattern is evident in a wide range of other industries. Another example is single-user personal computers. By now, a PC is practically an appliance. Technical improvements are adding only marginally to perceived user benefits. Low-cost products have achieved a major position in the market. The growth of strong cost competition is discernible in other parts of the computer market.

24

EXHIBIT 2-4
Electronic Calculator Output and Prices

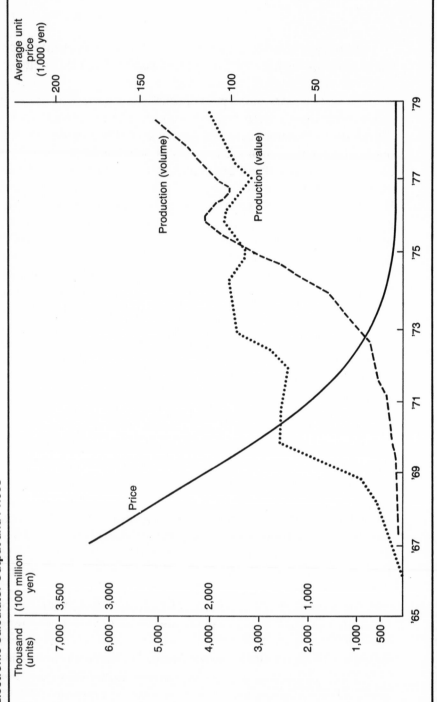

Even competition in airplane engines is becoming more and more about production costs, with manufacturers seeing little scope for real technical differentiation.

At the same time, the need to devote a high proportion of sales income to product development and process improvement does not diminish. Indeed, in most industries, R&D costs are steadily growing. As the technical complexity of products and processes increases, there are more and more areas in which a company must stay up with (or ahead of) the competition, and it becomes steadily more expensive to implement modifications in many more mature markets.

The declining opportunity for using product innovation as a competitive weapon does not mean that companies need not spend money on R&D. Far from it: falling behind current design-and-feature norms can still lead to loss of share, and feature-rich products can help boost performance. But as markets mature, customers make their decisions more and more on the basis of overall value. No single technical feature differentiates competitors' products, and quite small differences in price become important. Increasing levels of R&D are required to stay up to date, but they deliver relatively little in the way of positive competitive advantage. The main challenge in product development becomes simply being able to keep up with competitors. R&D efforts must therefore switch increasingly toward component reduction and improvements in the production process. Companies operating in mature markets therefore find themselves spending more and more on R&D to gain less and less product advantage.

The Japanese electronics companies have become masters at managing the product development process in this fierce environment. They are reacting to a consumer market that is the most competitive in the world and are marketing their products to customers who are probably the most discerning. Companies launching new products in Tokyo now expect to be followed by almost identical competitor offerings within a few months. Individual product lives are often less than a year and certainly shorter than the time it takes to develop and launch a new product.

As Michael Connors, Barclays de Zoete Wedd's Tokyo representative, has observed, ''Price competition has come to mean that these additional features are paid for by the manufacturer rather than the consumer.'' New product concepts like the Canon Auto Boy camera can offset the steady competitive pressure on costs for a time, but the easier they are for competitors to match, the shorter the period of remission.

The successful multinational of the future must develop strategies that recognize the importance of both cost leadership and innovation, and it must deploy the full arsenal of strategic weapons to achieve them. When it cannot match competitors' costs, it must seek other ways of competing.

And despite the fierce cost competitiveness of the largest and usually, therefore, the most mature markets, it must ensure also that its managers continuously keep watch for sudden new technological discontinuities. If ignored, these can torpedo its market position. If aggressively exploited, they provide the basis for leapfrogging competitors or the creation of entirely new business opportunities.

Bucking the Trend

One of the apparent implications of the analysis we have described is that companies without the ability to deploy global economies of scale cannot survive. This is clearly not true. There are many companies whose success is based largely on their performance as national suppliers.

An ability to buck the trend can derive from a variety of political, legislative, and strategic factors. Government influence and legislation have a powerful impact in many markets. Companies in many high-tech industries benefit from favored-supplier status with government agencies. In telecommunications, government regulations have helped preserve a highly fragmented industry from the competitive pressures that would otherwise exist in such a mature and highly R&D-intensive industry. The current spate of international telecommunications mergers has been triggered largely by the deregulation of national markets. Many governments have used import controls to protect their automobile industries.

Patents provide a further important source of protection in many markets. They help companies to extend their technological advantage well into the life cycle, though their use as a competitive weapon varies among industries. Patents provide very valuable protection in the pharmaceuticals industry, for example. In electronics and engineering, they often only tell competitors where to look for the reasons behind a company's secrets.

Many companies are concerned with manufacturing tailor-made products and systems for each customer. Markets requiring a high degree of customization do not offer the opportunities for economies of scale that exist with mass market standard products. Much of the software, defense, and scientific-equipment industries fall into this category. Consequently, it is easier to compete in purely national markets. Indeed, in the computer industry there is a continuing place for systems builders and value-added resellers that package standard products from international manufacturers to meet specific market needs.

Political and legislative action can impede the natural competitive processes we have described. Companies whose strategies incorporate a strong service element—as practiced by the builders of purpose-designed systems—can avoid the markets in which these pressures are strongest.

No company, however, remains insulated from competition forever. Few governments like to regard import controls as more than a temporary measure. There is steady pressure for more open markets all around the world. And all companies find themselves drawn into new product markets, where the protection they may have been used to in the past no longer exists.

Today, all CEOs must be prepared to fight their competitive battles in a world characterized by global competition and rapid innovation. They must have a clear view of the strategic imperatives confronting each of their businesses at different points in the development of their markets, and they must know what weapons to deploy to achieve these objectives.

Strategic imperatives change as markets mature. And the companies that are most successful in one phase of the life cycle are often ill equipped to compete in a different stage of market development. The next chapter shows how different forms of strategic partnership can contribute to achieving the goals associated with each stage.

CHAPTER 3

TARGETS AND WEAPONS: THE ROLE OF PARTNERSHIPS IN STRATEGIC DEVELOPMENT

> If all the world's economists were laid end to end, they wouldn't reach a conclusion.
>
> —George Bernard Shaw
> 1856–1950

Most major industrial companies consist of a spectrum of different businesses, each involved in markets at different stages of development, each facing different competitive threats, and each demanding a different management style. They include mature businesses under strong cost pressure from low-wage economies, as well as the growth businesses and major profit earners of the future.

Because of the increasing diversity of their operations and their markets, major multinationals will need to place an ever-greater premium on versatility and adaptability. While many of their businesses are based on a common set of core competencies—in terms of R&D, manufacturing and marketing skills—they will require quite different approaches to strategy in different businesses and at different times—particularly because, as Shaw was not the first to note, even the experts have trouble predicting the economy.

CHOOSING WEAPONS WISELY

The power of the product-market life cycle model is that it demonstrates how the areas in which a business must seek competitive advantage change as markets mature. But the compression of life cycles and globalization of competition mean that there is often little time to make the necessary adjustments in strategy. Managers must be able to *predict* how the competitive environment will change, and they must anticipate these changes in their strategic response.

This chapter examines the strategic imperatives that arise for businesses at different points in the evolution of their product markets, and in different competitive positions. The purpose is to provide an overall picture of the purposes of different forms of strategic partnership and to compare them with the more traditional means of achieving the same goals.

Goal One–Identifying and Obtaining New Technologies and Competences

The accelerating pace of business innovation means that companies must be able to exploit important new technologies rapidly. One of the primary objectives of any industrial company must therefore be to identify and monitor key technologies early in their development. This includes technologies that are likely to have a major impact on *existing* businesses and those capable of creating *new* commercial opportunities that the company is in a good position to exploit. In other words, every business must monitor emerging product-market life-cycle curves as they develop. Some will remain technological sideshows. Others could be the major income earners of the future.

Competition to be the first to exploit innovative technology is now so great that it is no longer possible to rely on in-house resources and the more traditional business development mechanisms of licensing and acquisition. Companies must get actively involved much farther upstream in the R&D pipelines feeding their industries.

A company must, of course, try to ensure that it maintains a leading position through ownership of proprietary technologies, and this will inevitably require in-house R&D. It is more than likely, however, that important technical breakthroughs will be made elsewhere, and there will be a great deal of relevant external R&D activity to which the company does not have automatic access. In any case, it will almost certainly be unable to afford all the R&D it would like. It must therefore devote a proportion of its R&D budget to building technology radar systems to monitor the research of commercial, government, and academic organizations. It can then step up its own in-house R&D activity once a specific area appears to be important.

Mechanisms to locate and exploit external sources of R&D include:

- Collaboration with university departments and other research institutions.
- Precompetitive collaborative R&D to spread research resources more widely.
- Corporate venturing—making systematic investments in emerging companies to gain a window on the technologies and market applications of the future.
- Joint ventures and other forms of strategic partnership that enable a company to acquire new competences by "borrowing" from a company with a leadership position.

Sponsored Academic Research

This is particularly important in industries where commercial developments are linked closely to advances in basic science, which can be readily transferred to industry and used to create commercial products or processes. Companies in some industries are now setting up small "listening posts" to monitor research in international centers of academic excellence.

As the pace of technology development accelerates and cross-linkages become more complex, companies are developing increasingly sophisticated strategies for gaining access to technology. They are also becoming more international in reach.

In a study of the semiconductor industry carried out at New York University, Carmela Haklisch examined 17 major centers of research supported by semiconductor firms, their combined annual budgets totaling $93 million. There were 96 corporate sponsors of this research, and 23 firms supported three or more groups. Non-U.S. firms were also actively involved. NEC supported work at Cornell; Philips was involved with Cornell and Stanford; and Hitachi was funding work at the Texas Microelectronics Research Center. In all, Japanese companies spend $30 million a year on research contracts at U.S. universities. They have endowed 16 chairs at $1.5 million each at MIT alone![1]

Precompetitive Collaborative Research

Although techniques for managing precompetitive R&D collaborations are still only very imperfectly understood, they are an important weapon in the armory of industrial companies.

In many areas of technology, major advances depend not on a single breakthrough but on experimenting with the design of complex systems incorporating a variety of technical improvements. This often requires continuous interaction with suppliers and potential customers, in many cases at both intermediate stages and the final level. This sort of research is a lengthy process, and it may take five or ten years to generate commercial products. Early phases may contribute little to the direct commercial advantage of the sponsoring company.

Yet collaborating with other companies in the early stages of the R&D process provides a way to spread the R&D budget more widely and reduce risks. Where collaboration is with customers or suppliers, it can also improve R&D efficiency and accelerate development times. This kind of precompetitive research is increasingly being carried out by consortia of industrial companies, often with government support. (The various forms of precompetitive collaborative R&D are examined in more detail in Chapter 8.)

Corporate Ventures

Corporate venturing gives companies access to some hotbeds of innovation. Many new ideas are exploited commercially first by small entrepreneurial companies, often set up by scientists to turn their own research ideas to practical use. The climate for entrepreneurial action varies within the triad: it is strongest in the United States and weakest in Japan; Europe lies somewhere in between. Even in Japan, an economy dominated by group thinking, some of the country's best known companies—Sony and Honda, for example—owe their success to precisely the kind of entrepreneurial founder that U.S. venture capitalists like to support.

The venture-capital community plays a pivotal role in the early stages of these new companies. By participating in the venture-capital process, multinationals can get up to two years' advance warning of new market trends and technological opportunities. Corporate venturing, as this process is called, has found special favor in the United States, where more than 80 major industrial companies have a dedicated venture-capital investment pool, and many more are actively involved in other ways. As the entrepreneurial culture spreads, corporate venturing is itself becoming a more international activity. Some companies have built up extensive international venture-capital networks. (The management of corporate venturing is discussed in Chapter 8.)

Forming a Partnership

Joint ventures and other strategic partnerships give the corporation access to a broad range of technical and managerial expertise. While corporate venturing provides a means by which larger companies can gain *new* technologies and steal a march on their competitors in exploiting them, companies are also faced from time to time with the problem of acquiring existing competences that they do not possess. The need for these competences can arise for a variety of reasons—for example, to maintain competitive strength in an existing business that has been affected by technological change, to build the portfolio of competences required to enter a new business, or to contribute to a catch-up strategy.

Building these skills by recruitment or internal training is often impossible. One cannot recruit an entire aircraft or automobile design team. Joint ventures, licensing, and joint development projects provide a means of acquiring these less tangible design and management competences. Companies in Japan and the newly industrialized countries have had the most practice in using alliances to acquire new skills from more advanced Western partners. Ever since World War II, NEC has systematically used alliances to acquire new technological and design competences. All three of the U.S. automobile giants have used alliances with Japanese companies as a means of acquiring manufacturing expertise.

Goal Two—Exploiting New Market Opportunities

The strategies just described concern research and development and gaining intelligence of market and technological opportunities. Some affect a company's existing product range; others, its production methods.

If well managed, they will, together with in-house R&D programs, also identify a steady stream of new commercial opportunities. Sooner or later, a company must decide whether those opportunities are attractive enough to warrant commercial involvement and, if so, where and how.

There are four main avenues by which a company can enter a new market:

1. In-house development.
2. Acquisition of an existing company.
3. Vertical supply alliances, that is, by licensing or buying product from an existing supplier.
4. Joint venture with another company.

In-House Development
In-house development is the traditional means of market entry at the early stage, when the key requirement is likely to be a suitable product. If the

company has developed proprietary technology itself, it can retain the initiative and probably have some control over the speed of commercialization. There will, however, usually be a number of companies with competing technologies and approaches. And, in many cases, in-house development is not the optimum strategy, at least not initially. The company may not have the skills and resources required, and it may not be able to move quickly enough.

Speed is of the essence during the early phases of new product-markets. Conventional large-company organization structures are ill suited to handling embryonic business opportunities, where the immediate outlook is rather uncertain and sales of only a few million dollars are likely over the first few years. Existing businesses and major contracts will always take precedence in decision making. It is difficult to allocate the best managers to business initiatives of this kind and hard to match the entrepreneurial environment of the thrusting start-up company. Conventional line management responsibilities in the largest and most visible divisions offer a more comfortable route to promotion than a five- or ten-year haul with a high-risk start-up venture.

The venture-capital business is all about moving fast to exploit these early, risky opportunities. Independent entrepreneurial startup companies can typically get new products to market in half the time and at a quarter the cost, as compared with the established multinational.[2] Some companies attempt to mimic this environment by creating a semiautonomous task force to develop the product. IBM's first PC was developed in this way. Often, however, the decision to try this is made rather late; recognizing the opportunity is as difficult as acting on it.

At the same time, the best solutions for technical problems are hardly ever apparent in the early stages of new markets. It may be much better for the large corporation to keep a watch on the start-up companies (often many of them) that are involved in the early stages of a new market and delay its own entry until the picture has become clearer.

Acquisitions
The financial power of the large company enables it to overcome its disadvantages by acquisition, once the most successful smaller companies have become apparent. Using acquisitions to effect late market entry is expensive, however, as P/Es are high at this point in the product-market life cycle. A suitable company is often unavailable, and even if it is, the integration problems associated with successful fast-growth companies are huge.

Vertical Supply Appliances. A more effective solution may be to buy into a product through a license or OEM* agreement with one of the more promising smaller companies. So it was that when IBM needed to add fault-tolerant computers to its product range, it did so not by developing a product in-house, but through a strategic marketing alliance with Stratus, a fast-growing Boston start-up company.

Vertical supply alliances, as an important option for entering new markets, are frequently associated with an equity investment. They may also provide the basis for later acquisition. Chapter 11 looks at this kind of relationship and examines the pros and cons of cementing them with an equity investment.

Joint Ventures

Technological change is becoming an increasingly complex process, with different technologies combining to open new product opportunities in a diverse range of market applications. In many cases, companies simply do not have all the skills and resources needed to exploit the opportunities available. Sometimes business opportunities take companies into new markets, requiring marketing skills they lack and access to distribution networks with which they are unfamiliar.

Forming a new joint-venture company with a partner offering complementary skills can provide an attractive way of tackling opportunities that might otherwise fall by the wayside. An important variant on this situation occurs when a company has developed technology with commercial applications outside its core business and that it is not able to market effectively itself.

The management of R&D is an imprecise art. All major commercial R&D facilities produce a steady stream of developments with commercial applications that are unlooked for or that lie outside the core business. Developments in manufacturing processes or testing techniques, for example, often have much wider applications than those for which they were originally intended. Such situations are especially common in the defense and aerospace industries, where the extent and quality of R&D are of the highest caliber, but where marketing capabilities are very specialized and cannot be applied elsewhere. Spin-off technologies are often not of a kind

*OEM is short for *original equipment manufacturer* customer. The OEM is, confusingly, the buyer of the equipment, not the supplier.

that can be readily patented or licensed. Sometimes the range of potential applications is so wide that a special exploitation company must be formed to pursue them.

Effective commercial exploitation may depend on teaming up with one or more joint-venture partners with strong marketing capabilities. BT&D Ltd. is an example of such a joint venture, created by British Telecom and du Pont to exploit optoelectronic component technology developed in British Telecom's U.K. laboratories. (The use of equity joint ventures to create new businesses is discussed in Chapter 9.)

Goal Three—Building Market Position Rapidly

As product markets grow, the secret of competitive advantage moves away from the best technical and marketing solution toward market power. Remaining competitive in the long term requires a scale of operations that is sufficient to support the high fixed costs of R&D, to maintain strong advertising campaigns, and to retain the commitment of distributors. High sales volume also usually delivers low manufacturing costs through scale economies and learning-curve effects.

With markets becoming increasingly international, it is important to have a strong presence in each of the major world markets, most notably the United States, Europe, and Japan. In mature mass markets, a share of at least 5 to 10 percent of the world market is typically required to remain in the first division. The leaders of the computer and aircraft industries have an even larger market share. Without this, a rather different set of strategies must be pursued—strategies discussed in detail later on.

Thus, one of the most important priorities for a company during the early growth period is to build market share before its competitors do and to provide the sales base from which to fight the rather different battles that will follow. In many new markets, the ultimate winners are the companies that succeed in powering up this growth curve most rapidly. Basing expansion entirely on 100-percent-owned marketing resources is often too slow and expensive. Strategic marketing partnerships have an important role to play in expanding sales during the growth period, and particularly in establishing a strong position in export markets.

Four types of strategic partnership can help a manufacturer build market position rapidly:

1. Vertical supply *alliances*—supplying product on an OEM basis for rebranding and resale by other companies.
2. Creation of value-added reseller *networks,* where different companies are involved in tailoring or augmenting the product for distribution to specialized users in various vertical markets.
3. Establishment of *local joint ventures,* with or without a manufacturing capability, to gain access to export markets.
4. Strategic *investments* in semicaptive local partners.*

In addition to helping a company maximize its own sales, these strategies can also help eliminate other companies as potential competitors by creating a network of captive distributors dependent on the manufacturer's technology.

There are also dangers. Many strategic partners are also potential competitors. Gaining the opportunity to resell or manufacture products could be the first step in developing their own. There is also a risk that, by selling through others, a company can lose direct contact with its ultimate users and become insensitive to changing customer needs and opportunities.

Companies choosing these routes must therefore structure their partner relationships carefully and take steps to maintain their technological edge. Direct contact with customers and independent market research may be required to ensure that products remain relevant to market needs. Chapter 9 examines the use of a number of different types of joint-venture strategies to build international market position, and in Chapter 11 we analyze the use of OEM relationships and strategic investments to achieve the same objective.

In many markets, it is essential to consider entry and growth strategies together. This is especially true where new categories of product are being developed for sale to markets with existing, well-defined customer bases or with well-established international distribution channels. Examples include new generations of civil airliners and most consumer electronics products. In these cases it is possible, by the judicious choice of development partners, to ensure global-market access from the start. The involve-

---

*Licensing is yet another option. It is particularly appropriate where strong patent protection prevails; licensing is extensively used in the pharmaceutical and semiconductor industries. In most situations, however, it does not generate high returns and is tactical or opportunistic rather than a form of true strategic partnership.

ment of European and Japanese partners in Boeing's 7J7 and V2500 projects is an example of this process.

In many areas of electronics, market success is also closely related to product and performance standards. Many competing standards are typical of the early growth phase of new markets, but as markets mature, standards with the greatest market share inevitably attract more attention from producers of associated equipment or software. This leads to a further dwindling in market support for manufacturers unlucky enough to choose the wrong standard at the start. In consumer electronics, telecommunications, and information technology, some collaboration on standards before market entry is often essential to minimizing risk. A careful choice of partners can create a de facto global standard, automatically easing entry to overseas markets while undermining the efforts of companies that have chosen to go it alone.

Goal Four—Survival through Specialization

As markets move through the shakeout phase, suppliers become divided into the strong and the weak. The strong companies, like IBM in mainframe computers, Boeing in jet airliners, and General Motors and Toyota in motor vehicles, have an enormous advantage. The scale of their operations enables them to achieve much lower manufacturing costs; they can afford more, and less efficient, R&D; they can sign up the best dealers; and they can wield enormous political pressure. They may also be able to use their size to gain other strategic advantages through the vertical integration of key component technology. For example, an in-house semiconductor manufacturing facility can enable companies to incorporate improvements in technologies into their products much earlier than their less vertically integrated competitors.

Companies that are not in the first tier in terms of sales cannot hope to match the product development capabilities of their larger competitors through internal R&D. They may also be unable to match their production costs. Weaker companies must therefore adopt strategies so as to avoid having to compete in the same territory as the market leaders. Possible options include:

- Specializing in specific market-sectors or subproduct areas.
- Switching to on-off contracts, in which scale economies are far less important.

- Buying key components on an OEM basis.
- Becoming a subcontractor to the industry leaders.
- Becoming a distributor for the industry leaders.

Strategic alliances are important in each of the last three areas and can extend the ability of a company to compete further into the life cycle. Aerospace, motor vehicles, computers, telecommunications, and consumer electronics are all industries in which such alliances have been adopted. However, the erosion of either R&D or marketing capabilities, which these strategies often imply, can have a serious long-term effect on innovation and competitiveness.

Goal Five—Reestablishing Critical Mass

As internationalization and competitive pressures increase, even quite sizable established companies may find it impossible to compete with the industry leaders and remain totally independent. At this point, the only options are disposal or the merger of operations, in one way or another, with another company.

Many companies are in fact active in several business areas, each at different points in the product-market life cycle and each subject to different competitive pressures. When a business unit is not of sufficient size to be internationally competitive, undertaking a partial merger with a division of another company can help strengthen market position and provide adequate R&D funding. In aerospace, collaboration on specific projects performs a similar function. In at least one case, Airbus Industrie, the collaboration has lasted long enough to produce what is essentially a new corporate entity.

Partial mergers are particularly important in the European content, where the existence of national champions in each of the European economies has prevented the formation of corporations with the ability to compete in global markets. (Partial mergers are discussed in detail in Chapter 10.)

Goal Six—Achieving and Retaining Cost Leadership

As we saw in Chapter 2, the impact of innovation on markets tends to decline as they mature. Some product categories achieve the status of near commodities, with competing offerings virtually indistinguishable in the eyes of the purchaser, and many companies able to replicate new products quickly. At this point, price tends to dominate buyers' purchasing decisions. Having a scale of operations sufficient to support world-class R&D becomes less important than the cost of manufacturing.

Achieving low unit product costs depends on a number of factors: economies of scale, learning-curve effects, quality of manufacturing management, and the costs of labor and capital. Many of these are under the internal control of individual companies. Japanese companies' successful response to the rise of the yen has, in large measure, resulted from their extraordinary capacity for setting and achieving tight cost-reduction targets.

One important factor is largely beyond direct internal control: the cost of labor. Over the last 20 years, a new group of aggressive industrial competitors has emerged. Their labor costs are much lower than those in the more developed nations, although increasing prosperity pushed labor costs higher as the '80s drew to a close. Led by the "four little tigers"—Korea, Taiwan, Hong Kong, and Singapore—the newly industrialized countries (NICs) offer a low-cost source of supply for many products in which the technology is reasonably stable and manufacturing skills are readily acquired. Leading suppliers in these countries can already match the quality of Japanese manufacture in many products. Just behind them stands a whole regiment of rather less advanced countries, led by Thailand, the Philippines, Malaysia, and Indonesia, with even lower wage costs. The emergence of a new economic and political order in Eastern Europe is likely to herald a similar group of industrial competitors there.

It is often argued that the development of advanced manufacturing techniques, involving far less direct labor than hitherto, means that it is as cheap to locate factories in high-wage economies as in low-wage ones. However, this is only part of the story. Advanced manufacturing techniques can reduce the impact of labor on direct costs, but they cannot counter the impact on indirect costs and the cost of components, raw materials, and services. Low-labor-cost countries will always offer tough competition when they can match product quality and use the same manufacturing techniques.

The four tigers' exports were estimated to be about nine tenths of Japan's in 1989. Korea is the largest and most powerful economically, although its per capita income in 1989 was still less than half of Singapore's, and barely more than half of Hong Kong's. Its development path has already led to strong textiles, steel, and shipbuilding industries, and it is an important manufacturer of automobiles and electronics, of which it now supplies some 5 percent of all world trade. Estimated 1990 vehicle production is 1.4 million, with manufacturers planning to raise production to 3 million by 1995.

To remain competitive as products mature, companies based in the Triad economies will increasingly need to source products from NIC suppliers, but in so doing they face the danger of creating their own competitors. Equity partnership provides an important means of internalizing this competition—either by joint venture or investment in the supplying company. Even here, there are pitfalls if relationships are not carefully structured.

Goal Seven—Orderly Withdrawal

As the key to competitive advantage in each product market moves progressively toward scale and cost leadership, some companies inevitably find themselves fighting losing battles. There may be only limited opportunities for refocusing the company as a specialist supplier or acquiring shared economies of scale. And the risks may be too great. The company's other businesses may offer better opportunities; there may be insufficient cash available to fund all the investment required.

The traditional options in this situation are two: to sell the business or gradually wind operations down. Partial mergers offer an additional choice—phased disposal, perhaps over three to five years, to a competitor of similar size that is determined to remain in the business. In many circumstances, this can make disposal easier and more remunerative.

DEPLOYING THE FULL ARMORY

Many multinational manufacturing companies are involved in a variety of product markets, each of which is at a different point on the product-market life-cycle curve. The increasing pace and complexity of technological change and the growing internationalization of markets mean that collaborative strategies are becoming more and more important to successful competition.

The corporation of the future will need to take a more dynamic view of its business. It must be prepared to deploy the full range of strategic weapons at its disposal—the collaborative and more traditional weapons sum-

CASE 3–1
JVC and the VCR: A Lesson in Building Global Market Dominance

The first commercial videocassette recorders were produced in 1956 by a U.S. company, Ampex. For 15 years, it remained an expensive and unwieldy technology of relevance only to television broadcasters and other professional users.

In the 1960s and 70s, however, as many as 40 companies began work on trying to produce machines for the consumer market. These included Matsushita, Japan's biggest consumer electronics company; JVC, its much smaller, partly owned associate; and Sony, the company run by Japan's best-known entrepreneur, Akio Morita. A series of products came out in the early 70s, each based on different standards. They included Sony's U-Matic and Philips' much-less-expensive VCR format.

The real consumer market breakthrough, however, came in 1975. Three important new products were announced in Japan in that year—Sony's Betamax format, the V-corded format developed by Sanyo and Toshiba, and Matsushita's VX 1000, launched the following year. Betamax quickly captured the lion's share of the market, and in fact "Betamax" became synonymous with "VCR"—for a time.

JVC did not launch its VHS format until December 1976. JVC's product strategy was based on consumer advantages—for example, a two-hour playing time, as opposed to Sony's one-hour—and ease of manufacture. As a small company, it recognized that it would need to work with a series of partners to build market share and acquire the credibility necessary to ensure a wide library of software titles.

Successive technical improvements and price reductions expanded the market rapidly, first in Japan and later in the United States and Europe.

Despite its late entry and small size, JVC's VHS format quickly overtook Sony's Betamax format in the United States. It immediately captured two thirds of the European market, and by 1979 it had replaced Betamax as the most popular format in Japan.

Sony's setback represented not just a loss of market share but also a fundamental loss of credibility. As a result, fewer software titles were produced for the Betamax format and fewer distributors were prepared to stock them. It was not until 1988, however, with VHS holding nearly 95 percent of the world market, that Sony conceded defeat and started manufacturing VHS machines.

The key to JVC's success in the United States and Europe was distribution, achieved primarily through a series of agreements to supply VCRs for rebranding that were negotiated by JVC and its parent, Matsushita. The most significant agreement in the United States was with RCA, which had the best distribution network of any U.S. consumer electronics company. Agreements were also signed with Magnavox, Philips' U.S. subsidiary, and a number of other suppliers.

The Japanese did not enter the European market, which had been dominated by Philips' VCR system, until 1978.

Both JVC and Sony knew that distribution would decide who would win the standards war in Europe. In 1977, both began to court suitable partners. However, this time there was a new twist, with JVC offering its partners the prospect of participation in manufacturing, once volumes reached a certain threshold. Britain's Thorn EMI, France's Thomson, and West Germany's Telefunken were all offered similar arrangements, each unknown to the others.

The outcome of these negotiations was J2T, a European joint venture company created to manufacture VCRs under license from JVC. JVC, Thorn, and Telefunken each owned one-third of the equity. Thomson was also involved for a short time before its nationalization in 1981; it returned to the venture when it acquired Telefunken several years later.

JVC provided considerable technical help in the establishment of J2T's three factories. These focused initially on assembly from Japanese-produced components, with progressively more manufacturing shifting to Europe. By 1987, J2T was producing 800,000 machines a year, equivalent to 60 percent of JVC's European sales for rebranding. The rest were supplied directly from Japan.

More recently, Thorn EMI pulled back from consumer electronics, selling its share in J2T to the other partners. Thomson, meanwhile, has consolidated its operations, acquiring General Electric's $3-billion U.S. consumer electronics business in 1987. It has introduced its own product designs and shows signs of becoming much more nearly equal of JVC in Europe.

marized in Exhibit 3–2. It must make sure that it identifies and enters new markets early, that it retains maximum competitive advantage as markets grow and mature, and, if necessary, that it withdraws gracefully if the competition gets too tough.

At the same time, the accelerating pace of business innovation and

EXHIBIT 3–1
Changing Strategic Imperatives

Strategic Goal	Weapons Available
1. Identifying and accessing new technologies	• In-house development • Corporate venturing • Precompetitive collaborative R&D • Academic links
2. Exploiting new market opportunities	• In-house businesses creation • Joint venture • Buying-in product from outside (OEM sourcing) • Acquisitions
3. Building market position	• "Conventional" distribution • OEM/VAR strategies • Local joint ventures • Strategic investments
4. Survival through specialization	• Specialization/contracting/ subcontracting • OEM sourcing • Distribution
5. Reestablishing critical mass	• Acquisition • Partial merger • Consortium
6. Achieving cost leadership	• Scale (through collaboration) • Cost improvement programs • Sourcing from NICs • Joint ventures with NIC-based companies
7. Orderly withdrawal	• Run-down operations • Disposal • Partial merger

the other macroeconomic trends we have described are compressing product-market life cycles. There is often insufficient time to switch from one mode of operation to another as markets evolve. Companies operating in embryonic and early-growth markets must try to put in place the strategies that will guarantee their competitive position later. And companies operating in mature markets must have the flexibility to react quickly to new technologies that bring either threats or opportunities to their existing businesses.

Companies will frequently have to address more than one of these goals simultaneously. From the very start of a new business, they must

44

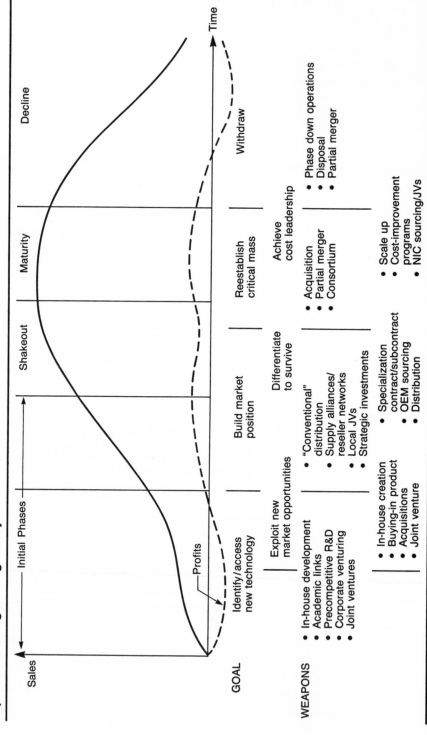

EXHIBIT 3-2
Imperatives Change During Life Cycle

find ways of building competence in each of the three main areas of competitive advantage—even if they are not well placed to do so on their own.

Even dominant companies do well to add partnerships to their strategic arsenals. True, companies that have achieved a position of market dominance during the growth and shakeout phases can often afford to be much more self-reliant. The advantages of dominance can last for decades. Brand loyalty works. Commercial agreements can lock in distributors. Proprietary technology can lock in customers that are eager to reduce upgrade costs and minimize risk. And financial muscle means that launching new products behind those of competitors—or misjudging the market— need not be fatal. There is always a second chance. Such companies have far less need to make strategic alliances. They can afford to be independent—for a time at least.

Industrial giants cannot, however, afford to become too introspective. Their very market strength sows the seeds of complacency. Major discontinuities are often difficult to spot in advance, and they can easily upset market positions. For example, the increasing power of semiconductors is redefining the market on which IBM's and other mainframe and minicomputer manufacturers' success is based. Japanese developments in the technology of manufacturing management have undermined the competitive strength of U.S. and European car manufacturers. Even the largest and strongest of companies must be actively seeking ways of identifying emerging trends likely to affect its business, and of introducing new skills and technologies into its core business. Strategic alliances can play an important role in this process.

The ability to think through such situations is essential to successful partnership. Chapter 4 looks at how management in five industries has used partnerships strategically.

CHAPTER 4

HISTORIC MANEUVERS

In strategy it is important to see distant things as if they were close and take a distanced view of close things. It is important in strategy to know the enemy's sword and not to be distracted by insignificant movements of his sword.

—Miyamo Musashi,
Samurai teacher, 1584–1645

International collaboration is not a new phenomenon. It has been common in some industries for many years. The structure and economic circumstances of industries vary, but many companies are clearly reliving the experiences of others in different sectors. There are therefore important general lessons to be learned from looking at specific sectors. The industries discussed here illustrate partnership among many different sorts of market and product types—from very new industries such as biotechnology to mature sectors such as automobiles; from high-volume, low-unit-cost products such as semiconductors to complex engineering systems such as aircraft. This chapter discusses the patterns of collaboration in five industries: commercial aircraft, automotive vehicles, telecommunications, semiconductors, and biotechnology.

THE COMMERCIAL AIRCRAFT INDUSTRY

Although the commercial aircraft industry came into being in the 1930s, the current structure is the result of a progressive process of concentration since the commercial jet age began in the 1950s. Both the airframe and engine sectors of the industry have been affected.

Before World War II, 28 major companies supplied aircraft to the world's airlines. Since then, the size of aircraft has increased substantially,

CASE 4–1
International Aero Engines—The V2500 Project

The V2500 project was set up in 1983 to develop, manufacture, and market a new jet engine with a thrust of 25,000 pounds for use in the new generation of 150-seat aircraft being developed for the 1990s— at the time, the Airbus A320 and McDonnell Douglas MD–89.

The V2500 project involved the same lead partners—Rolls Royce and Pratt and Whitney—as a previous short-lived project, the JT10D, which was dissolved after less than a year in 1977, following a change in customer requirements. Prior to the V2500 project, Rolls Royce had already been working on a slight, lower-powered engine with the Japan Aero Engine Corp., and Fiat and MTU had been involved in the development of the Pratt and Whitney PW4000 and PW2037.

The emergence of the new 150-seat aircraft designs offered attractive market potential. Projections indicated a market of 7,000 engines worth $30 billion over 15 years. However, both Pratt and Whitney and Rolls Royce were already heavily committed on other projects. This meant that neither team could really afford to develop a new engine alone. While both compete strongly in other power ranges, there was an opportunity to collaborate in the midrange market sector.

Unlike many other aircraft-industry partnerships, Pratt and Whitney and Rolls Royce entered their International Aero Engines alliance as equals, with key management split between the two companies. It was therefore essential to set up a strongly autonomous central management team. IAE has full authority for marketing, product service and aftermarket support, and financial systems. Nevertheless, the decision not to have a lead shareholder caused major problems, and project management has now passed to Pratt and Whitney.

The division of work has been carefully structured to build on each partner's technical strengths and minimize technology transfer between them. The existing relationships that Rolls Royce and Pratt and Whitney had with the junior partners helped to reduce the potential problems arising from such a large number of partners.

After the V2500 project was set up, a new opportunity arose—for a 30,000-pound-thrust engine to power long 150-seat jets like the A340 and Boeing 7J7. The IAE partners decided to promote the idea of a second project—an ultra-high-bypass engine based on the

> V2500 core. After a series of design studies and discussions with customers, it became clear that the new engine could not be produced in time, and the project was dropped, though with considerable damage to IAE's credibility.
>
> **Shareholders in International Aero Engines and Development Responsibilities**
>
> | | | |
> |---|---|---|
> | Rolls Royce | 30% | Forward section (low- and high-pressure compressors) |
> | Pratt and Whitney | 30% | Engine core |
> | Japanese Aero Engine Corporation Kawasaki Heavy Industries Mitsubishi Heavy Industries Ishikawajima-Harima Heavy Industries | 23% | Parts of forward section |
> | MTU | 11% | Low-pressure turbine |
> | Fiat Aviazione | 6% | Gearbox |

and the number of manufacturers has steadily declined. By the 1950s, only about 10 companies internationally produced large commercial aircraft (at that time, "large" planes were those that could carry more than 50 passengers). Today, just three manufacturers of big intercontinental jets survive: Boeing, McDonnell-Douglas, and Airbus Industrie (itself a consortium of European aircraft companies) together account for 90 percent of free-world demand. The number of independent engine producers has also declined steadily; now there are just three that are capable of developing a major turbo-fan jet.

Three Sources of Pressure

Pressure from three main sources has encouraged management to collaborate: the rising costs of development, the need to gain access to global markets, and political influences.

The R&D Escalator
The main reason for industry concentration is the steadily increasing cost of designing and launching new products. This is largely a reflection of the

growing complexity and breadth of the technology base on which the aircraft industry is built. Its companies are in fact complex system builders, integrating components and skills that lie at the frontiers of many diverse technologies—from materials to electronics to engineering.

The most popular civil aircraft before World War II was the DC3. It cost $3 million to develop, and more than 10,000 were built. The DC8, launched in 1958, cost $112 million to develop. The cost of developing the Boeing 747, which went into production in the early 1970s, was almost $1 billion. The development cost of a new aircraft with 135 to 160 seats is now around $3 billion, plus an additional $1 billion to set up production. Boeing's new widebody, the 777, is expected to involve an investment of $5 billion to $6 billion.

The cost of developing a new generation of engines for a plane of this size is an additional $3 million.[1] These sums are huge even by the standards of the giants of the industry: in 1989, Boeing reported net income of $973 million on sales of $20.3 billion, and McDonnell-Douglas earned $219 million on sales of $14.6 billion.

Realizing an adequate return on this kind of investment demands long production runs. And there are important learning-curve savings; production costs are reduced by as much as 20 percent with every doubling of volume. A "family" of aircraft must usually be produced to recover costs. Development of a stretched version typically requires about 25 percent of the original investment.

There are, however, many competitive and political barriers to achieving high volumes. Only 4 of the 23 large commercial jet aircraft launched since the 1950s have achieved production volumes in excess of 600 aircraft.

The concept development stage is lengthy, and success is uncertain as companies try to meet the differing and changing requirements of customers. Once the decision to go ahead has been taken, it takes four to five years to first delivery. Programs do not start to break even for 10 to 12 years.

No company can now afford to shoulder these kinds of risks alone. With the exception of the Boeing 757 and the Pratt and Whitney PW4000 engine, no major commercial aircraft or engine has been developed within the last 10 years on any basis other than a joint venture.

Global Access
Gaining access to markets has been a second, strong incentive for collaboration. The commercial-aircraft industry is probably more truly "global"

than any other. When an airline buys a commercial aircraft, it is making a 15- to 20-year investment. It must be able to obtain spare parts and service for the aircraft in any part of the world where it is likely to operate. And this support must be available throughout the aircraft's life. The high fixed costs of supporting such worldwide service and marketing networks represent a major barrier to entry for new firms and a strong incentive for producers to market a number of different aircraft or engines.

The international market has become increasingly important for U.S. manufacturers. Between 1950 and 1972, U.S. airlines bought 67 percent of the aircraft output of domestic manufacturers. A slowing of the U.S. rate of market growth, and significantly developing overseas markets, have since produced a substantial shift. The United States market accounted for only 40 percent of the world's aircraft orders booked between 1977 and 1982. Access to overseas markets has clearly gained in importance.

Political Influences

Collaboration has helped companies in different countries to tap each other's government-backed R&D and has weakened political trade barriers. All the governments of the industrial nations regard the aircraft industry as strategically important—from both the military and the economic points of view. Besides the importance placed on having a strong, independent source of military hardware, the aerospace industry is also a substantial source of employment. In the United States, it is responsible for some 2.2 percent of U.S. GNP and directly employs nearly 800,000 people. More important, the aerospace industry represents one of the high spots of technology. Because of this, it can support high wage costs and generate substantial spin-off opportunities.

As a result, the aircraft industry receives a high degree of financial support from governments. Defense expenditures provide a continuing baseload of work for most companies. Roughly three quarters of U.S. manufacturers' R&D is paid for by the government. Most of this is directed to the military arena and, while the spin-offs into commercial work are now thought to be far less important than they were in the 1950s and 1960s, the underpinning of fixed costs is still very important to the overall economics of the major companies.

Other countries strongly support civil projects. It is estimated that the French government provided as much as $500 million in support of SNECMA's CFM56 engine collaboration with General Electric. Airbus

Industrie has received some $14 billion in aid from European governments since its creation two decades ago. And the Japanese government has provided loans covering up to 75 percent of the cost of early development work carried out by the Japanese partners on the Boeing 767 and V2500 engine products. The ability to tap overseas sources of "soft" finance through collaborations has proved highly attractive for manufacturers in the United States, where government support for the industry is more indirect.

Besides the direct benefit from sharing costs, government-backed partners are better able to cope with financial crises, and they have political leverage when it comes to getting orders. The CFM56 project would have been disbanded in the mid-1970s but for SNECMA's contribution, and French participation helped secure contracts with Airbus.

Patterns of Collaboration

These three major sources of pressure have led to a steady process of industry concentration, first on a national basis and then, in the case of Europe, regionally. Much of the restructuring has taken place through mergers and acquisitions, such as the merger of Douglas with McDonnell in 1967. In other cases, companies have simply pulled out of large-scale commercial aircraft manufacturing to concentrate on military contracts, subcontracting, and smaller aircraft.

With only three major players in the industry worldwide, the conventional concentration process has now reached its limit. It cannot go any further without, in effect, destroying competition in the industry. Now, collaboration is the only way in which companies can shoulder the huge investments required.

During the entire period of contraction since World War II, commercial airline companies have collaborated in a number of ways.

Coproduction Licenses
Collaboration first emerged in the military sphere, when U.S. companies granted licenses for overseas production of aircraft and missiles. Between 1947 and 1986, more than 20 countries were involved in nearly 50 such projects. Production was generally restricted to the assembly of components shipped from the United States; more sensitive equipment was supplied as "black boxes." Contractors were not involved in design or marketing.

While this process helped many countries to build (or, in the case of Japan and West Germany, rebuild) a basic aircraft industry, the amount of technology transfer was limited, and little benefit spun off to the commercial sphere.

Military Offsets

In the end, coproduction licenses delivered huge export earnings to the major U.S. weapons producers, while starving licensees of the opportunity to develop in-house technology. As a result of European government pressures, the United States therefore introduced a policy of providing "offsets"—giving subcontract orders to a country's aircraft industry in exchange for weapons orders.

In Europe, the most successful of these arrangements, from the purchasers' point of view, was the F16, produced by General Dynamics in collaboration with companies in the Netherlands, Belgium, Norway, and Holland. When the deal was signed in 1976, it was agreed that European purchases should be offset by coproduction of 58 percent of the total expenditure. The success of the project internationally—well in excess of 4,000 aircraft have been sold—means that the actual figures have been even higher.

The learning benefits of participation in these offset programs have given a substantial boost to the international competitive strength of the participating companies.

Risk-Sharing Subcontracting

Subcontracting constituted less than 10 percent of aircraft production in the 1930s. However, escalating development costs and the need for an increasing range of special applications have led to a gradual increase in this figure—to about 35 percent in the 1950s and even more today. There is now a complex web of subcontracting arrangements right across the industry. Six major subcontractors accounted for 70 percent of production of the Boeing 747.

This trend has led primary contractors to ask subcontractors to participate in project risks by providing some of the development capital. The Boeing 767 project was established on this basis in 1978. Boeing's partners were Italy's Aeritalia and the Japanese Commercial Transport Development Corporation, itself a consortium of Kawasaki, Mitsubishi, and Fuji Heavy Industries. The memorandum of understanding stipulated that each of the subcontractors was responsible for development and production tooling costs to the extent of 15 percent of the total value of the aircraft. In return for this investment, the Italian and Japanese partners get a set price per unit. Ultimate profitability depends on the number of aircraft sold, and early sales were below the level originally anticipated. Both partners received government subsidies for up to half of the development costs incurred.

For Boeing, this collaboration offered a number of important benefits: the opportunity to spread financial risk, access to the Japanese market, and insurance against cooperation between the Japanese and Boeing's rivals—notably, Airbus Industrie. Boeing retained control of all the key decision-making and management functions, including design, production, and marketing.

The management of such subcontracting programs is relatively straightforward, with a clear lead contractor and well-defined subcontracting arrangements. However, the extent of technology sharing is very limited, generating pressure for greater involvement by the junior partners.

European Consortia

The European aircraft industry is highly fragmented, and the support that individual governments gave national champions in the 1960s and 1970s meant that none of the companies was ever able to compete with the scale economies of the large U.S. manufacturers. Europe's share of the commercial aircraft market fell from about 25 percent in the early 1960s to about 10 percent by the early 1980s. However, this trend has been reversed by the emergence of pan-European collaborations—most notably Airbus and the Panavia military Tornado consortium. The Tornado is the largest military aircraft project outside the United States. The British, German, and Italian venture hopes eventually to sell in excess of 800 aircraft to the major participating countries, with significant exports in addition. Panavia, the controlling consortium established in 1970, had 1986 revenues of $3.3 billion.

Airbus is the first large European commercial aircraft venture since World War II to come close to commercial viability, with more than 1,400 orders by 1990 and 20 percent of the free-world market. In both cases, project management has been turned over to a new joint organization, the participating companies acting as its subcontractors. The ability to divide an aircraft into discrete subassemblies (e.g., wings, fuselage) greatly facilitates this process.

International Joint Ventures

As the process of concentration increases, major projects are increasingly being undertaken on a truly international basis. The primary examples are the Boeing 767 and 7J7 projects and the V2500 jet engine being developed by International Aero Engines. Each has involved U.S. and European companies together with a consortium of Japanese manufacturers.

The Missing Competitors

> It is hoped that Japan will build up a system for basic research and development of aircraft engineering so that it may be fully ready for the expected technology innovation in the 1990s for the manufacture of the next generation aircraft.
> —Japanese Ministry of International Trade and Industry Report, 1982

An unusual aspect of the aircraft industry is the almost complete absence from the international scene of the non-Communist world's second- and third-largest industrial nations—Japan and West Germany. The aircraft industries of both were largely destroyed after World War II. Japan's domestic aircraft industry remains dominated by military sales, at 80 percent of the industry total (compared with 50 to 60 percent in the United States). However, the defense sector has been severely constrained by the informal but well-established bans on Japanese military exports and the historical ceiling on defense spending of 1 percent of GNP. West Germany found itself in a similar, if slightly less severe, situation; it was prohibited from building aircraft until 1955 and is still Europe's third-largest manufacturer.

In both cases, subcontracting and manufacture under license have been important to the rebuilding of the aircraft industries. The Japanese government has, through MITI, taken a particularly active role in the development of a strong aerospace sector, seeing it as a key plank in the building of an industrial structure based on high technology. The approach has been largely a catch-up strategy, involving the acquisition of overseas technology through joint ventures and other forms of collaboration. Unlike other industrial sectors, MITI has taken a lead in setting national goals and evaluating strategic options.[2]

The extent of Japanese participation in major collaborations has increased steadily. A consortium of Japanese manufacturers held a 15-percent interest in the Boeing 767 project, begun in 1978. By 1984, their share in the 7J7 project (later cancelled) had risen to 25 percent.

Collaborative projects such as the V2500 have generally been carefully structured to impede the transfer of technology and skills between partners, and the nature of the aerospace business as a complex system-integration process facilitates this. However, the emergence of Japan as a major competitor in this market cannot be delayed indefinitely. A key advantage of Japanese manufacturers is likely to be the development of the advanced product-development and manufacturing-management techniques that have been demonstrated to such effect in other industries. For this reason, Japan will probably have more impact in engines than in airframes. Competition is likely to take the form of stronger participation in multinational joint ventures rather than the creation of a totally independent force.

Special Management Challenges

The formation of international consortia like those created for the 7J7* and V2500 projects is the logical outcome of the process of international concentration. Pooling skills and resources on a project-by-project basis enables companies to acquire scale and international market access without giving up total control. Nevertheless, managing these complex ventures is immensely difficult. Major companies are often unwilling to give up control, and the desire to share tasks fairly creates inefficiencies and extra costs. There are frequent false starts as potential customers change their specifications or design and commercial differences emerge between partners.

> We now see that we should have had a lead shareholder. It was diplomatic to have the two principal shareholders as equals. But it was a management nightmare having, for example, the engineering department in England and other functions 3,500 miles away.
> —Nicholas R. Tomassetti, President and Chief Executive Officer, International Aero Engines[3]

---

*The Boeing 7J7 project was aimed at developing a medium-range, narrow-body airliner with an energy-efficient engine. After heavy investment by Boeing and its collaborators, the fall in oil prices forced the project's cancellation.

The Japanese Commercial Aircraft Consortium was a full partner in the program, with a 25-percent investment to finance development and sales. Shorts of Great Britain and Saab-Scania of Sweden were risk-sharing subcontractors. Boeing was responsible for project management.

Programs must be developed in a way that separates engineering and design responsibilities carefully to enable companies to retain their own areas of technological leadership without danger of seepage. And the marketing strategy must avoid conflicts between partners who continue to compete closely.

Toward this end, networks of alliances have sometimes been formed with companies choosing different partners for different projects to spread risk, maintain independence, and widen their product range. In some cases, this has led to conflict. In April 1990, General Electric filed a $1.15-billion lawsuit against Daimler-Benz, its partner of 25 years, after Benz announced that its Motoren-und-Turbinen-Union subsidiary was to pool its airplane engine activities with Pratt & Whitney. GE was particularly incensed that it had been providing MTU with detailed research data under a memorandum of understanding to cooperate on the development of 50,000-pound engines. It feared that the new partnership between MTU and Pratt & Whitney would make this knowhow available to its principal U.S. rival.

The new forms of collaboration—like Airbus and the V2500—are responsible for both marketing and project management. They have been set up as separate corporate entities: in the case of Airbus, as a Groupment d'Intérêts Économique, a French vehicle that passes liabilities through to participating companies; in the case of the V2500, as a jointly owned company. This is an important departure from the earlier and looser forms of collaboration and suggests a more permanent arrangement. As we have seen, the ability to stretch aircraft and designs to produce a family of related products is crucial to long-term cost competition. Once successful, ventures such as these create their own momentum, and it may not be easy to go back.

THE AUTOMOTIVE INDUSTRY

The automotive-vehicle industry is the single most important industrial sector in most advanced economies, and it exercises a powerful multiplier effect on other sectors. At the manufacturing level alone, it is worth more than $450 billion, consuming 20 percent of all steel products and making up 5 percent of total GNP within the OECD countries. This excludes the components industry and related downstream operations.

The world market is almost 50 million vehicles, 30 million of which

CASE 4–2
New United Motor Manufacturing Inc. (NUMMI)

NUMMI is a joint venture between Toyota and General Motors to produce subcompact cars at a plant in Fremont, California.

While Toyota is Japan's leading car manufacturer and the third largest in the world, it was relatively slow to invest in capacity overseas. The rising tide of protectionism made a U.S. plant increasingly necessary, and Toyota decided to seek a partner with which it could learn to operate in this very different environment. After initial discussions with Ford, Toyota approached General Motors in late 1981.

For GM, the proposal represented an ideal opportunity to learn Japanese production methods at first hand and to test their usefulness in a unionized U.S. environment. It also promised to provide a superior subcompact—a segment of the market in which U.S. manufacturers had been weak and in which price competition from imports was toughest.

Negotiations to establish the joint venture were protracted. Besides the agreement between GM and Toyota, it was also necessary to satisfy the Federal Trade Commission and negotiate new union agreements. Objections to the proposed deal came from other car manufacturers, notably Chrysler, and the FTC gave approval only after it was agreed that:

- The duration of the joint venture would be limited to 12 years;
- Output for GM should not exceed 250,000 cars per year; and
- The joint venture would be limited to production with no direct marketing of the cars.

FTC approval was finally given in April 1984. By this time, work on commissioning the plant was well advanced. The first cars were produced in December of the same year.

NUMMI is a 50/50 joint venture, incorporated in the United States. Each partner contributed $100 million toward startup costs. Toyota gave $100 million in cash; GM $80 million in plant and equipment and 20 million in cash. A further $250 million was raised in loans.

Originally opened in 1963, the old GM plant now used by NUMMI was closed by GM in 1982 after many years of industrial unrest and general inefficiency. Today, it is run according to the Toyota production system. The president and executive vice president are appointed by Toyota. Of NUMMI's 11 vice presidents or general managers, four are from Toyota, one is from GM, and the others are NUMMI appointees. Line managers are all U.S. nationals; Toyota personnel are coordinators.

The automobiles produced at NUMMI are based on the Toyota Corolla. Engines and transmissions are imported from Japan, but more than half of the parts are purchased from U.S. firms. NUMMI produces between 200,000 and 250,000 cars each year. These are mainly GEO Prizms distributed by GM, but it also produces the Corolla sedan for the Toyota dealer network.

Since NUMMI began production in December 1984, it has developed one of the best records for efficiency and labor relations of any of GM's North American operations. And for the partners, the venture has proved to be a valuable stepping-stone in their longer-term strategies: GM has been able to apply the lessons learned to its other plants around the world, and Toyota has gone on to construct wholly owned plants in Kentucky and Canada, with a total start-up capacity of 300,000 vehicles a year.

are passenger cars, the remainder light and heavy commercial vehicles. Western Europe and the United States each account for more than 30 percent of the world market. Japan accounts for a further 14 percent.

This huge sector bears the markings of an industry in a mature stage of the product-market life cycle. Capturing economies of scale is very important; concentration is the general trend.

Capturing Economies of Scale

There are powerful economies of scale in the automobile industry. As in the aerospace industry, there has been a steady increase in the cost of R&D. Fiat spent $330 million to bring its new Fire 1000 engine into production in the mid-1980s. The cost of designing and tooling for a new "world car" has been variously estimated at between $700 million and $1.5 billion.

It is not simply that R&D costs have risen, but also that the incremental gain from the investment has fallen under the weight of a mature and highly competitive market. The ratio of company profits to R&D investment had fallen from about 1:5 in 1945 to lower than 1:1 by 1970.[4] Given the margins that have been available in the overcrowded markets of recent years, it can take production of up to two million units to recoup these costs.

Production
Historically, there have been important economies of scale in production. These apply to all stages in the production process, although the impact varies from process to process. Economies of scale continue through to high-output volumes—with a minimum efficient annual production capacity of 250,000 for final assembly, at least 500,000 for engines, and 1,000,000 for stamping. However, the traditional picture is beginning to be challenged by the adoption of flexible manufacturing and developments in Japanese manufacturing practice. The minimum plant size is therefore falling; Japanese passenger-car makers are aiming at developing assembly plants that are profitable with a production capacity of just 40,000 units a year.[5]

Distribution and Promotion
There are also economies of scale in distribution and promotion. To sign up and retain the best distributors requires a wide product range and an aggressive promotion campaign. A minimum market share of about 5 percent is needed in most national markets to retain distributor commitment. The entry of Japanese manufacturers into the European market in the 1970s was partly facilitated by dissatisfaction among dealers acting for certain local manufacturers.

International Integration
The increasing economies of scale in production have led to progressively larger and more focused plants, designed to achieve a much higher level of integration within international operations. Integration took place first in Europe, led by Ford, which, between 1969 and 1974, developed a common European product range involving just three basic automobiles (a fourth was added later). Different plants specialize in particular design engineering and product tasks. This integration process is now extending to a truly global scale, with the U.S. multinationals obtaining components and vehicles from their Japanese, Korean, and other affiliates.

This trend is demonstrated most obviously by the growth in vehicle exports, which has risen by more than 500 percent since 1960 (against an increase in production of 200 percent). The commercial-vehicle market also demonstrates this growing internationalization. Exports, primarily of light commercial vehicles and vans, have grown by more than 400 percent since 1960.

The process of international integration has been greatly assisted by the development of so-called "world cars" that can be sold, with local variations, in all the major markets. Until the 1970s, the automobile markets in the United States, Europe, and Japan were very different. The U.S. multinationals had a major share of the European market, but the products they sold were very much smaller and less powerful than their own U.S. models. Japanese manufacturers still had only limited success in Europe, while their own market was effectively closed to imports.

The 1973 energy crisis, coupled with trends in Europe and Japan, led to a convergence of demand patterns, and the 1,300-to-2,500-cc segment emerged as the core in all three markets. Assisted by substantial cost differentials and by the slowness of U.S. manufacturers to respond to the changes taking place at home, the Japanese were able to take over one fifth of the U.S. car market by 1980.

This development was led by General Motors and has been taken up by Ford and the Japanese manufacturers.

Other Responses

Among the other ways in which manufacturers are attempting to realize economies of scale is a move to limit the number of key subassemblies used for different products. For example, by 1977 Volkswagen used only three types of gearbox for its entire range. Some companies have sought to stretch the lives of the most development-cost-intensive vehicle components and extend the volume on individual models. For instance, the small Nissan engines of the early 1980s were still based on the original British mini engine, which dates back to the 1950s.

Some of the weaker motor manufacturers have entered partnerships to spread R&D investment costs and gain production economies. Where there are holes in their product ranges, companies have also brought in products on an OEM basis from overseas suppliers. Examples include the Festiva, manufactured by Kia, Ford's Korean affiliate.

Concentration

Like the aircraft industry, the motor-vehicle industry has experienced increasing levels of concentration. The process took place first in the United

CASE 4–3
IVECO: The First Pan-European Company

IVECO was formed from the merger in 1975 of five European truck manufacturers—Unic, Magirus Deutz, OM, Fiat, and Lancia VS.

Fiat's main strength was in heavy trucks, OM's was mainly in light trucks, and Lancia was particularly strong in the military market. UNIC had been 100-percent-owned by Fiat for many years and had integrated production facilities in France. The real newcomer was Magirus Deutz, the truck assembly operation of Klockner Humboldt Deutz (KHD), the diversified German industrial group.

A new holding company was established in Holland, with KHD holding 20 percent of the combined company's equity, and Fiat holding the remaining 80 percent. KHD also negotiated an option to sell its remaining shareholding to Fiat in 1980.

While KHD remained active in the management of IVECO for several years, it eventually decided to withdraw from the company completely, the sale price being agreed after a two-year arbitration period.

The merger gave IVECO 20 percent of the EEC market for heavy trucks, and it offered Fiat, the dominant partner, three further important benefits:

* An opportunity to rationalize production.
* A strengthened international marketing organization, including access to the difficult German market.
* Product-line enhancement through use of KHD's air-cooled engine.

IVECO's units were initially given considerable management autonomy. Rationalization was really triggered by the downturn in the European truck market in 1980 and the transfer of full management responsibility to Fiat after the withdrawal of KHD.

In 1986, IVECO undertook a further important partial merger with Ford's U.K. truck interests. This gave IVECO access to the U.K. market, the one remaining major European country in which it was relatively weak. There was also strong product synergy, with Ford's successful Cargo medium range products fitting well with IVECO's strengths in heavy trucks.

Ford continues to supply engines for the Cargo under an OEM agreement.

IVECO Ford is 48-percent-owned by IVECO, and 48-percent-owned by Ford. The remaining 4 percent of the equity is held by

Credit Suisse First Boston. Management control rests firmly with
IVECO.
Today IVECO is Europe's second-largest commercial vehicle
manufacturer, selling a full range of vehicles across its European
home market.

States, with the emergence by the end of World War II of General Motors,
Ford, and Chrysler as the dominant suppliers.

Restructuring was slower in Europe. There were 26 manufacturers after
the end of the war and 11 in the 1970s, only 5 of which produced a full range of
cars. More rapid concentration was hindered by differences in national tastes
and by the political protection accorded national champions. Indeed, it was the
U.S. multinationals, Ford and General Motors, that were first to integrate
their operations across Western Europe as a whole. Despite the restructuring
of the European industry over the last 20 years, in 1987 GM and Ford still had
10 percent and 11 percent, respectively, of the European automobile market.

Progressive concentration has taken place primarily through conventional acquisitions and mergers, often triggered by overcapacity and financial difficulties. Today, more than 70 percent of world vehicle production
is accounted for by just 10 suppliers (see Exhibit 4–1).

Much of the restructuring in Europe has been triggered by overcapacity (25 percent in cars in the late 1970s, up to 50 percent in commercial
vehicles).[6] The United States will shortly be suffering from a similar problem, in large measure a reflection of increased penetration by Japanese
manufacturers and other overseas companies.[7]

The concentration process is not yet complete. There is particular
scope for restructuring in Japan, which still has nine major automobile
companies: Toyota, Nissan, Mazda, Mitsubishi, Honda, Suzuki, Isuzu,
Fuji, and Daihatsu. The Japanese government has been trying to bring
about a reduction in numbers since the 1960s.

New Low-Cost Producers

The Japanese automobile industry was one of the three major development
areas of MITI's plan during the 1950s to transform Japan's economy
through export-led growth (the others were steel and shipbuilding). The

EXHIBIT 4-1
World's Largest Vehicle Manufacturers (1988)

	Units produced (thousands)
1. General Motors (U.S.A.)	7,831
2. Ford (U.S.A.)	6,376
3. Toyota (Japan)	3,969
4. Volkswagen (West Germany)	2,850
5. Fiat (Italy)	2,375
6. Chrysler (U.S.A.)	2,361
7. Nissan (Japan)	2,164
8. Peugeot (France)	2,103
9. Honda (Japan)	1,869
10. Mitsubishi (Japan)	1,261

Source: *Automobile Industries,* April 1989

vehicle industry is the last of these sectors to face the challenge of low-cost producers in the newly industrialized countries such as Korea, Taiwan, and Brazil, which have labor costs a fifth or less than Japan's.

In Europe, the Eastern-bloc countries seem likely to become another source of competition. Making motor vehicles is an appealing way of earning hard currency, and the sophisticated car companies of Germany and other Western European countries are natural partners for them.

In Southeast Asia, the nature of the challenge has begun to change as currency appreciation and rapidly escalating unit costs have sharply reduced—in some areas even wiped out—price advantages of NIC-produced vehicles. Between 1987 and 1990, for example, Korean car makers saw their price advantage over U.S. and Japanese competitors fall from about $2,000 to $1,000. The prospects for further currency appreciation have lessened, but the pressure on labor costs has not. Though increases of between 15 percent and 20 percent in recent years have not yet brought Korean auto workers' wages up to Japanese levels, the gap is narrowing rapidly.

Still, the most aggressive of the low-cost competitors have been the Koreans. Aided by government support and a series of strategic alliances with U.S. and Japanese companies, Korean manufacturers increased production from 220,000 to more than 1.1 million vehicles between 1983 and

1989. Car exports more than doubled every year until 1989, when sharply higher labor costs and rapid currency appreciation took some of the shine from Korea's international competitive position. Exports are now likely to ' return to 1988 levels, about 580,000 units, with 94 percent of these shipped to the United States.

The growth in Korea's automobile industry has so far relied heavily on strategic alliances with existing multinationals, drawing on partners' model designs and on help with setting up modern manufacturing facilities and component suppliers. For example, 25 percent of the value of Hyundai's Excel is spent on components imported from Mitsubishi. The most important of these relationships are summarized in Exhibit 4-2.

Korea's first real export success came with the launch of Hyundai's Excel in the United States. In 1987, 264,000 Excels were sold, making it the best-selling import. Hyundai's success was followed by those by Daewoo, with 68,000 Pontiac Lemanses (a modified Opel Kadett) sold through General Motors, and Kia, with 60,000 Festivas moved through Ford.

Korean manufacturers are taking great care to avoid the trade frictions that the Japanese have encountered, with a rapid buildup of exports in each target market before selective import barriers can be introduced. They are also working hard to build up in-house R&D and develop a local components industry.

International Trade Barriers and Government Intervention

The automobile industry is such an important part of any advanced economy that government intervention in the market is inevitable. Changes in domestic production have a major impact on both employment and the balance of payments. Imports of Japanese vehicles were responsible for more than half of the $50-billion 1986 U.S. trade deficit with Japan.

Government restrictions have taken various forms. The EEC has a "voluntary" restraint of 1.1 million vehicles on EEC imports from Japan. The tightest restrictions in Europe, the French and Italian quotas of 3 percent and 2,500 Japanese vehicles, respectively, were negotiated before Japanese exports to Europe gathered momentum.

The automobile companies have all used inward investment and flexible procurement to get around these restrictions. By 1991, Japanese manufacturers will have 20 percent of their capacity in the United States, and by 1993, their U.S. production is likely to exceed 2.5 million units, doubling

EXHIBIT 4–2
Foreign Relationships with Korean Automobile Companies

Manufacturer	Estimated 1988 Automobile Production Capacity (000 vehicles)	Overseas Equity Interest	Technical Tieups and Parts Supply
Hyundai	647	Mitsubishi (15%)	Mitsubishi passenger cars bus and truck
Daewoo	163	General Motors (50%)	Opel (Germany) passenger cars Isuzu & Nissan truck and bus
Kia	249	Ford (10%)	Mazda passenger cars
		Mazda (8%)	Mitsubishi express bus
		C. Itoh (2%)	Shinmeiwa special cars

the volume of exports to which the U.S. government has limited them. Much of this production seems destined for the European market. The total capacity of the 12 Japanese-owned U.S. plants recently built or under construction could eventually reach 3.4 million units.

Governments have influenced competition in other ways. Safety and pollution regulations have a great impact on the industry and further serve to raise development costs. And there has been direct government intervention, especially in Europe, to encourage mergers or to support manufacturers that would otherwise not be viable.

New Manufacturing Paradigms

Ever since Henry Ford introduced the Model T, the key to competitive advantage in the automobile industry has been manufacturing. Ford's introduction of mass-production techniques and scientific methods replaced the skilled craftsmen of the early 1900s with low-skilled, assembly-line workers and labor-saving equipment. By 1913, manufacturing in Ford plants has been largely broken down into tasks taking between ten seconds and one minute.[8] Companies like Ford and General Motors built their competitive strength between the wars on large-scale plants, each dedicated to a narrow range of models.

The strength of the Japanese automobile industry is based on a third manufacturing paradigm, largely developed after World War II, through the work of Toyota engineer Ohno Tai-ichi. By introducing participative management techniques based on team problem solving and multitasking, and combining them with just-in-time inventory control, Toyota was able to improve productivity dramatically. By 1983, it was producing 120 percent more vehicles per worker than U.S. manufacturers. Landed cost differentials between U.S. and Japanese producers were between $1,000 and $1,600 per vehicle.

More remarkable, this performance was achieved with higher quality, smaller production lots, and greater product diversity. In 1987, quality, in terms of defects per 100 units, was still three times better in the best Japanese plants in the late 1980s than in the best U.S. and European plants.

The Toyota system has now been taken up in some form by all the Japanese manufacturers and has been successfully transplanted to Japanese-owned factories in the United States. It is now spreading to U.S. manufacturers, but European performance still lags in both productivity and quality.

The strength of the Japanese competitive advantage has been maintained by continual attention to ways of improving performance targets. There are now signs that a new manufacturing paradigm is emerging, with the development of miniplants capable of achieving the same high levels of productivity and quality and continuing product diversity, but giving much greater flexibility for tackling overseas markets.

Shortening Product Lives

The competitive advantage gained by Japanese companies in manufacturing has been coupled with a move to shorter product lives, with frequent facelifts and a proliferation of variants in order to widen consumer appeal. Western producers have been slow to follow this trend.

The domestic Japanese automobile market is intensely competitive. The adoption of greater model variety and shorter product lives as a competitive weapon has in turn directed attention to the product-development process itself. For example, Honda has instituted a "rugby" approach to product development, in which the design, prototype, engineering, and production-engineering tasks overlap. Suppliers are integrated fully into the development program. Product development times are typically $3^{1}/_{2}$ years, compared with 5 years in the West, and the model replacement cycle is 4 years rather than 8 or 10.

Collaborative Strategies

Against this background, different forms of strategic partnership have emerged in the vehicle industry. As with many industries, collaboration was relatively rare before the mid- to late 1970s. Since then, the number of tie-ins has grown, with the result that most manufacturers now have a complex web of international partnerships.

The most visible are the many full and partial mergers that took place in the late 1970s and early 1980s, particularly in Europe. Examples include the formation of Iveco in 1975 from the truck interests of Fiat and Klockner Humboldt Deutz. This was originally an 80–20 venture, with Fiat the majority shareholder, but it is now entirely owned by Fiat. Other recent examples include the mergers between General Motors and Volvo heavy trucks in the United States in 1986 and between DAF and British Leyland trucks in 1987.

Many of these arrangements, although called "joint ventures," are better described as phased withdrawals or exit strategies by one of the partners, with full control eventually passing to the other. Such strategies are an alternative where acquisition would be politically difficult or commercially damaging. One of the key advantages is that this approach makes it possible to change brands over a period of time; but the primary objective is the achievement of scale economies, usually through a combination of cost and ultimately model rationalization, together with the reduction of overcapacity and penetration by the more aggressive partner into new geographic markets.

The objective is similar in various joint development projects. An early example was the Club of Four, set up by DAF, Volvo, Iveco, and Renault to develop light- and middle-weight truck chassis. Fiat and Peugeot collaborated on the development of a fuel-efficient, electronically controlled engine in 1980. In 1990, Renault and Volvo announced a complex series of cross-shareholdings that would underpin future joint development. Volvo expects to achieve savings of some $400 million a year from the deal before the decade is out.

Perhaps the most extensive collaboration to share development costs and pool expertise so far has been that between Austin Rover and Honda.

The relationship started in 1979, with Austin Rover importing a Honda model, the Ballade, for assembly in the United Kingdom as the Triumph Acclaim. Honda earned a license fee and supplied major components and production machinery. The relationship developed further through the modification by Austin Rover of the Honda Accord for the British market, and the joint development of the XX Luxury car. The latter is sold as the Legend by Honda, and as the Rover 800 by Rover. Another joint development—to produce a medium-size car—is in progress.

This relationship is one of the most enduring strategic partnerships of the period. It satisfied Austin Rover's objective of filling vital gaps in the range of models at relatively low cost, and it helped Honda, a company that did not begin to manufacture cars until 1962, to acquire much-needed skills in large-car design and manufacture, particularly for the European market. It is a fascinating example of an alliance between two companies in sharply contrasting competitive positions. Austin Rover was steadily falling behind in international competitiveness and needed urgent short-term action to prevent collapse. Honda was rapidly increasing its international competitive strength and wanted to accelerate long-term growth by acquiring new design capabilities.

Automobile companies also cooperate to gain access to difficult export markets. A strategic partnership with a local manufacturer is not generally necessary for overseas companies wishing to sell into the U.S. and European markets. In several cases, however, Japanese companies have chosen to enter the United States market in this way. Toyota, for example, the largest and most cautious of Japanese manufacturers, negotiated a joint manufacturing venture with General Motors (NUMMI) as a first step in its U.S. manufacturing strategy. This was followed by a wholly owned plant. Mitsubishi has a similar joint-venture project with Chrysler.

The problem for Western companies selling into Japan has been more difficult. Three of the major U.S. manufacturers bought into Japanese companies in the 1970s, but the results have been disappointing. In 1988, Japan still imported only 131,000 vehicles; VW/Audi, a company without equity links, held the largest share.

The greatest benefit that U.S. companies have gained from these investments has probably been the opportunity to learn Japanese manufacturing skills. Certainly, the evidence suggests that U.S. companies have come closer to Japanese productivity and quality levels than European manufacturers that do not have these links. General Motors entered its NUMMI joint venture with Toyota with precisely this objective. Chrysler is drawing similar benefits from its Diamond Star joining manufacturing venture with Mitsubishi. After its 25-percent investment in Mazda in 1979, Ford launched an "after Japan" program in 1980 to introduce Japanese manufacturing methods into its factories.

Finally, strategic partnerships have an important role to play in securing low-cost sources of production of more basic models. In Europe, General Motors and Ford have long been accustomed to adjusting the balance of production in response to medium-term cost and exchange-rate movements.

If competitive advantage is inevitably flowing to companies like Korea's Daewoo or Taiwan's Lio Ho, and foreign companies are not allowed to establish 100-percent-owned subsidiaries, it can make sense for them to acquire an equity participation. General Motors' 50-percent investment in Daewoo may be a clear indicator of the way to survive in a global economy. However, giving up a part of a company's core business is not a decision to be made lightly, and gaining the financial benefits of this kind of relationship is more difficult than it looks.

Two new twists have recently been added to this story. When the Japanese yen continued to strengthen and cost-cutting measures at home ran out of steam, the Japanese were forced to move production to offshore plants for cost reasons, especially in the fiercely cost-competitive small-car segment. For example, Honda, Mazda, and Mitsubishi all either announced or were known to be considering exporting cars from their U.S. plants to Japan, and Mitsubishi is procuring its entry-level Precis range for the United States from its Korean affiliate, Hyundai.

Meanwhile, there was a flurry of activity as the European manufacturers rushed to take advantage of new opportunities in Eastern Europe. EEC car makers had long been active in the Soviet-bloc economies. In particular, Fiat helped the U.S.S.R. and Poland set up factories to make replicas of one of Fiat's designs; the same models, largely unchanged, are still exported by Russia today.

A string of new deals has opened the 1990s—involving Volkswagen, Opel (General Motors' West German subsidiary), Daimler Benz, and Peugeot. The opportunity is twofold: a market with as many consumers as Western Europe but currently buying only a fifth as many cars, and a source of low-cost manufacturing. Spain, currently the low-cost European production base for VW and General Motors, may need to re-examine where its competitive advantage really lies.

THE TELECOMMUNICATIONS INDUSTRY

By the 1960s, the telecommunications industry, rather like the automobile industry, had reached a position of maturity, at least in a technological sense. There were only gradual changes in the design of electromechanical exchanges and transmission technology, and product lives were long. The industry was characterized by national players, supported by the government-controlled network operators. Profitability was guaranteed largely by the internationally incompatible equipment and the long-term supply contracts that followed.

International trade was very limited (it remains only about 12 percent of world production), and the only real multinational was ITT, a company operating largely through highly autonomous, partly owned local subsidiaries. The only significant competition for orders was in the developing-country markets where there were no local suppliers.

The last 15 years have seen two dramatic changes that torpedoed this cost environment—the appearance in the mid–1970s of the microprocessor-based digital switch and the beginning of progressive deregulation in national markets. The result is an industry structure largely out of step with international market conditions.

Discontinuities of this magnitude occur only occasionally in most industries. They provide an opportunity for major changes in market position, as the traditional keys to long-term competitive advantage are replaced. In this case there were two discontinuities simultaneously—one technological, one marketing. The result was to send companies scurrying to form new partnerships that take advantage of the opportunities and adapt to the new environment.

Technological Discontinuities

Highly complex changes in technology came at a dizzying pace in this sector in the 1980s and '90s. R&D costs have soared against the background of a shift in the economics of competition, and the way has been opened for new competitors to challenge the established players.

The broadest development, digital technology, affects all parts of the telecommunications network—public-exchange (PBX), private-exchange (PABX), and terminal equipment. Software is the key to good products, and steady improvements in the power of semiconductor components have made it possible to develop increasingly feature-rich equipment.

CASE 4-4
AT&T and Philips Telecommunications (APT)—A Lesson in Taking Control

APT is a new company established in 1983 to develop, manufacture, and market telecommunications equipment outside North America.

By the beginning of the 1980s, Philips, with only 1.5 percent of the world telecommunications market, was having increasing difficulties in financing the level of R&D needed to remain competitive. The new digital public switch being developed in-house was behind schedule, and it was decided to shelve the project and look for an outside partner.

Philips was in constant touch with a number of industry players and had for many years maintained a close relationship with Bell Laboratories. Discussions in a quite different area opened the way for negotiations on a joint venture with AT&T.

For AT&T, the timing was ideal. The end of its U.S. monopoly and the liberalization of overseas telecommunications markets triggered a search for means of expanding overseas. Philips's existing marketing network appeared to provide the entree AT&T needed into the potentially lucrative European market.

The negotiations to create APT took some 18 months, and formal agreement was finally reached in March 1983. Originally as a 50–50 joint venture incorporated in the Netherlands, the new company took over all of Philips Telecom International's assets, together with its 4,000 development, production, and marketing personnel. AT&T's principal contribution was the 5ESS public switch.

For AT&T, APT provided access to the European market. Although equipment was initially imported from the United States and adapted for the local markets, all manufacturing was subsequently moved to the Netherlands, and the venture was given a high degree of autonomy in product policy and marketing.

Performance during the first four years of APT's life was disappointing. Significant orders were restricted to the Netherlands and the United Kingdom, and attempts to become France's second supplier were thwarted by the French government. In April 1987, a consortium bid for CGCT led by APT was rejected in favor of Ericsson and Matra. The decision was a bitter disappointment to both APT and AT&T.

APT has instead turned to attempting alliances with other national players. Despite long discussions with Italy's STET, its first success was in Spain, where in 1987 it took a 51-percent holding in a new company formed with Amper SA to handle orders from the Spanish national telephone company, Compania Nacional Telefonica de España. Under the agreement, the new company took on 450 employees from the troubled Spanish telecommunications company Marconi España.

Meanwhile, AT&T had decided that it wanted to take more direct control of APT's fortunes. After negotiations lasting 12 months, it was agreed that AT&T should buy a further 10 percent of APT's equity from Philips, thus increasing its shareholding to 60 percent. At the same time, it was agreed that APT should have much greater access to AT&T technology across a broader product range. The move was followed by a change in name to AT&T Network Systems, because Philips does not allow companies in which it has minority interest to carry its name.

Additional outside shareholders are still being sought among Europe's national telecommunications companies, although from now on AT&T will retain a majority shareholding.

The greatest impact has been on public switching equipment, the "flagship" product of most large companies and the entrée for sales of end-user equipment. While unit costs have fallen (switch prices fell from $1,000 to $300 per line in just four years), by the mid-1980s the cost of launching, supporting, and continuing the ongoing development of a public switch was estimated at $100 million a year. It was widely argued that companies needed at least 8 percent of the world market to achieve an adequate return on investment.[9] The next generation of public switches to be developed in the 1990s is expected to cost $2 billion to $3 billion, not far short of the cost of a big commercial jet. By that time, companies will also have to come to terms with a new discontinuity—optoelectronic technology.

Companies are spending up to 12 percent of sales on R&D to maintain their positions. Many of the smaller players do not have the resources to stay in the business alone, and the realignments that have already taken place are likely to be followed by a further sharp reduction in the number of companies currently manufacturing PBX equipment.

Some players have responded better than others to the challenge of new technology. L.M. Ericsson, heavily dependent on competitive overseas markets, has perhaps been the most successful. Many companies found themselves at the beginning of the 1980s without strong products, their position preserved largely through the protected nature of their markets.

The shift toward digital technology has also changed the economics of competition. The fixed costs of R&D are now more important than the variable cost of manufacturing, and companies have had to switch their emphasis from manufacturing cost reduction to generating sales sufficient to finance R&D. As a result, there has been strong pressure on margins as companies scramble to build market share. The resulting downward pressure on prices still further undermines the smaller companies' ability to fund the high levels of R&D required to remain competitive.

At the same time, the opportunities in the worldwide telecommunications market are enormous, as countries all over the world step up programs to replace analog switches with digital technology. World demand is forecasted to grow by about 10 percent a year until 1995.

An additional effect of developments in digital technology is that the public networks will offer higher capacity and greater intelligence. New offerings called value-added network services (VANS) are emerging. Many hardware suppliers have established joint ventures to exploit these opportunities.

In the PABX and terminal-equipment sectors, digital technology has created a convergence of the computer and telecommunications markets. The computer manufacturers recognize that, as hardware costs fall, their future lies in system integration. Networking and telecommunications will be an important part of their business. And by the same token, the networks provided by the telecommunications companies will support an increasingly sophisticated and wide-ranging mixture of information-processing equipment.

For example, the opportunities offered by the convergence of information technology and telecommunications were already clearly recognized in the motto "Computers and Communication," adopted by NEC more than 10 years ago. Since then, NEC has steadily built up the internal technological competences required to compete in the new markets it expected to emerge, both by internal investment and through joint ventures with Western partners.

Other important technical developments are accelerating the convergence between the telecommunications and IT industries, and involving new technologies beyond those traditional in telecommunications. Optical fiber has radically altered the nature of the transmission sector. Its superior band width and data-carrying capacity is leading to the displacement of copper wire for long-haul voice and data transmission in information-intensive sectors. And its advantages over conventional cabling systems is in turn making possible the development of the next generation of telecommunications network technology—the integrated services digital network (ISDN). This will allow the simultaneous transmission of speech, computer data, text, images, and video over the public telecom network. By the early 1990s, it is estimated, 5 percent of telephone users will be ISDN subscribers. Trials are already taking place in Europe. Fujitsu is one of the most active companies in developing products for the new market. It has been estimated that by the early 1990s, 5 percent of telephone users will be ISDN subscribers, although recent evidence suggests that ISDN will not be as attractive as originally expected—underlying again the risks of investing in new technology.

The increasing sophistication of digital technology has fostered the development of new types of services in mobile communications. Originally dominated by the vehicular communications market, the early 1990s is seeing a variety of personal communications equipment and services emerge. These developments are enabled by improvements in digital technology in subscriber equipment and by the availability of digital switches in the mobile network. Some estimates predict that by the year 2000, more than half the subscriber terminals sold in Europe will be mobile.

Taking advantage of these opportunities often requires levels of competence and investment that are not readily available for individual companies.

Market Discontinuities

The pace and complexity of technological change are fundamental reasons for the establishment of strategic partnerships in the telecommunications industry, but the whole vast process of restructuring has really been triggered by the deregulation of the U.S. and European markets.

Deregulation of the U.S. market began with the breakup of AT&T in 1984, opening the U.S. to overseas suppliers, and encouraging U.S. manufacturers to seek overseas markets more vigorously. The result was a strong telecommunications deficit ($1.3 billion by 1985) and political pressure for liberalization elsewhere.

Within Europe, the deregulation process started first in the United Kingdom, where liberalization of the equipment market began in 1981. The process has spread gradually to other countries, and the EEC Telecommunications Green Paper of 1987 sought to eliminate all barriers to telecommunications trade. Its first target is the monopoly exerted by many of the French Telecommunication agencies over the sale of customer-premises equipment. The liberalized European market, worth some $20 billion in equipment, will be a honeypot attracting European and non-European suppliers alike. The European industry, highly fragmented among protected national suppliers, was ill equipped to join battle in this new competitive war. It has therefore been rapidly restructuring to position itself to compete in the more open markets that are emerging.

Deregulation of services is also a growing trend within Europe. The British pioneered this approach by granting a license to Cable & Wireless in 1983 to offer public telecommunications services through its subsidiary, Mercury Communications, and the subsequent privatization of British Telecom a year later. This new attitude generates opportunities both for manufacturers through the fostering of competition, which stimulates market demand, and also for operators in the provision of services. This has been most noticeable in Britain's mobile communications sector, where cellular radio boasted more than 800,000 subscribers divided between two operators in 1989—the largest of any single European country.

This trend is proceeding more slowly in other European countries. A major advance occurred in 1989, when West Germany shed its ultra-conservative approach by breaking up the old Deutsche Bundespost. All services, including mobile and satellite, with the exception only of the base network infrastructure, were opened up to competition.

Deregulation of the Japanese market has been slower, although the agreement in 1987, after much political pressure, to allow Britain's Cable and Wireless to participate in a consortium to provide international telecommunications services represented an important step. On the domestic side, three competitors to the former monopoly carrier, NTT, have been approved and there are signs of increasing price competition in the domestic market.

A further aspect of the internationalization of telecommunications products is the growth of low-cost suppliers in the newly industrialized countries. As some telecommunications products acquire near-commodity status, NIC enterprises are likely to displace manufacturers in the industrial countries, forcing them to procure under OEM contracts if they wish to maintain a full product range. This process is already evident in handsets and more basic equipment. As the technology stabilizes, this pattern will be repeated with higher-cost equipment.

Patterns of Collaboration

Against this background, two broad types of strategic partnership are appearing. The first involves alliances between players already operating in the telecommunications market. The second is alliances between telecommunications firms and companies in other sectors.

Intra-Industry Partnerships

One or more of three specific objectives are involved in intra-industry partnerships. Alliances often contribute to the achievement of all of them:

- Reciprocal market access (especially where regulation hinders free competition).
- Economies of scale in R&D (particularly in the case of large public switches).
- Divestiture. Some forms of partnership provide a relatively painless fadeout strategy. For example, the formation of Alcatel allowed ITT to withdraw from public-switch manufacturing while maintaining a 37-percent stake in the new venture.

Some restructuring has been through conventional acquisitions and mergers. However, many situations require more subtle forms of strategic partnership. When GTE decided to reduce its exposure in the industry in 1986, it chose to sell an 80-percent stake in certain operations to Siemens. Both companies decided to continue selling their existing public switches in competition in the United States—at least for the time being.

An early move in the European restructuring process was the creation of AT&T and Philips Telecommunications (APT). This equity joint venture was established in 1983, initially on a 50–50 basis. The largest new European grouping is called Alcatel, formed by the merger of the telecommunications interests of ITT and the French government-owned CGE (Compagnie Générale de'Électricité).

One of the most fiercely fought battles in this arena was over the French government's denationalization of CGCT, France's second-largest telecommunications manufacturer. Bidders included APT, Siemens, and Northern Telecom. After much debate, the government chose a consortium involving L.M. Ericsson and Matra.

The arrangement is a superb example of the creative exercise of national industrial policy. Arguably the strongest force in the European industry from a technical point of view, Ericsson was given management control and access to 16 percent of the French PBX market. However, its equity stake in the new venture is limited to 25 percent, the majority going to Matra, its partner in the consortium. In return, Ericsson has agreed to set up an R&D facility in France and to develop a new European mobile telephone system jointly with Matra.

Many telecom companies also make wide use of OEM agreements with other suppliers to fill gaps in product range. Major players need a presence across all market segments—PBX, PABX, and terminal equipment. Some choose to manufacture themselves for just one or two of these sectors. Besides supplying through OEM customers, the stronger companies have also used local joint ventures and made strategic investments to strengthen their international marketing networks. For example, Northern Telecom of Canada has made a major strategic investment in Britain's STC, seeing it as a means of gaining access to the European market.

Partners in Other Industries
The second type of partnership involves collaborations between telecommunications companies and firms in other sectors, such as the computer industry and consumer electronics. Such partnerships seek to achieve:

- Access to new and complementary skills such as software development in the case of PABXs, manufacturing skills in the case of fiber-optic cable, and microwave technology in the case of cellular radio.
- Access to new distribution channels. Firms that develop technology from outside the telecommunications sector will often have to rely on established telecommunications companies to distribute their products.

Some of these inter-industry partnerships have taken the form of new companies established as equity joint ventures to exploit new or growing market opportunities. Examples include BT&D Ltd., set up by British Telecom and du Pont to exploit the optoelectronic-component market, and Siecor, a fiber-optic cable joint venture involving Siemens and Corning.

The investment necessary to participate in Europe's new mobile telecommunications industry, $1.5 billion, makes a consortium approach virtually mandatory, and the choice of partners defines the competitive strategy for Europe and the United States. One entrant, Unitel, is a good illustration. Its four shareholders are STC, a telecommunications equipment manufacturer; Thorn EMI, a leading consumer-products retail and rental company; Deutsche Bundespost Telekom, the West German telecommunications network; and U.S. West, a telecommunications and cable-television operation.

Where convergence affects a company's core business, other means of acquiring new technological competences have had to be sought. Some of these alliances have been fraught with difficulties. For example, in an attempt to acquire PABX technology, IBM first negotiated an OEM agreement with Mitel, a fast-growing Canadian telecommunications equipment company. When Mitel's product, the SX 2000, slipped behind schedule, IBM canceled the agreement and switched to Rolm, taking a 15-percent equity stake in 1983. IBM acquired Rolm outright the following year.

The emergence of more-aggressive private network owners through deregulation and privatization—such as NTT in Japan, the Bell operating companies in the United States, and British Telecom in the United Kingdom—will provide a new source of venture partners. In fact, over the next few years the whole pattern of competitive advantage in the telecommunications industry is likely to change, with the development of increasingly feature-rich customer-premises equipment and the emergence of truly global mass markets. The factors for success in the telecommunications markets of the 1990s are likely to be quite different from those of the 1970s and 1980s.

THE SEMICONDUCTOR INDUSTRY

The semiconductor industry differs in many important characteristics from the others discussed so far. The commercial economies of the industry are dictated by three fundamental factors: short product lives, continuous innovation that leads to repeated technological discontinuities, and high investment costs. (See Exhibit 4-3). Together, these factors mean that survivors exploit new products rapidly, building up maximum sales while margins are still high.

The speed with which a technical lead is eroded and the high R&D expenditures required for technology renewal give international market exploitation and urgency virtually unparalleled in any other industry. This has led to companies forging extensive networks of global alliances and means that the speed with which new plants are brought on line can be a critical determinant of overall profitability. It also creates

EXHIBIT 4–3
Investment Required for Memory-Chip Production

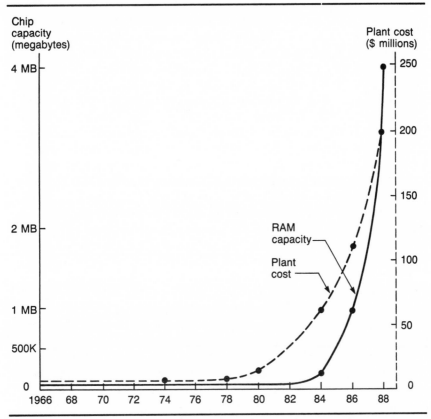

strong pressure on prices and provides a huge financial incentive for companies to try to achieve maximum plant utilization.

The economics of the industry are also affected by two important relationships. The first is the interdependence of the memory- and logic-chip parts of the business. Continuous process improvement is an important feature of the industry. This is essentially a learning process linked to production volume. The high-volume Dynamic Random Access Memory (DRAM) chip business, the most price-competitive sector of the market, offers particular opportunities for honing manufacturing skills and improving quality. Lessons learned can then be applied in other sectors. By giving up this market to the Japanese and later to the Koreans, U.S. manufacturers' ability to improve competitive

CASE 4–5
The Motorola–Toshiba Alliance

The year 1986 was a watershed in the world semiconductor industry, with a deep recession and aggressive pricing by Japanese companies leading to claims of dumping in export markets. In July, the U.S–Japanese Semiconductor Trade Agreement was signed. It had two objectives: to improve access for foreign manufacturers to the Japanese market, and to prevent Japanese companies from dumping products at prices below fair market value. Japan's Ministry of International Trade and Industry administered the agreement with rigor, effectively imposing production controls on Japanese producers.

Not surprisingly, price competition had been strongest at the commodity end of the semiconductor market. Successive U.S. manufacturers, including the leader Motorola, had pulled back from this segment, concentrating instead on the more lucrative microprocessor market, where its share was approximately 50 percent. However, in the long term this is a dangerous strategy, as the high volumes involved in chip production yield important process technology improvements, which spill over into other parts of the industry.

This situation provided the background to the most imaginative alliance signed by any semiconductor company.

Motorola's two key aims were to re-enter the memory-chip market and to strengthen its position in Japan, the largest market in the world for semiconductors and therefore crucial to overall global competitiveness. Though Motorola already had one Japanese manufacturing plant, sales were growing much more slowly than it wished and stood at less than a half of those achieved by Texas Instruments.

In contrast, Toshiba's strength was in memory chips, in which it was the world's leading producer, with 17 percent of the market. Toshiba's position in microprocessors, however, was much weaker, leaving it behind NEC and Hitachi.

Yet Toshiba recognized a strategic need to strengthen its position in mainframe computers and telecommunications. For this it needed access to microprocessor technology.

The agreement between Motorola and Toshiba involved exchanging Motorola's microprocessor technology for Toshiba's chip technology and its help in penetrating the Japanese market. Toshiba has agreed to provide access to its own sales and distribution channels to help Motorola achieve its objectives. The speed at which Motorola's technology is made available, however, is carefully governed in the agreement by the rate at which its share of the Japanese market increases.

The first step involved Motorola assembling Toshiba memory chips and marketing them in its own name. Motorola reciprocated by supplying Toshiba with 8-, 16-, and 32-bit microprocessors.

The next important stage in the technology transfer process was the creation of a jointly owned manufacturing plant, Tohoku Semiconductor Corp., which began operating in Sendai, Japan, in July 1988. Each company has committed $120 million to the venture, and each supplies 50 of the venture's 340 employees.

Under the agreement, production initially focused on memory chips that used Toshiba's process technology, and on 8- and 16-bit microprocessors. This would later be expanded to include Motorola's 32-bit microprocessor technology.

Toshiba's process and design technology was also supplied to other Motorola plants, and full-scale production began in 1988. Further technology exchanges are envisioned until the agreement runs out in 1991.

strength in the logic-chip business has been impaired. Motorola's alliance with Toshiba is in large measure aimed at rebuilding its competence in DRAM manufacture, and other U.S. semiconductor firms are also considering how to reenter the business.

The second area of interdependence is with customers. Advances in semiconductor technology provide a continuing stream of opportunities for companies in a wide range of industries to introduce new products and improve existing ones. The computer and consumer electronics industries are particularly responsive to these changes, and individual product lives are short.

The interdependence between customer and manufacturer gives the integrated electronics groups, such as NEC and Philips, a number of important advantages over companies not so linked. First, it enables users to get early access to new generations of semiconductors so that they can be designed into products early. Second, and by the same token, these internal sales enable the semiconductor producer to crank up production more rapidly. And third, it enables both producer and user to ride out the extreme cycles to which the industry is prone, the users having greater security of supply during periods of shortage and the manufacturers having a baseload of market demand during periods of overcapacity. Consequently, a number of alliances have been formed between users and suppliers, especially in the United States, aimed at reducing vulnerability to intermittent shortages and the high prices associated with these cycles.

An important development in the 80s was the introduction of Application-Specific Integrated Circuits (ASICs), which represent a dramatic departure from traditional semiconductors in that users produce their own designs that are tailored to specific products which may be produced in relatively small volumes.

From the beginning, the ASIC market has been dominated by small companies, often started by people from the traditional semiconductor plants who compete by offering more personalized service. In response, the established semiconductor manufacturers have had to modify their marketing approach, going head-to-head in the ASIC markets to protect their standard product lines.

Local Development Patterns

The semiconductor industry has developed in widely varying ways in different countries, so it is sensible to look at industry history in each member of the Triad and in the NICs before examining the types of strategic alliance that are prevalent.

The United States
The first companies to exploit the invention of the transistor and develop a semiconductor industry were U.S. companies, often with an established business in a related field or aiming at a particular application for electronic devices. Companies such as Fairchild Camera and Instrument, Motorola, and Texas Instruments developed their semiconductor divisions during the 1950s. In the cases of Motorola and TI, semiconductor operations have grown to become their major business activity.

As the market expanded in the 1960s, a second generation of U.S. companies appeared with a much more focused business strategy. They were often founded by groups leaving existing concerns, particularly Fairchild, to exploit a particular market or technical expertise.

Technological development and venture funding led to the founding of Intel Corporation and National Semiconductor. Both are now $1-billion-plus operations. They grew with, and established a dominance in, the logic sector of the market by developing families of devices that have secured strong positions in a wide variety of applications.

More recently, a third generation of companies has emerged that seek to exploit a particular technology or niche market instead of attacking the well-established leaders head on. They have often been founded by breakaway groups from established companies, with which they may retain close contact (and possibly even establish an equity relationship). LSI Logic and VLSI Technology have emerged as leaders in the new ASIC market discussed a moment ago. Altera Corporation, founded by a group from Intel, developed a technology for manufacturing programmable logic arrays (PLAs), which it subsequently licensed to Intel.

Still more recently, U.S. companies have taken the lead in developing and marketing Reduced Instruction Set Computer (RISC) microprocessors, which offer an improvement in processing speed of four to ten times over traditional designs. Again, this new development provides the opportunity for new entrants to the industry, such as Sun Microsystems, whose spare chip design is manufactured by an international network of licensees, including Fujitsu, Philips, and Texas Instruments.

In parallel with the growth of the mainstream semiconductor companies, a number of others whose core businesses lie elsewhere have developed in-house expertise to feed their internal requirements for semiconductor technology. The major example of this type of development is IBM, the second-largest manufacturer of semiconductors after NEC. All of IBM's production is consumed internally.

Other companies with a well-developed captive capability include AT&T, Matsushita, and General Motors, which owns Delco and Hughes Electronics. General Motors uses its products internally in addition to selling them on the open market.

Japan
Over the past 15 years, Japan's semiconductor industry has developed to a point where it now dominates many market sectors. Increasingly, Japanese suppliers are displacing U.S. manufacturers as the largest volume suppliers of integrated circuits. Three reasons for this success should be emphasized—the effectiveness with which Japanese companies have developed new-process technology, the effort put into general improvements in manufacturing performance, and the linkage with in-house customers.

CASE 4–6
Fujitsu's Mainframe Computer Alliances

Fujitsu was formed in 1935 as a spin-off from Fuji Electric, itself originally founded as a joint venture with Siemens under the aegis of the Furukawa group. Siemens still retains a 7.3-percent stake in Fuji Electric, which in turn owns 15 percent of Fujitsu.

Today, Fujitsu is Japan's largest domestic computer maker, with more than 50,000 employees and sales of some $15 billion.

After World War II, Fujitsu maintained close links with Siemens, which provided the basis for development of Fujitsu's early computer technology. However, the increasing dominance of world computer markets by U.S. manufacturers, led by IBM, made this an inadequate strategy on which to build an internationally competitive computer business.

In 1966, MITI launched the heavily subsidized Super High Performance Computer Development Project, the first program under the Large Scale Project described in Chapter 7. Participants included Fujitsu, Hitachi, Mitsubishi, Iki, NEC, and Toshiba. Fujitsu and Hitachi were assigned the task of developing IBM-compatible machines.

The next important move in Fujitsu's development was the establishment of a relationship with Amdahl Corporation, a U.S. venture capital-backed startup company founded by Gene Amdahl, designer of IBM's 360 mainframe computer.

Amdahl's strategy was to develop mainframes that would be compatible with IBM's 370 series, launched in 1971. The link with Amdahl provided the ideal opportunity for Fujitsu to acquire both product and design skills with which to ease its own transition into the IBM-compatible market.

The first agreement involved establishing the Fujitsu California Institute on Amdahl's premises. However, Amdahl's development costs turned out to be higher than expected, and Fujitsu's financial involvement gradually increased. In 1972, Fujitsu purchased 24 percent of Amdahl's stock, later increasing this to 49 percent when the venture-capital investment was sold.

Amdahl's financial problems forced a scaling down of the internal R&D program, and the companies agreed that Fujitsu should provide part of the product range on an OEM basis, a commercial arrangement that began in 1975. Since then, this technical and marketing collaboration has continued. Fujitsu manufactures core components for Amdahl-designed machines in Japan, while Amdahl has become Fujitsu's OEM outlet for Fujitsu-designed mainframes, supercomputers, and peripheral equipment in North America. A fifty/ fifty joint venture, Amdahl International Ltd., was created to market Amdahl products outside North America and Japan, and by 1987 30 percent of Amdahl's sales came from Europe. In 1988, Fujitsu also announced plans to import certain Amdahl machines.

In 1978, Fujitsu signed up a second major POEM customer, Siemens, providing an important distribution channel for Fujitsu IBM-compatible mainframes in Europe. By 1986, imported Fujitsu mainframes accounted for 10 percent of Siemens' 3-billion Deutschemark data-processing equipment revenues.

Fujitsu signed another European partnership with Britain's ICL in 1981. However, because ICL's business was based on its own proprietary operating system, a straightforward OEM sourcing agreement was not possible. Instead, Fujitsu provides the core for ICL's Series 39 mainframes, using semiconductor components manufactured to ICL's design.

Fujitsu's OEM relationships are important in supporting economies of scale, not just in mainframe manufacturing but also in R&D and in Fujitsu's semiconductor manufacturing business.

Many American companies complain that their Japanese competitors have been, in effect, dumping their products, although in an industry characterized by such rapidly advancing technology as semiconductors, it is difficult to distinguish unfair tactics from learning-curve pricing. In any event, competition is—for the time being—restrained by the U.S.-Japan Semiconductor Trade Agreement.

In the 1970s, MITI sponsorship of the VLSI project was crucial in accelerating investment in Japanese manufacturing technology. This was an extremely successful cooperative R&D venture in which many of the major Japanese electronics companies were involved. As a result, they now have a dominant position in the high-density-memory marketplace, forcing many U.S. companies to concentrate on more specialized logic chips and microprocessors. By 1988, five Japanese companies had an estimated share of about 85 percent of the world DRAM market; a year later, the Japanese had 90 percent of the emerging 1MB market.

In parallel with the thrust into high-density process technology, the Japanese have concentrated on refining general manufacturing techniques. This has further reinforced their position in commodity memory products where yields, and consequently, manufacturing costs and quality, are the key factors in determining success in the marketplace. The effects have been beneficial in other sectors of the industry as well.

The competitive effects of these technological strengths have been reinforced by the industry's structure. In Japan, most semiconductor operations are divisions of much larger, diverse electronic and industrial concerns. NEC, Fujitsu, Toshiba, and Hitachi are all major players in the semiconductor market, but they are also well established in the major user industries such as computers, communications, and consumer electronics. Other Japanese companies, led by Seiko, Sony and Sanyo, have also recently developed semiconductor capabilities, primarily to serve their internal product-development requirements.

Japan also has a number of recent entrants in the semiconductor sector as a result of corporate diversification by companies with no strong history in the electronics sector. NMB Semiconductors and Nippon Steel have both invested heavily. NMB is a particularly useful example of a Japanese startup. Funded by Minebea, a ball-bearing manufacturer, NMB invested $340 million in two of the most advanced production lines in the world before acquiring product licenses and design expertise by forming alliances with U.S. startups. Within four years, NMB had achieved sales of nearly $300 million.

Europe
In terms of industry structure, Europe more closely resembles Japan than it does the United States. While some pure semiconductor companies have developed—Inmos, the United Kingdom's developer of the revolutionary transputer (computer on a chip), and Italy's SGS are examples—the major European players are divisions of large, diverse conglomerates. Notable among them are Siemens, Philips, and L.M. Ericsson.

Europe has also benefited from a long tradition of inward investment by American and, more recently, Japanese technology companies. Investments have taken the form both of wholly owned subsidiaries of companies that include Motorola, TI, and IBM, and of joint ventures such as Matra-Harris and Eurotechnique, created in 1980 as a joint venture between National Semiconductor and Saint Gobain of France.

These joint ventures were typically a marriage of imported technology and European money. They have not been particularly successful.

Newly Industrialized Countries

Other important areas of activity include Korea and Taiwan. The Korean marketplace is dominated by four diverse trading conglomerates: Samsung, Hyundai, Daewoo, and Goldstar. All of them have recently invested heavily in developing a semiconductor capability. This has been achieved through a complex web of joint-venture agreements or other types of collaboration with U.S. and Japanese partners. Samsung has cooperation agreements with Intel, Micron, and Sharp, and by 1987 was already seventh in the world in DRAM production. Hyundai is closely linked with GI and TI. Goldstar's semiconductor operation is a joint venture with AT&T.

In Taiwan, the semiconductor industry has developed around ERSO, a government-funded research organization. In many cases, U.S.-trained Taiwanese have tapped the U.S. capital market to fund technically driven startup operations.

Patterns of Collaboration

This pattern of high risk and high reward, combined with rapid technological change, has a significant effect on the types of joint venture used. Four forms of strategic partnership predominate: precompetitive collaborative R&D, cross-licensing agreements, alliances involving investments by users, and joint ventures to transfer technology.

Collaborative R&D

As we have seen, progress in semiconductors depends largely on advances in process technology. New generations of semiconductors will be based on entirely new approaches to manufacturing, and advances are also closely linked with scientific discovery in the materials sciences. Research and development is therefore enormously expensive and very complex. As a result, there has been a growing trend toward collaborative R&D, led by the highly successful Japanese VLSI project in the late 1970s.

In theory, these activities are often carried out under the guise of "pre-competitive" collaborative R&D, a term that avoids antitrust problems and helps secure government financing. In practice, the dividing line between pre-competitive and near-market R&D is often obscure.

In Europe, the principal example was the Mega Project, a joint program of Philips and Siemens to develop 1MB and 4MB RAMS. The Mega Project, completed in 1988, was followed by JESSI (Joint European Submicron Semiconductor Initiative), a $5-billion project to develop 64MB DRAMs and logic chips. JESSI, which is operated under the EUREKA pan-European collaborative R&D program, at first involved Philips, Siemens, and SGS Thomson; IBM was admitted later. In the U.S., MCC and especially Sematech, a consortium of more than a dozen semiconductor companies, are similarly organized. However, the more ambitious joint venture to develop a 1-billion-byte chip plant—U.S. Memories—failed after the world shortage of DRAMs ended in the second half of 1989.

The patterns of collaboration on semiconductor development are becoming increasingly international. Besides its participation in JESSI, IBM also has a separate one-to-one agreement to work on 65MB DRAMs with Siemens, while in 1988, TI and Hitachi announced an important agreement to collaborate on the design and production of 16MB DRAMs.

There are also many smaller, more specialized collaborations. An example is AT&T Microelectronics' agreement with Nokia-Mobira to develop digital signal processing components for the new GSM pan-European cellular system.

In parallel with these activities, many companies have established linkages with university centers of excellence. The Semiconductor Research Corporation (SRC) sponsors research on behalf of a consortium of U.S. companies, but most also have direct linkages. A study in 1986 of 17 major U.S. university research groups showed widespread industry support involving 96 companies. The total of their technical budgets was $93 million. The companies involved included both users with in-house semiconductor capabilities (such as DEC, which sponsored five teams) and semiconductor merchants such as Motorola (with six). The list also included Hitachi and NEC, sponsoring one university each.[10]

Second-Source Agreements

The most common form of collaboration between semiconductor manufacturers is second-source agreements. A company with a new product faces a difficult marketing dilemma. As a monopoly supplier, the company will be in a strong position to dictate price once the product is introduced into the market. But because of this monopolistic position, customers are apt to be reluctant to make a commitment to the product. (In this context, it should be noted that in nearly all applications, a similar electronic function can be achieved with different sets of components. Once a particular design is adopted, however, the price of redesigning the circuit because of the non-availability of a key component is significant.)

In addition to extending market access, second-source license agreements attempt to overcome this problem. The licensor provides all the information, mask sets, and anything else required to manufacture the product. In return, the licensor may receive payment in cash or royalties, or in access to technology in which the licensee has an expertise. Just as important is the creation of alternative suppliers to the marketplace.

The original designer's objective is to encourage a number of second-source agreements without losing control or ownership of the technology. For example, an American company might aim for one or two suppliers in Europe and one in Japan. Some companies consistently manage to do this with great skill. Examples of the network of second-source agreements created by leading manufacturers included Intel's agreement for manufacture of the 8086 with Fujitsu (Japan), Matra-Harris and Siemens (Europe), and AMD and Harris (United States); and Motorola's agreement for manufacture of the 68000 with Hitachi (Japan), Philips and Thomson (Europe), and Mostek, Rockwell, and Signetics (United States).

Second-source agreements may develop into broader technology alliances, with several companies sharing the R&D cost of developing a product family. They have also been forged between companies with differing process expertise as a method of introducing, say, NMOS and CMOS versions of a device.

Investments by Users

As we saw earlier, access to secure sources of advanced semiconductor technology can give user companies important competitive advantages in the market. This has led a number of electronics companies to acquire or make strategic investments in suppliers. The best-known example is IBM's investment in Intel, its primary supplier of microprocessors for the personal computer. IBM was reliant on Intel both to fund high levels of R&D and to provide continuity of supply in a very rapidly growing market. But in 1983, IBM accounted for only about 10 percent of Intel's total revenue. To achieve its objectives, and preempt possible Japanese moves to gain control of Intel's operations, IBM acquired a 12-percent interest.

This was rapidly increased to 20 percent. Other examples of this strategy are Wang Laboratories' decision in 1984 to close its internal semiconductor operations in favor of a 15-percent interest in VLSI Technology Inc., and AT&T's 20-percent investment in Sun Microsystems to get its new RISC technology.

An interesting international example is European Silicon Structures (ES2), formed in 1985 to establish a pan-European capability in the emerging ASIC market. ES2 investors include a number of large European companies, all of which have a commercial interest as users of ASIC devices, but none of which wish to participate as an independent player in that market.

Joint Ventures to Transfer Technology

Alliances designed to achieve a permanent transfer of technology include those initiated both by *new* entrants to the industry and by companies wishing to catch up in a particular technology. Licensing, joint ventures, and venture-capital investments in new companies all have a role to play in adopting a technology acquisition strategy adopted.

Several joint ventures to build an indigenous semiconductor business have been organized in Europe. However, the results have not been markedly successful. Examples include Matra-Harris, a joint venture between Matra SA of France and Harris Corp. of the United States, and Austrian Microsystems International (AMI), a joint venture between American Microsystems Inc. of the United States and Voest Alpine of Austria.

A more complex strategy was adopted by Siemens in 1977. After disappointing results from technology exchanges and marketing agreements, it bought a 17-percent share in Advanced Micro Devices and formed a 60–40 joint-venture company to develop and sell microprocessors to OEM manufacturers of telecommunications equipment. The venture broke up a year later.

The companies that have been most successful at building on acquired technology are in Japan and Korea, where licensing and joint ventures have been supported by the aggressive development of indigenous capabilities. One of the most fascinating alliances is an agreement signed by Motorola and Toshiba in 1986. This involves the exchange of Motorola's logic-device technology for access of Toshiba's DRAM manufacturing capability. Motorola hopes in this way to be able to reenter the DRAM market, though the ultimate winner in this game of technology-transfer poker is anybody's guess.

CASE 4–7
The MEGA Project: Rebuilding Europe's
Semiconductor Capabilities

Siemens and Philips are Europe's two largest diversified electronics and electrical engineering companies. Together they employ nearly 700,000 people. Like other companies in these sectors, they face a rapidly changing commercial and technological environment and must make frequent adjustments to their business portfolios.

By 1984, both companies felt increasing pressure to strengthen their semiconductor capabilities, particularly in memory chips—a market that was dominated by their Japanese competitors.

Direct access to semiconductor technology is important for electronics companies for two reasons. *First,* it offers security of supply during the market's frequent periods of undercapacity. *Second,* it provides designers in user divisions with advanced knowledge of availability and technical capabilities. This makes it possible to reduce product lead times by several months. With technology changing so quickly, this often represents a significant proportion of the overall profit-earning window on electronics products.

Short product lives make an in-house capability particularly important in consumer electronics, one of Philips' major businesses. For Siemens, the creation of an internal semiconductor capability was part of a strategy to shift the overall balance of the company's business toward electronics. Automotive electronics and telecommunications were seen as particularly important users.

Philips and Siemens first began collaborative R&D in 1982, with the establishment of a 50-member project to carry out work in semiconductors, computer-assisted design (CAD), and speech recognition. The budget was a relatively modest $4 million. This early collaboration provided an ideal opportunity for the two companies to get to know one another's interest, capabilities, and culture, providing a basis for the much larger MEGA project, launched in 1984.

The aim of the MEGA project was to catch up to Japanese memory chip technology by jointly developing the next generation of manufacturing processes for one- and four-megabit chips. Siemens concentrated on 4MB dynamic RAMs, and Philips on 1MB static RAMs.

The total cost of the MEGA project, including construction of the manufacturing plants, was $1.3 billion. R&D costs were borne fifty/fifty by the two companies, with each receiving a 40-percent subsidy from their respective governments.

The project involved parallel development programs in the two companies. Each had separate project leaders for the four principal areas of R&D—equipment, CAD, technology, and design. It was only rarely that specific R&D tasks were allocated to one or other of the partners. Full-scale manufacturing plants were planned for Regsburg (Siemens) and Hamburg (Philips), each using different production processes. Intellectual property was assigned to the company directly responsible, with the other partner receiving a free license.

Although each company had a high degree of autonomy in the way it pursued its own development programs, there were regular exchanges of information between the terms. There were also a limited number of liaison assignments, typically for periods of six months. Overall coordination was the responsibility of a six-person board, drawn equally from the two companies.

The first prototype products became available in 1987, with full production starting in 1989. However, this was achieved only after key production technology for the 1MB chip was licensed from Japan. Siemens has acknowledged that it is still one to two years behind Japanese manufacturing technology. Moreover, Philips, which must sell 70 percent of its production outside the company if it is to justify the manufacturing investment involved, was forced to postpone plans for the production plant in Hamburg because of slack demand.

Philips and Siemens have widened the scope of their collaboration to include other projects under the EEC's ESPRIT program. They are also planning to collaborate with SGS Thomson, the Italian-French semiconductor manufacturer in the $3.3-billion JESSI (Joint European Semiconductor Silicon) project.

THE BIOTECHNOLOGY INDUSTRY

Biotechnology—the use of biological systems, processes, and products in industry—has been serving man since antiquity. Traditional applications may be so common as to be overlooked. Baking, cheesemaking, and the production of alcohol by sugar fermentation are probably the most pervasive examples.

The first half of the 20th century brought a series of discoveries that led to the creation of a second-generation biotechnology industry. Processing-technology development facilitated the production of penicillin and cephalosporins as antibiotics. Fermentation techniques were applied to produce a range of specialized products including amino acids and enzymes.

The last 15 years have seen the creation of a third-generation biotechnology industry based on genetic engineering. The scientific trigger for this development was the unraveling of the structure of DNA by Crick and Watson in 1953, a discovery itself made possible by advances in X-ray crystallography. DNA is the template by which hereditary information, coded as a sequence of amino acids, is passed down from generation to generation. Once this discovery was made, it was just a question of time before the means were established to manipulate that sequence.

Today biotechnology is, strictly speaking, not an industry at all but an enabling technology. Its applications cover a wide range of industries. They include human health care, agriculture and animal husbandry, and food and drink manufacture. Biotechnology has even been applied to the problem of waste disposal. In health care and agriculture, its influence today is pervasive.

The pharmaceutical industry and allied fields were quickly seen as areas in which the new biotechnology would make its greatest initial impact. For example, cancer research had identified some dozen or so proteins with powerful kill-and-cure abilities for tumors. Biotechnology offered the prospect of producing these proteins artificially. Synthetic insulin was produced after the genetic sequence of amino acids that code for insulin production was determined and incorporated into bacterial cells. Bioprocessing enabled the scale-up production of these insulin-secreting cells, providing relief from diabetes.

Biotechnology also provides a means of producing new diagnostic tests, using monoclonal antibodies to indicate certain clinical conditions. Over the last 15 years, a wide range of diagnostic tests has been developed, ranging from highly accurate pregnancy tests to indicators for multiple sclerosis and cancer.

Probably even more revolutionary in the longer term will be biotechnology's impact on agriculture. Besides the creation of the animal and plant equivalents of human health care products, biotechnology offers the ability to develop new forms of pesticides and herbicides, and the opportunity to affect the food-generating performance of existing species. Many developments are limited only by legal constraints.

Again, examples abound. Foot-and-mouth disease is endemic throughout most of the world. However, current vaccines are both expensive and haphazard in action. Genetically engineering the vaccine could mean a lower cost and more stable product, particularly valuable for the poorer cattle-breeding countries of South America and Africa. Bovine growth hormones control the growth of cattle and thus the profitability of raising them. Synthetic growth hormone synthesized by using recombinant DNA could greatly increase meat production. The use of selective propagation methods for plants is now widespread. Where it could previously take more than 10 years to develop new seed crops, the product lead time is now usually less than one year.

Yet the impact of third-generation biotechnology has so far been slight. Initial success has been achieved in identifying the genes controlling resistance to certain diseases and to herbicides, such as Monsanto's Round-up, and incorporating them into plant cells. A number of other commercial applications are in advanced states of development.

The Economics of Exploitation

More than any other modern technology, biotechnology has its foundation in academic research. In fact, nearly all the important enabling discoveries have come from universities or research establishments. Until the 1970s, the key area of scientific expertise, molecular biology, was virtually unrepresented in industrial companies.

The number of scientists with the skills to develop and apply the new techniques was at first small, and the careers of nearly all were in academic research. The companies whose markets were most likely to be affected by biotechnology suddenly realized that they lacked the technical competence to exploit the new opportunities. At the same time, many academic biotechnologists found that their work had suddenly become very commercial. They had skills that were in short supply and, in some cases, their research pointed toward specific commercial products. Some set up their own companies to exploit this expertise, especially in the United States. The climate in the late 1970s and early 1980s was especially conducive to this, when venture capital was readily available. Investors saw biotechnology as a high-tech industry offering the same potential for explosive growth as the then-new computer companies spawned by the microprocessor revolution just a few years before.

In other countries, without the same entrepreneurial culture, governments took a more active role in exploiting academic expertise. In the United Kingdom, two special exploitation companies, Celltech and Agricultural Genetics Company (AGC), were created and granted rights to government-funded research in medicine and agriculture, respectively. AGC attracted investment by a number of international companies.

Whereas the market entry costs for a new computer business are well within the reach of conventional venture capital, the cost of developing and launching a new drug is prohibitive. New products must be subjected to rigorous and lengthy clinical trials. Side effects must be investigated thoroughly. Every national drug authority has its own stringent approval procedures, and it is difficult to manage the process without a presence in each country. An international distribution and marketing network must be put in place to secure sales, and expensive litigation may be required to combat attempts to infringe on patents.

The challenges for new biotechnology companies concerned with drug development are therefore considerable. Entry costs are vastly greater than were those facing the wave of computer and electronics startups of the 1970s. Only a handful of the new biopharmaceutical companies are likely to grow beyond the research-and-development stage into fullblown pharmaceutical companies, marketing under their own brands and through their own sales forces.

For the established pharmaceutical companies, the scale of investment required to remain competitive is hardly less daunting. In 1988, U.S. drug companies spent $5 billion on R&D, while only 52 new prescription medicines were approved worldwide.

The major drug companies typically spend 10 percent or 15 percent of their revenues on R&D, for the rewards are high. Many large companies remain dependent on just one or two drugs, and continued success requires developing replacements before patent protection expires.

Against this economic background, completing the development and launch of a major pharmaceutical product and remaining competitive longterm is both expensive and risky. The costs and timescales involved in developing biotechnology engineered veterinary products are similar to those for human pharmaceuticals. In the case of plant biotechnology, delays arise from the length of time taken to grow plants—significantly longer than the time required to grow microorganisms in a fermenter. By the end of the 80s, no plant biotechnology products were being produced commercially.

Government regulations also have an important impact. Indeed some countries have regulations completely forbidding the release of engineered organisms. Trials on sugar-beet with disease-resistant genes, were held up in Denmark until 1990, and in Germany the regulations are so stringent as to be in danger of driving that country's biotechnology industry abroad.

Development of Collaboration

The ways in which collaboration developed in the biotechnology industry reflect the differing needs of the three major sets of players—academic institutions, which require cash to finance research; large pharmaceuticals and agricultural-products companies, which had the resources and capabilities to exploit the new technology but lacked the key technical skills; and entrepreneurial, R&D-based companies, which offered a bridge between the two.

Venture-capital backed companies often saw their role extending well beyond the R&D function into manufacturing and marketing—posing a long-term competitive threat to the established companies. As the magnitude of the entry costs and the inadequacy of their business expertise became clearer, however, many entrepreneurs had to settle for more modest objectives.

Strategic partnerships within the industry have been dominated by the desire of major companies in downstream industries to acquire technology and products. Two main forms of partnership have emerged: sponsorship of research programs in universities and subcontract joint-development and license agreements between major users and the R&D boutiques, often backed up by an equity relationship.

The extent of university research funded by the major companies is considerable, particularly in the United States. Both U.S. and overseas companies have made such investments: Hoechst guaranteed $70 million over 10 years to fund a molecular biology unit with a staff of 100 at Massachusetts General Hospital, Monsanto gave $20 million to Harvard Medical School, and du Pont gave $6 million to the same institution for research on molecular genetics.

The major pharmaceutical companies have virtually all created substantial networks of partnerships with new biotechnology companies. Hoffman LaRoche, for example, has 16 in the United States alone. Many have involved equity investments, either directly or indirectly through venture capital funds. Three phases can usually be identified in the development of the large companies' partnering strategies.

The *first* phase involves monitoring developments with commercial potential by funding university research and investing in small companies of potential strategic interest. In both cases, a hands-off approach is usually adopted, with relatively little attempt made to influence the direction of research programs.

A *second* phase typically involves targeted alliances focused on specific product developments, with agreements on intellectual property and marketing. The first generation of biotechnology-based medical products on the market was the result of licensing agreements between the established pharmaceutical companies and the new entrepreneurial biotechnology boutiques. For example, Schering Plough licensed alpha interferon from Biogen and Eli Lilly licensed human insulin technology from Genentech.

The *third* phase involves internalization of key technological competences by recruitment and by acquisition of leading companies.

The major companies are therefore now better placed to grow their biotechnology business organically, and the risks of their being caught out by new technology are smaller.

Few, if any, of the biotherapeutic products now under development are based exclusively on in-house research. Most pharmaceutical companies continue to deploy a wide network of alliances with academic centers of excellence and with smaller companies to gain access to leading-edge R&D and to augment their own discovery capabilities.

From the smaller company's perspective as it gets closer to market, an alliance allows it access to resources to assist with clinical trials, distribution, and possibly manufacture—without having to make an investment in downstream functions.

Many of these venture capital-backed companies saw their role extending well beyond R&D into manufacturing and marketing—potentially posing a long-term competitive threat to the established companies. But as the entry costs and the inadequacy of the business expertise they were able to deploy became clearer, many had to trim back their objectives. Half now expect to be acquired.

Most of the new biotechnology boutiques have sought to maintain partnerships with a number of companies, maintaining their independence and flexibility and protecting them from the threat of unwanted acquisitions.

The web of relationships established between the R&D boutiques and their larger corporate partners was even more complex. Most tried to make alliances with a variety of partners, each typically focusing on a particular R&D project. Between 1977 and 1983, 13 established U.S. corporations made early equity investments in 11 new biotechnology firms.

Genentech had alliances with Monsanto, Eli Lilly, and Corning (United

States), Hoffman La Roche (Switzerland), and Kabivitrum (Sweden). The Eli Lilly agreement, for example, covered the marketing of Genetech-produced insulin. Genex's strategic partners were Yamanouchi and Mitsubishi (Japan), Bristol Myers (U.S.A.), Schering AG (Germany), and Pharmacia (Sweden). The Bristol Myers contract gave it exclusive rights to Genex interferon. Biogen agreed to programs of work with Shionogi and Fujisawa (Japan), Merck and Monsanto (U.S.A.), and Kabivitrum (Sweden). The agreement with Monsanto also involved an investment of $20 million in return for a seat on the board and a 30-percent equity stake.

Perhaps more interesting than the form of individual relationships is the way in which the sponsoring companies have increased control and built up their own internal competences. The process has typically involved three phases:

* Monitoring biotechnology development with commercial applications by funding academic research programs and participating in venture-capital investments in small companies. In both cases there is little or no attempt initially to influence the direction of research programs.
* More-focused product collaborations involving the formation of stronger relationships in an attempt to influence research direction and ensure exclusive access to results and, in the case of the R&D boutiques, the signing of specific development and marketing agreements.
* Internationalization of the key technological competences by recruitment and acquisition of leading-edge companies.

Many of the leading biotechnology boutiques of the early 1980s have since lost their independence. In 1986, Eli Lilly acquired Hybritech; DNAX was bought by Schering Plough; Phytogen by J. G. Boswell, Cetus Madison by W. R. Grace; Agrigenetics by Lubrizol; and Biotherapy Systems by Damon.

Over time, the leading multinational companies have gradually built up their own in-house research capabilities, particularly in the United States. By 1982, both Eli Lilly and Schering Plough had biotechnology budgets of $60 million—larger than the combined budgets ($58 million) of the two leading biotech companies, Genentech and Cetus. While the large multinationals must continue to keep a watchful eye on basic research in the universities and elsewhere, through strategic alliances they have positioned themselves to dominate the future of the industry.

CASE 4–8
Amgen's Corporate Partnerships

Amgen, founded in 1980 as Applied Molecular Genetics Inc., took the name Amgen three years later. It has two principal corporate investors, Abbott Laboratories, with 8.3 percent, and SmithKline Beecham, with 3 percent.

Through its entire first decade, Amgen's financing requirements were met almost entirely by the proceeds of equity issues and by limited R&D partnerships with three corporations. In 1989, less than 4 percent of the company's revenues came from product sales.

Amgen's three R&D partners were:

- *Abbott*—In addition to its equity investment, Abbott entered into a five-year R&D agreement with Amgen in 1983, under which Amgen realized a total of $19 million. Amgen carried out research into several kinds of diagnostic products that, if developed, Abbott would manufacture and sell, with Amgen receiving a royalty.
- *Johnson & Johnson*—Amgen had two agreements relating to therapeutic products with J&J, with payment for R&D activities closely tied to the achievement of specific milestones. In the three years up to 1989, Amgen earned almost $16 million under these agreements. J&J received exclusive manufacturing and marketing rights in exchange; Amgen stood to benefit through royalties and profit sharing. (Some aspects of these arrangements, however, have been the subject of legal dispute.)
- *Kirin*—Amgen's third major partnership involved a fifty/fifty joint venture with Japan's Kirin Brewery. Again, Amgen received substantial payments—almost $12 million in the three years up to 1989—that were closely linked to performance.

Nine years after its formation, Amgen was on the threshold of bringing its first commercial product to market, a drug aimed at treating anemia in dialysis patients. A number of its other products were in the final stages of development and clinical trial.

Another interesting aspect of this industry is that the unexpected nature of the biotechnology revolution has provided an opportunity for some companies to change strategic direction and overhaul their competitors. For example, the whole shape of Monsanto's business has been changed by a determination to exploit the opportunities offered by biotechnology.

Meanwhile, the prospects for many of the remaining boutiques look bleaker. The new biotechnology companies came into being because of their research expertise. Most of their financial resources came from research contracts or equity stakes from established companies seeking a "window" into the new technology. The risk to the established pharmaceutical giants of losing business to the smaller companies has now greatly receded as the technology has matured, the expertise has become more widely available, and the entry costs have increased. Most multinationals—at least in Europe and the United States—have now acquired the skills necessary to manage and further develop their biotechnology business portfolios through strategic alliances in addition to organic growth.

With a scaling back of research contracts and equity investments in the United States, biotech companies have looked more and more to overseas linkages, particularly with Japan—for instance, those of Biogen with Teijum (for factor 8), Fujisawa Pharmaceuticals (tissue plasminogen), Meiji Seika Kaisha (agricultural chemicals), and Shionogi & Co. (gamma interferon interleukin and human serum albumen). Meanwhile, a new phenomenon has appeared in the late 1980s: mergers in the pharmaceutical industry, previously considered "takeover-proof."

Companies with revenue streams dominated by one or two drugs with limited patent lifetimes are vulnerable targets. Moreover, the costs of maintaining a world-class R&D capability and the risks involved in failing to find replacements are powerful arguments for mergers. In 1988, Sterling Drug merged with its white knight, Eastman Kodak, in response to hostile moves from Hoffman La Roche of Switzerland. This fueled U.S. fears of hostile takeovers coming from cash-rich foreign pharmaceutical companies. In 1989, Smith Kline Beckman, ranked seventh in sales, started a restructuring and cost-cutting exercise in an effort to avoid a takeover, but agreed in July 1989 to a merger with Beecham of Great Britain, at that time creating the second-largest prescription drug concern in the world. Smith Kline shareholders are equal owners with Beecham of the new conglomerate. The company has been rationalizing its operations and can benefit from economies of scale both in research and development and in marketing.

A further significant merger was also approved in 1989, that between Squibb and Bristol Myers, to create the world's second-largest pharmaceutical company. And in July 1989, Marion Laboratories agreed to a deal giving Dow Chemicals two-thirds of Marion's equity. Further mergers between western companies can be expected.

CHAPTER 5

PARTNERSHIP MANAGEMENT: THE EIGHT GOLDEN RULES

We have entered the age of alliances.

—Carlo de Benedetti

During the course of our study we examined many kinds of strategic partnership. In some maneuvers on the battlefield, entirely autonomous new businesses were created; in others, one partner retained management control. Despite the obvious differences, these various forms of partnership share one common feature: the conventional disciplines of modern management are quite inadequate. "Management by objectives," Peters' and Waterman's eight attributes of well-run U.S. companies, even Harold Geneen's simple "Management Must Manage"—none of the traditional formulas tell a strategic partner what to do. Perhaps this is why so many companies end up with egg on their corporate faces.

"A disaster waiting to happen" was how one manager described an alliance he had been told to make work. "Why do companies keep doing it, when they always go wrong?" asked another. The answer, of course, is that they must. Today's commercial environment often offers no alternative. And strategic partnerships *can* be made to work if a company approaches them in the right way—and if its executives are equipped to manage them.

Our study identified eight precepts of strategic-partnership management:

Successful Strategic Partnerships—The Eight Golden Rules

1. Plan, plan, plan.
2. Balance trust with self-interest.

3. Anticipate conflicts.
4. Clearly define strategic leadership.
5. Be flexible.
6. Accept cultural differences.
7. Orchestrate technology transfer.
8. Learn from your partner's strengths.

PLAN, PLAN, PLAN

Ideas for strategic partnerships can come from many sources—line management, the CEO, prospective partners. Alliances may form part of a coherent strategy for diversification, or they may represent an opportunistic response to a particular situation. A strategic partnership is just one way among many of achieving a company's objectives; there may be other, easier options.

Whatever the circumstances, and whoever first has the idea, it is essential that all proposals be carefully scrutinized. Managers are generally used to writing business plans for resources that are under their control or that can, one way or another, be purchased. In planning for strategic partnerships, these luxuries do not exist, and it is easy to assume that a plan is unnecessary or impossible. Many companies negotiate partnerships with only a vague idea of what they want (and can reasonably expect) to get out of them—and what they will need to put in.

Planning is, if anything, more important when there is that much uncertainty. While it may not be possible to produce the same kind of detailed operating plan as for a wholly owned business, there is a certain discipline that any company contemplating a strategic partnership must observe.

First, it must examine how the proposed partnership can help it achieve its strategic goals, and it must compare the partnership option with other approaches in terms of costs, benefits, risk, and speed of execution. The next step is to prepare an outline plan for the activities to be undertaken by the partnership. This helps determine what resources are required. Those not available must be sought from prospective partners or otherwise brought in from outside.

The venture plan must, however, go beyond a simple analysis of inputs and outputs. It must look at the broader relationships between the venture and the rest of the company's business, and it must look at the longer-term strategic impact. What is the objective of the partnership, and how does this relate to those of the parent business? What kind of trading flows does the company want? What financial return should it aim for, and how should this be achieved? How does it want the partnership to develop? What would be the effect of collaborating with partners of different kinds, and what are the important partner characteristics that will ensure success? What are the risks, and how can they be minimized? Only when these complex questions have been explored is it possible to set down appropriate partner selection criteria. Preliminary discussions with a number of potential partners may be needed in order to determine how they measure up against the ideal. Deciding whether to accept an external partnership proposal requires the same discipline.

Finally, a company must plan how the relationship is to be structured and managed for its own benefit. If the partnership is opened at the engineering level, will the company's marketing people be brought into the picture to ensure effective and rapid commercialization? If an important side benefit is the opportunity to acquire new skills for the core business, how is this to be achieved? And what is the company's ultimate goal for the venture? Is it a stable relationship expected to be viable over the long term, or is it intended to have a finite lifetime? If the arrangement is a joint venture, is ultimate acquisition contemplated? If it is part of a systematic business development program aimed at acquiring new competences, what is the next move, and how should it be triggered?

This kind of examination is essential, whether the partnership is about sharing R&D, setting up a new joint venture, or procuring strategic components through an OEM agreement. Without the answers to these and related questions, it is impossible to decide whether a partnership has the ingredients to be successful. There is no point in setting up a joint venture with a partner that lacks the needed technology or market access. It is pointless to set up an OEM agreement to supply the company with products if its sales people do not know how to sell them. A partnership that delivers neither strategic nor financial returns is just a distraction.

Golden Rule 1: Plan, plan, plan

- Establish clear strategic objectives.
- Evaluate alternative means of achieving them.
- Decide how best to structure and manage the deal.

BALANCE TRUST WITH SELF-INTEREST

If planning helps ensure that the right machinery has been constructed to make a partnership successful, it is mutual trust that oils the wheels. Virtually everyone we spoke to in our study put trust at the top of the list of factors underpinning success.

Genuine trust is a three-legged stool: an understanding of each other's business, an appreciation of each other's objectives, and good personal relationships.

The first leg of this stool is concerned with facts. It is about evaluating what a partner is likely to be capable of delivering and what it is not. Surprise is the surest way to destroy trust—discovering that a partner's technology is less advanced than it had led you to believe, that it cannot meet quality standards, that it lacks the distribution capability you need, that it has not made a proper market appraisal, or is not prepared to commit as many people as you want to a project. An honest exchange of information and a willingness to answer detailed questions are crucial to building this trusting relationship at the start.

The second leg of the stool of trust is about expectations. Companies must be sure that they have a clear understanding of each other's objectives for the partnership—in both the short and the longer terms. You need to understand the short-term objectives because you want your partner to achieve them; all partners must perceive that they are gaining if the strategic partnership is to get off the ground in the first place. Some concessions will probably have to be made in the negotiations to ensure that this is the case. Pushing for the best deal without regard to the other partner's interests merely sours the relationship before it has had a chance to bear fruit.

At the same time, you must try to determine how the partnership fits into your partner's long-term strategy. What are its aspirations with regard to your core business? How does this alliance relate to its other strategic partnerships?

The third leg of the stool is about human nature. Anyone who has been in business for any time knows that whom you know and how well you get on with people are as important as any management theory. Building trust takes time. This is why partnerships are often developed around existing commercial relationships. Collaborating in small things can often create the framework of trust for a more substantial project. Knowing that you can work effectively with another management team—getting the chemistry right—is an important component in successful strategic partnerships.

The negotiating period is critical to forming interpersonal relationships. You must make sure that your people go out of their way to help your partner's team members when they visit you, and get to know them well socially, so that potential difficulties can be aired frankly and resolved in an atmosphere of cordial self-interest rather than confrontation.

Golden Rule 2: Balance Trust with Self-Interest

- Make your objectives known, and assure yourself that your potential partner can satisfy them.
- Find out your partner's objectives, and be sure you can satisfy them.
- Establish good personal relationships.

ANTICIPATE STRATEGIC CONFLICTS

> Our company gained much, but . . . also gave things that they did not wish to. The weakest gained the most. Because this happens, the weakest became relatively strong, the relative position of the big firms changed. That is why our attitude towards joint research was slightly revised. We are more careful about what to do jointly and what to do ourselves.
> —Japanese VLSI program participant[1]

Building trust must not be allowed to distract from the realities of business. Many strategic partnerships involve collaboration with competitors. Sometimes companies with which you do not yet compete have ambitious aspirations.

A common situation is shown in Exhibit 5–1. Company A contributes technology or products to the alliance, and Company B provides market access. This is typical of many joint-venture, OEM, and strategic investment situations. In the short term, the companies' objectives are compatible; in the longer term, they invite head-on collision.

To develop its business, Company A wishes to obtain direct contact with end users and develop its own marketing network. It may also wish to maintain Company B's technical dependency by dissuading it from trying to acquire its own technology. Company B may have precisely the opposite objective, wishing to acquire in-house technology, eliminate dependence on Company A, and improve its share of the total value added. Its objective

EXHIBIT 5–1
Taking Precautions in Alliances with Competitors

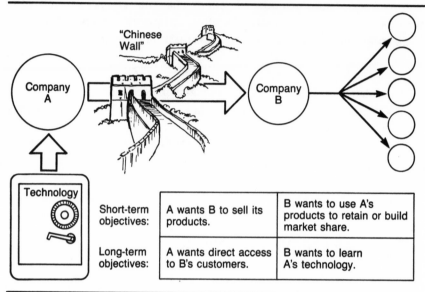

	Short-term objectives:	A wants B to sell its products.	B wants to use A's products to retain or build market share.
	Long-term objectives:	A wants direct access to B's customers.	B wants to learn A's technology.

is to learn Company B's technological skills and replicate its R&D and manufacturing functions, while discouraging Company B from building up its own marketing network.

Partners' intentions are not as Machiavellian as this in every situation. The growth of competitive rivalry may simply be an unplanned result of opportunistic moves by managers elsewhere in the company. However, a company entering a strategic partnership must be sure to identify the potential for conflict and be prepared for any hidden agenda.

You must look carefully at your partner's overall strategy—and at any other partnerships in which it is involved. There are two reasons for this. First, it is possible that the partner is trying to use a combination of alliances as a springboard to build up in-house capabilities and mount a competitive attack. Second, some of those alliances might involve your direct competitors, perhaps giving them a far greater long-term interest in your partner and posing a threat to your alliance.

Gaining an understanding of the webs of alliances that most multinational companies are spinning is a complex task. In some situations it will be impossible to find partners with which there is no potential conflict of some kind. However, this understanding is an important element in the management of any strategic-partnership program. It can and should influence decisions to collaborate, it can shape the legal agreement, and it can help establish areas where action must be taken to reduce competitive risks.

Once the decision has been made to negotiate a strategic partnership, competitive risks and conflict can be contained in a number of ways, depending on the nature of the partnership and the kinds of risk involved. The most straightforward is prescribing the geographic markets of each partner. This is, of course, illegal within the jurisdiction of the United States or the European Community, but it can work to the advantage of the partners in transatlantic collaborations. Companies adopting this approach, however, can still find themselves competing in some smaller national markets.

Another approach is for partners to operate in entirely different applications markets. This is difficult to build into any legal agreement, but it can be useful when there is a high level of mutual trust and a genuine difference in the focus of the businesses. For example, the very horizontally structured Mega project collaboration between Philips and Siemens was possible largely because of the small overlap in the applications interest of the two companies.

In a formal joint-equity venture, the scope of the venture's business must be clearly defined to make sure that the potential for competition with the parents can be effectively managed—not just in the first few years, but as technology and market opportunities evolve.

A significant risk is the unplanned seepage of technology. A strategic partnership may be viewed as a semipermeable membrane through which technology and expertise can flow unintentionally from the stronger partner to the weaker. The risk is obviously greatest in R&D collaborations. One way of reducing seepage is to divide the project into carefully defined components, that is, to make the collaboration as vertical as possible. This is an important element in the V2500 project, in which each partner has responsibility for clearly defined sections of the engine, thus minimizing unwanted technology transfer. In certain OEM situations, suppliers can restrict customers to older product models, reducing their ability to compete head on and making it more difficult for them to catch up and bring production in-house.

Whether any or none of these methods of reducing competitive risk is adopted, it is important to manage a competitor's access to personnel and resources carefully. Friendship and confidence building are important at all levels, but this must not be at the expense of normal commercial prudence. You must define the limits of the relationship carefully and make sure that your people know what information can be shared and what cannot.

It is, of course, always possible for partners to headhunt your key employees. This can sometimes be inhibited by an appropriate clause in the agreement.

Golden Rule 3: Anticipate conflicts

- Be sure you understand your partner's long-range interests.
- Identify areas of potential conflict in advance.
- Keep them in mind when screening partners.
- Include a mechanism to resolve conflicts in your agreement.

CLEARLY DEFINE STRATEGIC LEADERSHIP

One of the most important aspects of structuring a strategic partnership is the leadership decision. A specific, accepted leader is essential in any business or project. In strategic partnerships it is often tempting to try to side-step the issue, especially if the partners are of roughly equal size and neither is willing to cede control. Sometimes the easiest decision appears to be a political one, with responsibilities split between the partners in some way or with the creation of a cumbersome committee structure. In two of the mergers we examined, the participants retained their own boards, and each reported to its own central holding company. In one case, Fokker–VFW, the venture was ultimately dissolved. In another, the process of integration was delayed for several years, until one of the partners sold its interest to the other, which then installed a unified management.

Failure to create an effective leadership structure can be fatal; it makes coordination difficult and expensive, slows down development, and can seriously erode the decision-making process. Many avoidable partnership failures can ultimately be attributed to this cause.

Strategic leadership can be provided in two ways: by creating an independent leadership structure or by giving one of the partners explicit or de facto management control.

Independent Management

One option is to create an independent entity. To provide the effective management this requires, a strong, politically adept CEO or project director must be appointed. In precompetitive collaborative R&D programs, a completely independent manager from outside is often chosen. For commercial ventures, someone with relevant experience may be available from only one of the parents.

The general rule is to choose the best person for the job and, having done so, to give him or her strong authority. The manager's personal future and remuneration should be closely linked to the success of the partnership, as should that of the other senior members of the management team. The board to which the manager reports, usually drawn from the senior echelons of the sponsors, should interfere in operations as little as possible, once the overall strategic direction has been agreed on.

Control by a Partner

Choosing one of the partners to take on the role of project management is the easiest solution in major development projects, where complex contributions from many partners must be integrated. This shifts the role of the other participants much closer to that of risk-sharing subcontractors. It also helps speed the process of integration in partial mergers, provided that executives of the partner companies are valued on their own merits.

Exceptions

In certain forms of partnership, the establishment of a single strategic leader is less critical: where the role of the partnership is to facilitate trading (OEM or strategic investment situations) or where it has been decided to collaborate on R&D through a program of parallel development. Here, the prime need is rather for strategic leadership among the partners, so that they are equipped to exploit the potential of the partnership fully for their own shareholders. Parents must be sure that they have the management machinery to coordinate inputs from different parts of the business.

Golden Rule 4: Establish Clear Leadership

* Choose leaders solely on merit, and give them plenty of power.
* Tie their rewards directly to the success of the partnership.

BE FLEXIBLE

I don't want any surprises.

—H. G. Geneen, President of ITT, 1959–79

The traditional approaches to business-building—in-house development and acquisition—have the advantage of offering total control. Particularly in the West, wholly owned subsidiaries are the norm. Many multinationals have set up sophisticated planning and control systems to manage such structures, an approach tuned to a fine art in Harold Geneen's ITT.

Strategic partnerships require a different approach. Objectives may differ between partners, and they may diverge over time. Plans and budgets must at best be negotiated; at worst, they may be devised by a management team over which you have no formal control. It may be difficult to obtain adequate information about performance, and there may be little possibility of directing it in the conventional sense. Companies involved in strategic partnerships must therefore learn how to manage without control.

In each case, attention needs to be paid to the interests of the other partners. Management must be predominantly by persuasion and influence, with a willingness to adapt as circumstances change. The degree of influence available depends very much on the type of partnership and on the power balance between the partners. It can also change over time. For example, a minority investor in a company that is doing well has little or no influence over its management. A company that is doing badly, and in need of sales or an injection of capital, must listen carefully.

Venture capitalists are accustomed to this kind of situation, and their degree of involvement in investee companies fluctuates accordingly; advice and the injection of key business skills during periods of development, an arm's-length relationship when things are going well, and a willingness to demand changes in management if things are going badly. Companies practicing corporate venturing must at the very least learn these hands-on management skills. Many choose to delegate the process to a professional venture-capital team. In joint ventures and collaborative R&D, taking the gloves off is even more undesirable. Unless the venture is to be dissolved, you have to continue to work with your partner afterward.

Strategic partnerships seldom continuously deliver benefits. Companies must be flexible in their responses to changing circumstances. They must be prepared to tighten the degree of control when required or seek other means of achieving their objectives. In 1988, when AT&T's joint venture with Philips failed to deliver the European business AT&T wanted quickly enough, it negotiated an increase in equity from 50 to 60 percent, giving it a greater degree of control. Managers involved in partnerships must be both diplomatic and astute, and the importance of working constructively together with the other partner must be understood at all levels within the team. At the same time, the limits of cooperation must also be clear; sensitive information must be identified and isolated. Self-interest must always come first—even to the extent of being prepared to change partners if the alliance is not delivering the benefits sought.

Partnerships call for new kinds of skills—skills not taught in the business schools. Companies active in strategic partnerships must devise their own training programs to make sure that the lessons learned are shared.

Golden Rule 5: Be Flexible
- Balance astuteness and diplomacy.
- Be prepared to alter control agreements as circumstances change.
- Always put self-interest first.

ACCOMMODATE CULTURAL DIFFERENCES

The potential for cultural conflict abounds in strategic partnerships. There are four principal sources:

- Differences in management styles of large and small companies.
- Differences in the styles of management appropriate to product markets at different points in their life cycles.

- Differences in national business cultures.
- Differences between the established management styles of individual corporations.

Differing management styles of large and small companies are one of the major causes of difficulty in corporate ventures. Large companies tend to have established procedures for making investment decisions, and complex organization structures with multiple tiers of management. Usually, many different groups have an interest in any given project. In small companies, decisions can be made quickly by one or two people. Small numbers and regular day-to-day contact between employees make informal communications the norm for exchanging information.

We have already touched on some of the differences between Japanese and Western cultures, but there are as many differences among Western nations. U.S. companies tend to get into legal discussions at an earlier point in negotiations, and their executives are often more direct than a European manager would be. Many French companies have a reputation for independence and a management style that permits only limited consultation. Many large British companies are seen as slow and unimaginative in taking new business initiatives. Within these broad national generalizations, there are great variations from company to company.

Evaluating a prospective partner's culture is an important part of the courtship process. It may be necessary to start preliminary discussions with a number of potential partners before settling on one. Broken engagements are inevitable—and a lot better than divorce. Despite the most careful selection process, there are bound to be important differences in culture. Bridging the cultural gap requires understanding and forbearance, and it is important that all members of the partnership team know what is entailed, how the partner makes decisions, how it plans and measures performance, where the limits of authority lie, and how to behave socially and in business in order to avoid giving offense and causing misunderstanding.

Golden Rule 6: Accommodate Cultural Differences
- Know your partner's management style.
- Behave appropriately in shared social and business spheres.

ORCHESTRATE TECHNOLOGY TRANSFER

Many partnerships have the explicit objective of developing technology that will then be used or marketed by the sponsors. Technology transfer is notoriously difficult, particularly in the West, where attitudes of not-invented-here are prevalent. The problem is aggravated when a long period of time elapses between starting development work and the production of marketable technology, and changes must be made in communication channels as the project progresses. These difficulties are common to many strategic partnerships, and communication problems are often aggravated by wide geographical separation.

All strategic partnerships need sponsors in the parent companies. Since it is not uncommon for management people to move to new positions every three to five years or so, it is often necessary to find new sponsors between the beginning of the partnership and delivery of marketable technology. If the partnership is a new joint venture with responsibility for marketing, this may not be a problem. Where the benefits of the partnership depend on a sponsor's taking an active marketing role, real difficulties can arise if the lines of communication become weakened.

Collaborative R&D programs are the offspring of their sponsors' R&D departments. Lines of communication in corporate-venturing relationships are first formed at a technical level, to enable the investors' R&D people to evaluate the technology that is being created and perhaps to contribute practical help.

Commercial exploitation requires communication in the opposite direction—and to different audiences. The investors' business units and the planners, marketers, and production people must take the lead—after they are convinced that the technology to be exploited is worth their time and effort.

The creation of channels of communication at the commercial level is often left until too late, and great distances can complicate the transfer of technology back to the sponsors. This is one of the major disadvantages of basing collaborative R&D programs in central laboratories, and it is one of the limitations on international corporate venturing.

Where the success of a strategic partnership depends on technology transfer, special mechanisms must be set up at the planning stage to make transfer effective. Seminars and the circulation of reports, though important, are not enough. The most important element in a technology-transfer program is establishing early commitment and involvement of the sponsor's people who will be responsible for commercial exploitation—the planners, engineers, and marketing professionals in the business unit involved. They must therefore be directly involved in the planning stage.

The key to transferring detailed technical knowledge, and applying it commercially, is people. A plan of long-term and temporary transfers and briefing meetings must be drawn up with the object of bringing the technology back to the sponsors and making sure that the commercial opportunities it offers are well advertised internally. This requires a clearly identified receptor team, with the technical skills to understand and use the technology gained. As the technical and marketing uncertainties are reduced and the technology or product comes closer to commercial exploitation, contact between joint venture and sponsor must increase. Ultimately, a self-standing group must be created in the sponsoring company, with the skills to use the technology developed with, or by, its partner to exploit market opportunities.

Golden Rule 7: Orchestrate Technology Transfer
- Recognize the organizational problems.
- Identify a commercial sponsor.
- Create a receptor group.
- Build transfer mechanisms into the plan.

LEARN FROM YOUR PARTNER'S STRENGTHS

Acquisitions are easier than joint ventures, but you miss the chance to learn something from a new partner.
—Finance Director, European multinational.

Strategic partnerships offer other opportunities for learning from partners. Every company has its own way of doing things. Partnerships provide the opportunity to observe differing practices at first hand—R&D programs, business development programs, management information systems, methods of managing overseas subsidiaries, even remuneration packages.

In the 1950s and 1960s, joint ventures gave Japanese companies the opportunity to learn and improve on Western technology. Many Western companies underestimated their learning capabilities. Since then, Japanese companies have developed approaches to product development, manufacturing management, and strategic management that enable them to outperform the West repeatedly. Today, Western companies should be trying to learn from Japan. While Japanese companies keep close control over technology and products under development, there is much less reticence about discussing management methods.

At the same time, some Japanese companies are using partnership experiences to change to Western techniques—in budgeting, for example. As they expand overseas operations, they will need to absorb other aspects of Western management practice, particularly in human resources.

Learning from partners as a company takes place only if at least some of the individuals involved are receptive to new ideas and able to promulgate what they have learned throughout the organization. Spreading the knowledge calls for internal seminars, special programs to evaluate its relevance to the company's particular circumstances, and the planning of career patterns to ensure that ideas are passed on and implemented rapidly in key locations.

Ultimately, it is direct experience that teaches best. The more people who can be involved in the learning experience that strategic partnerships provide, the more quickly useful changes will be made back home.

Golden Rule 8: Learn from Your Partner's Strengths

- Choose your own participants partly for receptivity to new ideas.
- Create ways of spreading the partnership's good news within your organization.

CHAPTER 6

THE NEW STRATEGIC MANAGEMENT: LIBERATING THE RED QUEEN

"Well in our country," said Alice, still panting a little, "you'd generally get to somewhere else—if you ran very fast for a long time as we've been doing."

"A slow sort of country!" said the Queen. "Now, here, you see, it takes all the running you can do, to keep in the same place. If you want to get somewhere else, you must run at least twice as fast as that!"

—Alice and the Red Queen in discussion; from Lewis Carroll's *Through the Looking-Glass and What Alice Found There.*

SPEEDING TOWARD THE MILLENNIUM

In Chapter 5 we identified the keys to using individual partnerships effectively. The chief executive of the 1990s must be able to choose among the different forms of partnership we have examined and to trust his or her managers to negotiate and oversee them in a way that brings the company financial and strategic advantages.

The growth in strategic partnerships is really just a response to a series of more fundamental trends—trends that are putting continuous competitive pressures on virtually every company today. First, the increasing pace of technological change means that companies must devote more money to R&D just to maintain their position in existing product markets and stay in business.

And they must, one way or another, be able to demonstrate competence over a broader range of technologies.

Then, the ability to take a broad view of technology must be matched by a wider view of markets. As economies of scale in R&D come increasingly to outweigh national preferences and distribution costs in the cost equation, global marketing is becoming a prerequisite of commercial viability. And there are the new competitors. More and more countries are emulating the Japanese model of accelerated economic development, with highly focused industrial specialization and export-led growth as the cornerstone of strategy.

Today we see a range of producers with different wage costs and different technical and managerial abilities, all trying to climb the economic ladder. No longer is there such a clear dividing line between the advanced industrial nations and the rest. Now to be reckoned with are countries like Singapore, Spain, Korea, and Brazil, with a transformed Eastern Europe offering potentially the most important addition to the list.

Such countries can be powerful competitors, especially once a technology has stabilized and markets have matured. By this point, manufacturing skills can be acquired relatively easily. Product designs can be licensed or copied and, as technical competence increases, improved. Low costs enable these countries to undercut those with higher wage costs, driving their companies out of established core businesses. Many manufacturing processes can be applied as readily in Bangkok as in Boston.

These trends mean that the factors that determine competitive advantages shift more rapidly—from technological innovation to market access and to cost leadership. They are shrinking the window of commercial exploitation through which premium profits can be made from new products. And they imply that companies will need to manage a faster turnover of business units as competitive advantage is won and lost.

They also mean that there will be more new business opportunities each year. To stay ahead, companies must be faster at identifying and exploiting them. If the initial entrée is technology, the reduction in product-market life cycles means that developing competitive advantage through market access and cost leadership is also more urgent. Companies must plan how they are going to achieve this, even before new products are launched.

Global markets offer profit opportunities for the best-managed multinational companies but, with converging international tastes and standards, the primary defensive reason for global marketing is that it offers the most cost-effective way of generating sales volume and cash flow from an existing product portfolio. The cost of rejuvenating the product base is now so great that a company needs all the cash flow it can get to plow back into R&D and the development of the businesses of the future. The remainder of this chapter examines the implications of these challenges, particularly for corporate management.

Actions to secure competitive advantage cannot be left entirely to business-unit managers. It is up to the CEO to provide them with the tools, including strategic partnerships, to build competitive advantage on all three fronts, and to make sure that the company environment encourages them to use these tools.

It is also the job of the CEO to see that the corporation's portfolio of business is replenished—that promising new opportunities are effectively exploited and unprofitable businesses are removed. We therefore examine the role of partnerships in diversification strategy and indicate the way in which the business development function of the 1990s must be organized.

The net of it is that the multinational of the 1990s will need to manage its business portfolio more actively and deliberately than ever. Top management must keep its hands on the levers of competitive advantage, know when and how to quit or diversify, and pull everything together internally to create the multinational of the 21st century.

HANDS ON THE LEVERS

The three sources of competitive advantage keep shifting in the fiercely competitive global marketplace. Managing them presumes an understanding of the relationship between the internal corporate R&D function and external sources of technology, the role of the company as a whole in securing international marketing networks for its business units, and what must be done to maintain cost leadership.

Managing the R&D Pipeline

Since the 1870s, when the first specialized laboratories were established in industry, R&D has become more and more professionalized. By 1980, there were some 1.5 million scientists and engineers working in the R&D system of the OECD countries. Companies that have set up their own well-equipped R&D laboratories (a process that started in the chemical and electrical industries),[1] have come to place great reliance on them to develop new products or improve existing ones. Many, however, have found that their in-house facilities have not had the impact on corporate performance that was hoped for: they are frequently located away from the main operational businesses, and establishing an effective interface with commercial operations is a constant problem.

Despite these shortcomings, the role of the corporate R&D function remains unchanged: to secure competitive advantage for the company by the development and application of technology. The ability of an in-house function to discharge this responsibility alone is now more limited, however, as the complexity of technology increases and the cost per innovation rises. A company must now take a much more comprehensive view of the overall R&D pipeline feeding its business, and develop strategies that use each part of it effectively.

Phase I: Basic Research and Development
As technology flows through the pipeline, it passes through three distinct phases. The first is the R&D carried out more or less within the public domain—in universities and government laboratories, for example. This activity is not focused on developing new products, but on improving scientific understanding and breaking fundamental engineering constraints. Some of the more basic research in corporate laboratories also falls broadly within this category.

It is almost impossible to predict when and how research at this level will produce breakthroughs with important applications, and a good deal of further development is usually required before the commercial impact begins to be felt. This fundamental research, however, results in some of the most important discontinuities, and it is these discontinuities that provide the opportunity for major changes in competitive positioning or the creation of whole new businesses. Furthermore, there is strong evidence that the pace at which scientific discovery produces commercial spin-offs is accelerating.

Modern commercial R&D thus requires a much deeper scientific foundation than before. A theoretical understanding of materials science and of physical, chemical, and biological processes is required to produce the next generation of products and industrial processes. Tapping into the academic research community is increasingly important, especially to companies in nations with higher wage costs. Their success depends more and more on the exploitation of leading-edge technology. Wherever possible, they must try to gain proprietary rights to it.

This is particularly important in industries in which strong patent protection is possible, such as pharmaceuticals. Monsanto spends some $15 million to $20 million a year on university research collaboration. This is about 3 percent of its total R&D budget, but about 15 percent of its discovery activities. It works with a number of leading universities, including Oxford in England and Washington University in St. Louis, Missouri, its home base. Hoechst, the West German chemical company, started its huge pharmaceuticals business on the back of a collaboration with Erlangen University in painkilling drugs 100 years ago. Today, it has some 250 academic collaborations around the globe.[2]

Public R&D is by definition widely published.* A company wishing to tap into this research can gain no sustainable advantage at this point over its competitors. If preemptive rights are to be retained, strong linkages must be established between the corporate laboratories and academic centers of excellence in technologies of relevance to the company's business. Bridging this particular gap is notoriously difficult.[3]

Scientists have motivations that are quite different from those of commercially oriented technologists, and their output is measured in terms of publications and contribution to scientific knowledge. Technologists in commercial companies, on the other hand, are concerned with making things work and with obtaining private or proprietary knowledge from which premium profits can be generated. Cultural barriers, pride, and the momentum of existing projects must be overcome if outside ideas are to be absorbed and acted on. Direct access to original research results is extremely important, and the access achieved is closely related to the degree of participation.[4] Funding research programs and joint R&D projects helps ensure that scientists maintain close and frequent contact. If the contract is large enough, and structured in the right way, it can provide preferential access to technology.*

Phase II: Opportunity to Secure a Lead
The centerpiece of the next segment of the company's R&D pipeline is the R&D department itself. Its role, as we have seen, is to use technology to

---

*The only real exception to this is work in government defense and nuclear laboratories, where access is more limited.

secure and maintain the company's competitive advantage. Internal research priorities are usually determined by the needs of existing business units. Their managers always respond to those who shout loudest for help. Embryonic technologies offering long-term opportunities may at first appear to offer insufficient commercial benefits to justify much R&D investment. In any case, technological change is now so complex that it is more and more difficult to cover all the areas of potential relevance. As a result, the smaller, more entrepreneurially driven company is often first to exploit new technology commercially.

Companies must therefore know how to collaborate with external R&D-driven businesses that, while not now direct competitors, are exploiting new technology of relevance to the corporation. The technology may be helpful in improving the company's manufacturing processes, or it may provide the boost for products with the potential to compete with, augment, or improve the company's own product range. In both cases, competitors initially have equal access to their output. Competitive advantage may, therefore, go to the company that is first to gain access to this technology and secure some control over its use. Corporate venturing provides a mechanism for identifying developments in these smaller companies and for gaining a strategic lead in applying them. Joint ventures can provide access to R&D in larger companies.

Also included in the second phase of the pipeline are competitors' R&D functions. The spread of strategic partnerships means that access to these is no longer as difficult as it used to be.

> The nature of the uncertainty associated with innovation is such that most firms have a powerful incentive most of the time *not* to undertake the more radical type of product innovation and to concentrate their industrial R&D on defensive, imitative innovations, product differentiation and process innovation.
> —Christopher Freeman, *The Economics of Industrial Innovation*

Phase III: Commercial Exploitation

Here we have to look at process and product separately. Responsibility for process improvement lies with a company's production engineering function. Close interaction between production engineering and R&D is relatively easy to achieve, though even here there are problems. Communication does not come as naturally as one would wish; not-invented-here attitudes can impede the acceptance of good ideas.

New Technologies can enable commercial advantage in three ways:

through the improvement of existing products, the introduction of new products, or the creation of new businesses. Responsibility for the first typically falls to the marketing departments of each of the company's business units, working through the design function. The difficulties of integrating marketing with R&D are well known. Their resolution is outside the scope of this book, but note that the communication channels required are at least predominantly internal, and the company's commercial managers have a clear interest in sponsoring work of this kind.

The development of new products is more difficult. Many companies are not organized in a way that provides a natural sponsor for the building of new businesses or the development or acquisition of new products. External sources of ideas are likely to be as important as internal ones, and new products are often more effectively exploited through spin-off companies.

This is not to say that large-company in-house R&D is wasted. On the contrary, the evidence suggests that established technology-based corporations are highly inventive. It is merely that, while they are adept at using new technology for existing applications, they are less than 100 percent efficient at exploiting it in very new markets—markets that are inevitably small, specialized, and risky.

Those trends are making weaknesses in conventional R&D management more significant than ever. The increasing complexity and interconnectedness of technological change mean that no laboratory can afford to have in-house all the technical skills it may need. Developments in many areas affect its products and processes. Companies must therefore focus their internal R&D efforts on technologies over which they need internal control—that underpin the performance of existing businesses or allow them to move into important new areas. They must be prepared to buy in where this is not the case or where better technology is available. Responsibility for acquiring external technology is an important but underemphasized role of the modern R&D department.

Companies must also cast their nets in a way that allows them to maintain surveillance of technologies that, while not at present a priority, could become relevant in the future. This requires machinery to search out potential sources of technological advantage—in universities, research organizations, other companies. As competition becomes more global, a company's antennas must stretch to all parts of the world, at least to those parts with centers of excellence in key technologies.

The relative importance of different sources of technology varies from company to company, of course as do the mechanisms best suited to acquiring it. The chief executive officer of the 21st century will need a clear understanding of how the R&D pipeline works in the company and the industry. He or she must know where ideas originate, how they are developed, and what external resources a company can tap in order to maximize its share. The company must be equipped to exploit all parts of the R&D pipeline on which it can draw, both those over which it has direct control and those on which it can only exert influence. Strategic partnership provides the means to exert influence—by working with universities and research centers and through precompetitive collaboration, corporate venturing, and the other tools of business development.

This approach will be possible only if there is the organizational apparatus to manage it, with a strong business-development function that has close links with R&D. The organization of this activity will determine the long-term winners in the battle to exploit new technology.

Building Market Access

One of the keys to continued success in technology-driven markets is the ability to generate sufficient sales to finance R&D that will renew the product portfolio. For most companies, building the requisite global marketing networks represents an enormous challenge. Only a very few have the management, infrastructure in place to orchestrate global strategies, and each new business or product category is likely to require access to new channels of distribution.

The critical period occurs at the start of the product-market life cycle, when the market is growing quickly. Executives are focusing on more immediate priorities, and because fast-growing markets are highly profitable, the need to build share overseas does not become apparent until later on. Delay can be deadly. National patterns of supply are established quickly, and breaking into major export markets becomes progressively more difficult.

Competition may be restricted by trade barriers. There may be political pressures for buyers to purchase from national suppliers. Product standards may vary. Distributors may have become locked into existing local companies and may even be under their effective commercial control. They may want overseas companies to commit themselves to major investments in advertising and after-sales service before they are prepared to handle new products. In some markets, distributors must be offered a full product range before they are prepared to sign up for a new product. The cost of establishing a brand name or company image may be prohibitive, especially in the consumer goods industries.

Even though managers of new business units will not usually give priority to building overseas marketing networks, there are powerful reasons why a company should invest in building a strong international market position as rapidly as possible once it launches a new product, instead of taking each major market step by step. This should form a part of the launch plan of any product or business offering rapid growth where global competition is expected. It requires a five- or ten-year view of competitive strategy—which, though it may *seem* to be a luxury at this point in the new business—is, in fact, essential.

The onus is therefore on the CEO to provide this long-term vision. The top management team must make sure that businesses that are subject to global competition adopt global strategies, and must provide the machinery for their execution. For the large corporation, this means action at two levels—the individual business unit and the corporation as a whole.

Each business unit requires its own global marketing strategy, reflecting the structure of the distribution chain, the resources the company has available, and the characteristics of the market. The strategic partnership options—licensing, OEM contracts, and joint ventures—must be evaluated in comparison with distribution routes offering greater control. The costs and risks must be weighed. In some cases a staged approach must be developed, using OEM contracts as a route to eventual own-branding or negotiating strategic investments in distributors with a view to later acquisition.

This is a job for the individual business unit manager. But carrying it out requires knowledge and planning—knowledge about how distribution channels work in different markets and knowledge of potential partners. It is unlikely that the manager will have the knowledge, and it is unlikely that he or she will have the time or resources to acquire it quickly enough. It is often sensible to put in place some of the strategic building blocks in advance, making investments in overseas companies to understand how they operate, and building relationships on which distribution agreements can later be based. Such investments may be justifiable at the corporate level, even if it is hard for any single business unit to make a financial case for them. This is why action at the level of the corporation is so important—to provide the strategic management framework and organization within which business unit managers can implement global strategies.

At a minimum, it means making available an experienced business development team to help prepare and execute plans. The true multinational must have members of this team permanently resident in major markets to search out opportunities and to identify, investigate, and woo potential partners.

It may also mean making acquisitions and partnerships at the corporate level, to ease access for the products of a *number* of business units or to acquire some experience and competence in local marketing, upon which a more substantial organization may later be built.

For the smaller company, many options are unavailable. They must rely on strategies requiring less investment (OEM deals, license agreements, local distribution arrangements) to reach overseas markets. As a result, they have less control over their distribution channels and are more vulnerable to actions of their partners. The need to develop a strategy for global marketing at the planning stage remains strong.

Cost Leadership

The third dimension of competitive advantage is cost leadership. Production costs are relatively unimportant during the early stages of any new-product market. Even if a drop in unit cost triggers the new market, it is usually major discontinuity in technology that creates the cost-reduction opportunity, not the fine tuning of cost structures. During the early growth phase of new markets, competitive advantage is achieved primarily through product differentiation, and sales volume is closely related to market access. The main purpose of production is to make products that work and that satisfy quality and volume requirements.

Time changes all that. As markets mature, competitors become more capable, and the technology is more established; price and cost increasingly dictate market share. However, not only market share is at stake. As the market grows, the cost of rejuvenating the business through innovation increases. Gross margins need to be brought as high as possible, as quickly as possible, to finance this investment in the future. Furthermore, the shrinking of product-market life cycles makes this need more and more urgent. This means that achieving cost leadership must be a priority from the start of any new business, and improving costs must be a continuing, unrelenting task.

With a given volume of sales, there are essentially five ways in which unit costs can be reduced:

- Improvements in technology.
- Management action to improve efficiency—for example, value engineering and better production management.
- Manufacturing in locations that benefit from lower costs (labor, finance, components).
- Subcontracting elements in the value chain to organizations with a lower cost base.
- Collaborating with other organizations to achieve shared scale.

Identifying opportunities for improving the cost base requires continual reappraisal of each business and each element in the value chain—R&D, raw materials and component supply, manufacturing and assembly, distribution, and after-sale service. CEOs must make sure that these improvement programs receive continued attention at all levels of the organization and in all business units. The pursuit of cost improvements and the elimination of waste are not disciplines just for periods of adversity.

Much attention must be directed at a very detailed operational level—identifying areas of the business's operations where improvements in quality or in efficiency could deliver significant benefits, and then setting up task forces to find ways of achieving them. But strategic partnership can also have an important role to play. The objective is to pinpoint activities where sharing or subcontracting can reduce unit costs, either by setting up combined operations with competitors or by disposing of assets that can be reinvested more effectively elsewhere in the business and using outside companies to fill the gap.

Effective strategic cost-reduction programs require a detailed understanding of the relationship between volume and cost in different parts of each of the company's businesses. For example, in automobiles, the greatest economies of scale are achieved in engine and gearbox manufacture. The key to market share, however, lies in factors such as styling and overall value for money. It is therefore possible to collaborate on R&D in a way that does not inhibit companies from differentiating their products or adopting independent marketing strategies. Programs to develop and manufacture these hidden components jointly make sense for all but the largest manufacturers.

Opportunities for saving money in this way might be in R&D, in the manufacture of certain components, or in distribution. In essence, they provide a means of building shared economies of scale without an increase in sales volume—particularly important for second-tier companies in terms of global market share. The push for vertical integration—appropriate, perhaps, to a company that has already achieved cost leadership and market dominance in its core activities—may well need to be reversed when the advent of global markets has undermined that leadership. Specialization, focused plants, and subcontracting may be more appropriate.

At the same time, the cost benefits of subcontracting and collaboration must be weighed against the strategic risks of dependence on others and the encouragement of competitors. Core skills and technologies must be closely guarded. Strategic investments and joint ventures can play a part in mitigating risks, enabling a company to exert some degree of control over suppliers and distributors as well as to participate in their success.

KNOWING WHEN TO QUIT—AND HOW

Despite management's best efforts to improve technology, widen the market base, and reduce costs, there may come a time when cost pressures make a business no longer viable. This may happen because the company is not large enough to compete and cannot acquire scale through collaboration, or because of the growth of competitors, perhaps in the NICs, with lower costs.

This situation will become increasingly common, and many companies will need to learn the skills of orderly market withdrawal. As we have seen, partial mergers have an important part to play in this process, providing a solution when straight disposal is not an option or when the effects on customers, employers, and brand image would be too disruptive.

DIVERSIFICATION

The trends we have examined demand a new approach to diversification in which strategic partnerships can play a major role. Not only must the multinational of the future focus on growth markets much earlier in its life cycle; it must also be more innovative in its use of business-development weapons to enter those markets. This demands regular and formal mechanisms for scanning for market opportunities. It means being prepared to take a long-term approach to building new business units and, if necessary, it means acquiring the competences required to exploit the opportunities of the future through a series of incremental moves. A variety of strategic building blocks may have to be put in place over several years, in a gradual accumulation of all the components that will ultimately be needed for a fully fledged business. These might include market access, critical product and process technologies, an in-house R&D capability, and key management skills.

Diversification typically takes place through a mixture of systematic and opportunistic moves. Opportunistic moves are likely to be effective, however, only if the necessary strategic direction and organizational apparatus have already been established. Only then can opportunities be identified and analyzed quickly and investment decisions made in the light of strategic priorities. This is true of all business development, but the enormous potential that now exists for forging strategic partnerships, and the complexity of their impact, make it particularly important in today's environment.

The more aggressive practitioners of strategic partnerships—companies such as Nippon Steel and Olivetti—use alliances not just to preserve an existing competitive position, but to gain entry into new areas of business.

In many Western countries, diversification is associated with acquisition. It reflects the strong financial orientation of large-company top management and stock markets, especially in the United States and the United Kingdom, where acquisitions are easy. In Germany and Switzerland, the opportunities for acquisition are far fewer. In Japan they are largely restricted to so-called "dogs."

In reality, acquisitions frequently fail to deliver the expected financial and strategic benefits, and using them to enter growth markets is expensive. Potential candidates, where they exist, are traded at high price/earning ratios. The most successful acquirers tend to be those who are good at spotting bargains and realizing short-term improvements in operating performance.

Strategic partnership offers a more flexible means of diversification. It makes it possible to combine external and internal competence in a way that can be both more precise and less costly. Compared with these new weapons, acquisition is a blunt tool indeed.

The dividing line between natural organic development and diversification is a thin one, of course. While setting up or acquiring a business to sell new products in new markets is generally regarded as a diversification, selling new products into existing markets may not be.

The key point about today's commercial environment is that many of the most exciting business opportunities are enabled by new technology, with no single company perfectly placed to exploit them. In this situation, new opportunities are open to exploitation by companies currently operating in any number of different markets. To take advantage of these opportunities, each must acquire new skills and resources. Strategic partnerships, therefore, provide the only means of early market entry.

The greatest pressure to diversify comes when a company's traditional business is in severe decline; it is therefore particularly instructive to examine the approach of one such company, Nippon Steel.

Japan's modern steel industry was founded on an approach to steel production that left traditional manufacturers out in the cold. By building mammoth, integrated coastal steel works and making better use of labor, it was able to achieve huge productivity advances over most Western steel companies. Japan's lead remained largely unchallenged well into the 1980s; in 1984, it produced 106 million tons of steel, more than the EEC countries combined, and a quarter more than the United States.

By 1986, the wheel had come full circle. Japan's economic success had pushed the yen so high that its steel was no longer competitive. In tight markets at home and abroad, volume fell by 8 percent and income per ton by 13 percent. The new cost leaders were the newly industrialized countries such as Korea and Brazil. Japanese wage costs increased by 83 percent, in dollar terms, between 1984 and 1986. In Korea, they increased by just 10 percent.

Nippon Steel is the world's largest steelmaker. Its sales in 1987 were $15 billion, four-fifths of it earned directly from the sale of steel products. Nippon Steel's reaction to the crisis was dramatic. First, it increased the already strong efforts being put into rationalization and cost saving. Fixed costs, product yields and raw materials consumption, labor expenses, and administration efficiency were all targets of efficiency improvements under the company's third rationalization plan, begun in 1985. These efforts were redoubled, with a 30 percent cut in production capacity planned over the following three years. Nippon also established programs aimed at moving to higher-value-added steel products. One area in which it believes margins will remain good is high-quality automobile sheets. Eager to gain an inside position in the U.S. market, it has negotiated a 40–60 joint venture with Inland Steel Industries, the United States' fourth-largest steel company. Two thirds of the plant's $450-million startup costs are being financed with loans from Japanese trading companies.

But the plan did not stop there. Nippon Steel also announced plans for a huge diversification program, its aim being almost double company revenues in 10 years and reduce dependence on steel from 80 to 50 percent. Target industries were those based on the wide-ranging technological strengths that the company believed it had amassed as a steelmaker. They included electronics, urban development projects, computer software, biotechnology, and some other growth industries. Nippon had already had some success in engineering and new materials.

The foundation of this strategy was the creation of a number of new divisions within the company. A New Material Projects Bureau was set up in 1984. By 1987, there were five new companies, including:

- A $33-million joint venture with Philips to manufacture and market ceramic tip capacitors.
- A $35-million composite-material R&D consortium.
- A joint Ceramic Development Center with Kurosaki Refactories Co. Ltd. (a 40-percent-owned subsidiary).
- Nippon Micrometal Corporation, a joint venture with Matsuda Precious Metals Company to produce gold bonding wire for semiconductors.

A standalone Electronics Division was established in 1986, with the broad objective of seeking out and evaluating business opportunities in electronic devices, computer and data-transmission equipment, and electronic equipment systems. Nippon Steel's push into electronics involved widespread and imaginative use of strategic partnerships. It included joint ventures and OEM agreements with overseas companies to acquire product and manufacturing technology, the taking of equity stakes in innovative small R&D companies, and the establishment of in-house development and engineering laboratories. Progress within the first year was encouraging:

- A 40-percent holding in a joint venture to import and sell superminicomputers from Concurrent Computer in the United States.
- A 40-percent stake in Soliton Systems KK, a Japanese company involved in ASIC semiconductors.
- A 51-percent holding in Tau Giken Inc., a company specializing in database systems, data transmission, and LSI-design technology.

- An agreement to manufacture and market Automatic Drawing Recognition Systems produced by GTX Corporation (United States), backed by a 21-percent equity stake.
- An OEM agreement with SUN Microsystems Inc., which will enable it to market workstations under the brand name NISSUN.
- Establishment of an Electronics Products Center to produce production prototypes of in-house-designed electronic systems.

To develop service-based businesses, Nippon Steel formed a separate Service Division. In the first 20 months of its existence, it established companies to sell technologies related to nondestructive testing, financial services to company employees, classes in the Japanese language and culture to foreign businessmen, and other training programs. A more recent venture is Sunvenus Corporation, a joint venture with other Japanese companies to provide accommodation and other services to Japan's growing legions of the elderly. Space World, a $226-million educational theme park in which Nippon Steel is the lead investor, will open in 1990. Divisions for Biotechnology and for Information and Communications Systems have also been established.

On paper the strategy looks highly fragmented, but by working with these different partners, Nippon will be able to acquire all the skills and resources it needs to build complete businesses. Each of its partners contributes a small component of this total competency. None of them need think that it is helping to create a major competitor. Ultimately, Nippon will be able to build an internal R&D and manufacturing competence—the key to sustained competitive advantage over the long term.

Nippon's plans are impressive—some would say over-optimistic. Japanese companies are under greater pressure than companies in the West to retain their workforce, and in the steel industry this demands radical action. Japan's other steel companies have made similar moves.

Nippon's philosophy is clearly stated in its 1987 annual report: "The company recognizes the vital importance of timely judgment and action in pursuing good business opportunities, such as joint research projects with other companies, introduction of technologies, joint ventures, equity participation and corporate acquisition. To this end, Nippon Steel is ready to pour money, men and other resources into priority target areas. . . ."

Despite heavy pressures for cost cutting and rationalization, Nippon's management was determined to make a long-term commitment of money and resources for new business development.

MAKING IT HAPPEN

The trends we have outlined in this book and the new strategic responses we have described put new demands on corporate management. They mean that clear, imaginative strategic thinking must be embedded in corporate culture. New technological and market opportunities must be actively and continuously sought out. Companies must carefully analyze the resources needed to develop new businesses, and they must be prepared to acquire or borrow them through partnerships. Developments in the competitive environment must be anticipated earlier. And to help in achieving their objectives, companies must identify the best partners from all over the world. They must have staff who are able to negotiate with different business cultures, and they must understand how different kinds of strategic partnerships can be structured and managed for success.

All of this must be achieved within a coherent framework of strategic development for the company as a whole—one that focuses rather than dissipates management efforts, while encouraging entrepreneurial action. The accelerating pace of change has elevated the strategic-management function to a position of primary importance in the multinational company. The question is when and how to discharge this function effectively.

Delegating strategic management entirely to operating-unit level has the advantages of immediacy and of direct, intimate knowledge of the market. However, it also means that partnerships may be undertaken by unskilled negotiators, with little experience and a poor appreciation of the pitfalls. Uncoordinated action can also lead to internal policy conflicts and can undermine relations with key partners. More important is the danger that opportunities will fall between existing operating units. Working at the operating-unit level also makes it difficult to build coherent international partnership networks. It is likely to lead to a series of short-term expedients that fail to put in place the strategic building blocks upon which major business developments can be constructed later.

At the same time, a large, central strategic-management function risks creating a bureaucratic structure that actually impedes business development. Many multinationals have demolished the huge corporate planning structures they created in the 1960s and 1970s after they failed to do much more than fill filing cabinets with consolidations of five-year financial plans. By dismantling this resource, many companies have left themselves without the capability to orchestrate growth or implement the major strategic changes that will be a continuous feature of the 1990s. These are tasks outside the day-to-day operational management responsibilities and experience of line management in operating divisions. Having to reach difficult goals in existing businesses is a strong disincentive to creating new ones. The cutbacks and efficiencies of the recessionary 1970s and early 1980s have left many companies with all hands pumping out the bilges and no one to set the sails.

Many companies now need to reconstruct this central strategic-management function, but in a way very different from the old corporate planning departments. The new need is not for strategic planning, but for strategic action. Without an adequate strategic-management resource, opportunities will be missed, decisions delayed, and implementation bungled.

One company that has made extensive use of alliances is the U.K. computer manufacturer, ICL. ICL has a complex matrix organization that links vertical and geographic market sectors to product-development and manufacturing centers. Many parts of the organization have an interest in negotiating strategic partnerships. To coordinate this activity, ICL has appointed a full-time Collaborations Director with a small central staff and a network of collaborations coordinators spread across the company. To help in identifying and monitoring potential partners, it maintains a regularly updated database of partnerships involving other major computer companies.

Models of Strategic Management

Two companies that have used strategic planning to engineer particularly radical changes in direction are Monsanto and Olivetti. In each case, as Exhibit 6-1 shows, the approach adopted to the strategic management function has been crucial.

Monsanto
In the early 1970s, Monsanto was heavily dependent on low-value-added products, predominantly chemicals and plastics selling in near-commodity markets. The search for more profitable income streams began in 1972, the year that John Hanley was brought from Procter & Gamble to lead the company. This is also the year when the company began investing in venture-capital funds.

Those venture-capital investments were pivotal in focusing attention on biotechnology and the life sciences, and helped to identify a new strate-

EXHIBIT 6-1
Strategic Business Development Organization Structures

Monsanto (1979)

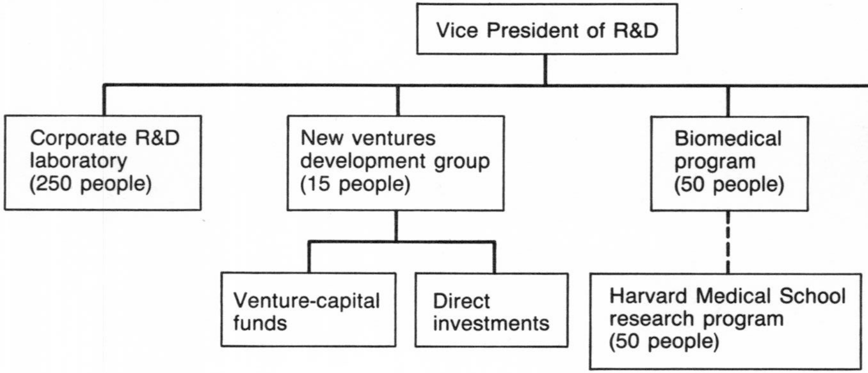

Olivetti

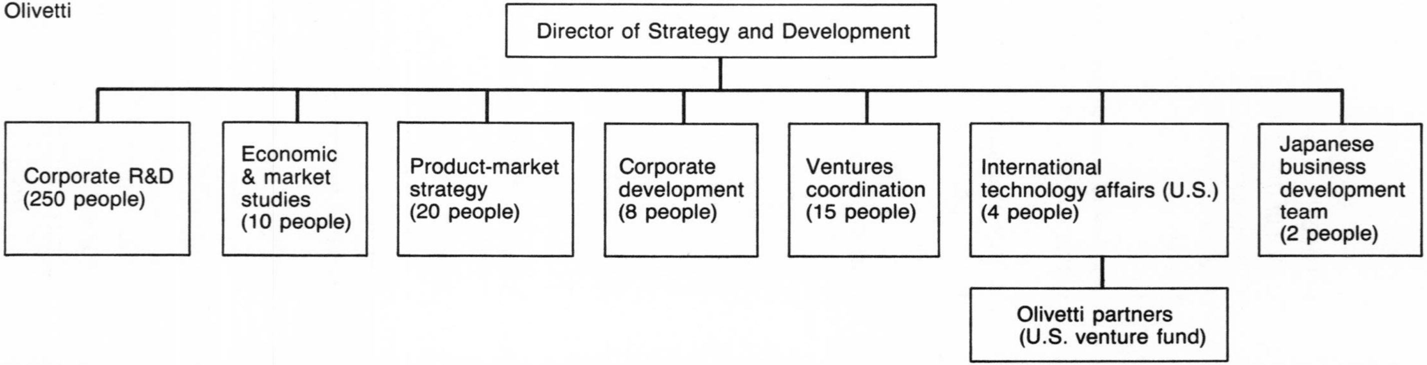

gic direction for Monsanto. In 1977, a new internal structure was set up to develop the new businesses. One of its most important features is the bringing together of strategic R&D with other, more commercially oriented business-development units.

Responsibility for Monsanto's ambitious program was given to Dr. Allen Heininger, Vice President of R&D. Heininger's organization consists of four units. The first was the corporate R&D laboratories, employing some 250 people. Monsanto's total commitment to R&D was about nine times this, but most of its R&D people worked for individual business units. The main role of corporate R&D was to use leading-edge research to help develop key technological competences that would be useful to more than one of the company's business units.

The role of the New Ventures Development Group, some 15 executives strong, was to identify new areas of business and obtain access to technologies and external businesses of potential interest to the company— not to carry out research or operate the businesses itself. In this capacity it was responsible for liaison with Innoven, the U.S. venture-capital fund in which Monsanto invested, and it also took direct equity positions in various start-up companies. Later on, as Monsanto's international ventures activities expanded, a small team was established in Brussels to provide more direct contact with the European venture-capital community.

Once the New Ventures Group had obtained support to move into a new area of business, a special unit was set up to achieve this. Two major units were rapidly created—in hollow fibers and biomedicine. The Hollow Fibers Separations Group was a full-function business team set up as an incubator for an invention created in Monsanto's corporate laboratories. Some 35 people were involved. The Biomedical Group was initially set up purely as an R&D group and consisted of about 50 scientists. However, this was also the core in-house resource for exploiting Monsanto's very substantial collaborative R&D program with Harvard Medical School. Monsanto invested well in excess of $20 million in the Harvard program over 12 years. In 1982, however, Monsanto switched its support to Washington University, which is located much closer to the main corporate facilities, thus improving communication with Monsanto's own scientists.

About the same time, Monsanto also began a long-term funding relationship with a team of scientists at Oxford University. In 1989, the company decided to set up its own center of competence in glucose research, called glucobiology (glycobiology in Britain), which had begun to offer useful applications in therapeutics, agricultural products, and physician diagnostics, all of which are important to Monsanto's core businesses. To secure the necessary expertise for its own center, Monsanto sent its researchers to Oxford to take part in glucose research activities there.

Meanwhile, a new venture-capital-backed company, Oxford Glycosystems, was established to exploit the technologies developed at the University. Initially, it provided research service and produced fine chemicals, but it also planned to offer instruments and diagnostic services. Monsanto was a major shareholder, both directly and through venture-capital investments.

One of the reasons Monsanto found biotechnology attractive was the potential synergies with the company's highly tuned process-engineering and molecular-manipulation skills. In this respect, Monsanto's interest in biotechnology differed from that of the many pharmaceuticals companies that had taken a similar path. While it had an established agribusiness, it lacked in-house clinical testing skills and had no capability in pharmaceuticals marketing and distribution.

By 1984, Monsanto had made a substantial investment in biotechnology R&D, with many highly attractive product and process developments moving through the R&D pipeline. However, one key building block had to be obtained before an integrated business could be established—an international marketing and distribution network. The acquisition of Searle Pharmaceuticals in 1985 completed the picture. Monsanto used $2.8 billion of the $3 billion it had obtained from the disposal of its commodity petrochemical businesses to fund the investment.

Many years go by between the development of pharmaceutical products and marketing. Thorough clinical trials are required to obtain government approval. This provided a window of several years or more in which Monsanto was able to put in place the foundation for its move into biotechnology-based pharmaceuticals. Strategic partnerships with other companies played a key role in the early days of the new strategy.

The key benefits of Monsanto's venture-capital investments were the knowledge and understanding of the biotechnology business that they provided. Collaboration with universities and a greatly strengthened in-house R&D capability, offering the benefits of technology ownership, became much more important later on.

Olivetti

For Olivetti, the time pressures were more acute. Olivetti's transition from an ailing typewriter maker into an international information-technology company required aggressive action on several different fronts—the acquisition of products, the rebuilding of a strong R&D capability, and the exploitation of both vertical and geographic markets.

To achieve this, Olivetti has made imaginative use of the full range of business-development weapons—strategic investments with AT&T and Toshiba; joint ventures with Bull, Canon, EDS, and YE Data; acquisition of majority shareholdings in Acorn and Triumph Adler; and the minority equity positions in dozens of small technology-based companies.

This would not have been possible without a major strategic-management resource. The man responsible for setting up this network of partnerships is Elserino Piol, Olivetti's Vice President for Strategy and Development.

Olivetti's Corporate R&D Laboratories were for a time headed by Dr. Hermann Hauser, founder of the U.K.'s Acorn Computers, in which Olivetti acquired a majority stake in 1985. The work of its 250 scientists and engineers is designed to complement that of the nearly 4,000-person R&D staff based in Olivetti's operating divisions. A major strategic objective is the development of equipment for the "office of the future" by integrating a variety of different leading-edge technologies: VLSI, voice synthesis, image processing, and optical mass storage. The role of Corporate R&D is to develop innovative prototypes, transfer know-how to the operating divisions, and support them in subsequent commercial exploitation. In a bid to foster innovation and get access to local centers of excellence, the number of staff in any one research group was limited to 25, and separate teams were located in different parts of Europe and the United States. As a means of securing access to a first-rate team, this approach worked well, though later, more formal reporting relationships were established.

The structure of Olivetti's strategic management function is designed to ensure that R&D is closely wedded to market opportunities. A team of 10 economists and market researchers provides information on current and potential markets, while another 20 staff members are responsible for developing corporate product-market strategy. Similar skills exist at divisional and operating group levels. The role of Piol's team is to take an overall corporate view, working with the divisional staff.

The business end of the strategic-management operation lies with the Corporate Development and Ventures Coordination Groups, together made up of some 25 staff. The role of Corporate Development is to identify partnership opportunities and carry out detailed investigations and negotiations. Altogether, Olivetti evaluates about 1,000 partnership propositions a year, roughly two thirds of them proposals from other parties. Once investments are made, the job of monitoring and, if necessary, organizing troubleshooting operations passes to the Ventures Coordination Group.

Olivetti's predominant market strength lies in Europe. For this reason, the primary vehicles for business development tend to be acquisitions and joint ventures which help to open up specific product-markets by the acquisition of product-development, manufacturing, and sometimes specialist marketing resources. Olivetti's position in the United States and Japanese markets has traditionally been much weaker, and its strategic partnerships with AT&T and Toshiba were designed to help provide access to these important markets.

The acquisition of technology and product has to be global in reach. The company has small teams in New York and Tokyo, therefore, to search for and negotiate with partners in these two countries. In the United States, venture-capital investments are the primary vehicle. In Japan, joint ventures are more important, a reflection of the greater importance of larger companies in product innovation and the relative lack of venture-capital opportunities.

Many of Olivetti's venture-capital investments have a dual purpose. First, they provide an opportunity to get involved in emerging product markets at an early stage and to gain experience with how they develop. Second, if things work out well, they provide the basis for negotiating OEM deals later on. Technology that is clearly destined to provide a base for future Olivetti strategy may be involved, but often the company does not yet have a clear idea of how and where it will be used. In this situation, Olivetti's Corporate Development team is the first principal point of contact with the partner. Permanent responsibility for managing the partnership is later passed to one of Olivetti's operating divisions, once the strategic relationship has become clearer.

In some cases, alliances provide a means of filling product gaps while internal capabilities are rebuilt. Olivetti's first word processor was supplied on an OEM basis by Syntrex, a U.S. company in which Olivetti had invested in 1981. The competing in-house development was judged to be inferior and dropped. Later-generation products were developed inside the company.

Olivetti's corporate-development function is one of the most sophisticated in the world. It has to oversee the huge range of strategic partnerships in which the company is involved and integrate them firmly with the development of its core internal capabilities. Olivetti has made very much greater use of strategic partnerships than has Monsanto, a reflection in part of the faster product turnover and greater complexity of the IT business. Nevertheless, both companies needed to bring about dramatic changes in strategic direction. The situation Olivetti faced in 1978 was in many ways very similar to Monsanto's. Both needed to introduce new technology and refocus their in-house R&D capability. Both needed to put into place new means of distribution.

The similarity of the organizations that the two companies established to achieve their objectives is striking. Both chose to establish a close relationship between corporate R&D and the business-development function; both made significant venture-capital investments and set up pivotal in-house teams to manage this activity. Both have sought systematically to gain access to technology in all parts of the Triad—Europe, North America, the Far East. Both have, in different ways, provided incubators for new business ideas. They offer role models of relevance to companies in many other industries.

Designing the Multinational of the 21st Century

It is just a decade since Harold Geneen's reign over ITT came to an end, signaling the demise of the tightly controlled diversified conglomerate as the role model for multinational management. Many companies had already taken the ax to their headquarters' staff, starting with the corporate-planning department.

In Search of Excellence[5] offered a new paradigm, placing emphasis on individual action, teamwork, and corporate culture. Razzmatazz rather than ratios was the key to motivating the workforce. Acquisitions and portfolio management got hardly a mention; the watchphrase was "stick to your knitting."

Of course, both paradigms have important lessons for today's management, but the more international, faster-moving markets of the 1990s demand something extra. Staying ahead is no longer just about how you run your company. It is also about how quickly you can change it to take evolving threats and opportunities into account. Sticking to one's knitting is an inadequate strategy when no one is wearing sweaters.

We stated our research by looking at the structuring and management of individual alliances, our interest triggered by the rapid growth in the strategic-partnership phenomenon and spate of massive partial mergers. It soon became clear that there were major implications for the very structure and corporate management of multinational companies.

What will manufacturing multinationals look like in another decade? Will more companies go the way of Corning Glass, with more profits generated outside the core business in autonomous joint ventures than within it—a sort of R&D investment bank? Will companies be linked up through networks of minority shareholdings like Northern Telecom's stake in STC or GM's stake in Isuzu, to form global versions of the Japanese Keiretsu? Or is growth in strategic partnerships just a transitional pattern that will ultimately lead to a restoration of majority control, once the battle to build global business is over?

And how will the globalization that is taking place in financial markets influence this pattern? Will the Japanese and West Germans open up their markets to hostile takeovers? Will U.S. and U.K. companies discover that by making increasing use of joint ventures and cross-shareholdings they can create powerful poison pills to deter raiders? If adopted, will such practices overcome the financial pressures on companies to concentrate on short-term policies? It is too early to provide a clear answer to these questions, and the rich diversity of corporate practice will no doubt always remain.

But what is clear is that the 1990s will be a period of major change in the structure of international business. The process of globalization is moving apace. What is also clear is that the pace of business innovation is speeding up. Companies must focus on better ways of staying ahead—on being first to exploit new technologies and markets, on building global distribution networks before their competitors, on continually finding new ways of reducing operating costs.

An inevitable result of this acceleration is that there will be a faster turnover in companies' business portfolios. Today's technological lead soon begets tomorrow's price war. Today's cash cow soon turns into tomorrow's dog. No company can expect to have all the resources—technical, financial, and managerial—to respond to this fast changing environment quickly enough. Acquisition is a tool too flexible and too unwieldy to achieve every business-development objective.

The problem for the modern multinational is that the strategic priorities are likely to differ for each business unit under its control. It must find a way of imposing tight cost control in some parts of the corporation, while providing an environment that promotes long-term investment and risk-taking elsewhere. Strategic partnership offers an increasingly important response to this more complex, more urgent, and less forgiving competitive environment. And the companies that move the fastest will get the best partners.

Strategic partnership is appropriate only when you don't want control, you can't afford it, you don't need it, or you are not allowed it—or where it provides a temporary expedient to help you bring new competences into your business that will make it stronger in the future. Running good alliances is not the same a building as strong corporation; it's just a part of the story.

When it comes right down to it, business is about making money for your own shareholders, not somebody else's. It's a tough, competitive world out there, and it's up to you to build the competences that help you stay on top, whatever the other guys decide to do. Being able to control your own destiny is a prerequisite of achieving this position.

While widespread use of strategic partnerships will remain a permanent feature of the changing commercial world, it is only one means to an end. In many cases, strategic partnerships will continue to provide the only way of realizing corporate objectives, but there will be a steady turnover of relationships as the relative strengths and interests of partners change. Wherever possible, partners will ultimately want actual or de facto control.

Retaining the initiative in this more turbulent and faster-moving environment puts new demands on management. It requires new levels of understanding and new management skills. Strategic thinking is no longer a luxury for the few; the dynamics of international competition have an effect on every manager in business. Strategic-partnership skills may be required at any time right across the corporation.

It is the job of the CEO to make sure that managers are equipped to deal with the strategic realities of business as well as the operational ones—through training and staff development programs and by providing appropriate levels of central support when executives are in difficult territory. And the process of continuous innovation for which corporations must now strive demands a much more aggressive and more carefully structured approach to business development than has hitherto been common.

It is often only in adversity that the business-development activity receives real attention. The creation of a fully supported business-development function rescued Olivetti from disaster in the early 1980s. It allowed Monsanto to refocus its business on higher-value-added products. In the same way, Japanese companies such as Nippon Steel and Kobe Steel have set in motion imaginative diversification programs to recover from the decline in the profitability of their core business.

These companies are the exception. There are strong pressures to defend position by improvements in *existing* technology. The most important improvements in the sailing ship occurred after the introduction of steam-driven vessels.[6] The response of many thermionic-valve manufacturers to the introduction of the transistor was to develop better valves.[7] Today's multinational must react to change as aggressively as Nippon Steel, but it cannot wait as long.

To ensure that the corporation is continually being rejuvenated, a new form of strategic-management organization is required—one that can:

- Identify markets for new business formation and put in place the skills and resources required to exploit them.
- Gain access to external technologies while also engineering effective commercial exploitation of those in-house.
- Make and manage investments in new ventures.
- Ensure that the distribution networks are in place to exploit products worldwide.
- Manage continuous strategic cost-reduction programs to maintain competitive edge.

The strategic-partnership tools described in this book are some of the most important weapons for achieving these objectives. They are also often controversial. Success is not guaranteed, and there are plenty of people around to say "I told you so" when problems arise, but radical changes in the competitive environment demand radical action.

Many of the examples we examined hold lessons for every CEO in industry. General Motors' decision to create the NUMMI joint venture as a means of acquiring Japanese manufacturing skills shows a willingness to learn that is only too rare in the West. Corning Glass's use of joint ventures to start more than a dozen successful new businesses points to how many diversification opportunities other less-imaginative companies may be missing. Philips' and Siemens' commitment to rejuvenating their semiconductor businesses through the Mega and JESSI projects represents one of the few high spots of the European electronics industry. Fujitsu's alliance with Amdahl and its OEM agreements with Siemens and ICL provide a model for any company seeking late entry into a highly competitive world market. And the success achieved by Olivetti demonstrates how strategic partnerships can help rejuvenate an entire corporation.

These strategies require vision—and patience. They require recognition by shareholders and top management that investment in new businesses is as important as investment in R&D—and as risky. Such an approach is not popular in the West. No one gets the credit for building a business over a 10-year period, and investments in new businesses are judged quite differently from investments in R&D, where there is no revenue figures to cause argument. The structure of Olivetti's strategic-management organization underlies the extent of the commitment required.

Putting into place the mechanisms to achieve these objectives— providing the organizational investment for the future, while dealing with more short-term cost and market pressures—is the most important challenge facing today's CEOs.

CHAPTER 7

PRECOMPETITIVE COLLABORATIVE RESEARCH AND DEVELOPMENT

Science clears the field on which technology can build.
—Werner Heisenberg

The idea of a group of companies getting together to collaborate in research and development was first put into practice in a substantial way by the British, early in the 20th century. Groups such as the British Pottery Research Association were formed to serve the members of a wide range of industries. These associations were strongly supported with government finance from 1917 on, and the other industrialized nations emulated the practice.

The role of these traditional trade associations tended to be relatively pedestrian, focusing on standards, testing, troubleshooting, health and safety, and training. A principal objective was usually to support small- and medium-size companies whose R&D capabilities were limited. Some associations also carried out longer-term research or funded research in universities. Programs with more strategic objectives were left to the individual companies.

The acceleration in the pace of technological change and the increasing cost of maintaining a world-class R&D program have engendered a new model of research collaboration. Some of the major players in an industry get together to undertake substantial R&D projects that will produce a long-term technological advantage for the participants; other such programs are organized by governments.

These new forms of R&D collaboration have a national or, in the case of Europe, regional perspective. Strictly speaking, the Japanese and U.S. projects lie outside the scope of this element of our study. It is only in Europe that precompetitive collaborative R&D has frequently had a major international dimension (though an international element is being introduced into a few Japanese programs). Companies that collaborate on

R&D, however, frequently do so to leverage their international competitive strength.

Since precompetitive collaborative R&D is not aimed at producing marketable product designs, such projects avoid many of the antitrust problems associated with downstream collaboration.* In practice, however, the lines between research, development, and engineering are getting progressively thinner. Many of those involved in precompetitive collaborative R&D would agree that their programs are actually much more commercially oriented than the label would suggest.

The first part of this chapter describes in some detail the different approaches to precompetitive collaborative programs in the Triad. Management of this kind of partnership is discussed in the second part.

JAPAN

The role model for many collaborations around the world is the Japanese VLSI project, to which is often attributed Japan's dramatic entry into, and subsequent domination of, the world semiconductor market. Thus, it is the Japanese approach to collaborative R&D to which we first turn our attention.

The Japanese government is sometimes criticized in the West for giving excessive financial support to industry. In fact, the government funds only about 20 percent of R&D related to science and technology (see Exhibit 7-1). That is much less than in the United States and many European countries, and down from about 27 percent a decade earlier.

The real R&D force in Japan is industry itself. In 1989, industry spent some $30 million on R&D, less than 2 percent of it funded by government. Many Japanese companies have been steadily increasing the proportion of R&D directed to sales over the last 10 years.*

The whole science and technology infrastructure is much more commercially oriented in Japan than in the West. For example, the proportion of research devoted to basic science in Japanese universities is only 57 percent, compared with 95 percent in the United Kingdom. In the engineering

---

*For example, the European Commission allows EEC member states to make subsidies of up to 50 percent available for precompetitive research, as against lower levels of support for R&D that is more directly market oriented. Joint exploitation of the results needs special permission, although since March 1985 prior participation in precompetitive R&D collaboration may remove this constraint in certain situations.

EXHIBIT 7–1
Comparative R&D Expenditures, 1987

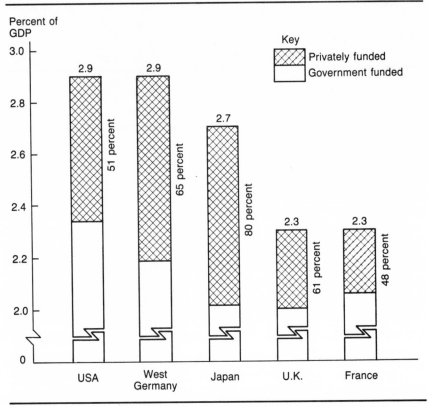

sciences, students commonly undertake doctorates from a company rather than a university base. The standard of science at Japanese universities is mixed, and there are complaints from some universities about the amount of support they get from Japanese companies.

One of the main differences between Japanese R&D spending and that of most other advanced nations is the small proportion devoted to defense—about 1 percent of the total, as compared with 33 percent in the United States. Roughly two thirds of U.S. government R&D funding goes to defense. The Japanese figure is 5 percent. By funding research on demanding, leading-edge projects, the U.S. defense program has been the progenitor of much of the country's high-tech industry. The Japanese government's civil R&D programs have had a similar purpose.

Industrial collaboration has played a major role in the Japanese government's R&D program since the early 1950s. Japan's industry was virtually destroyed at the end of World War II. Its major conglomerates (Zaibatsus) were broken up by the Allied Powers, and it was forbidden for many years to produce aircraft and heavy machinery.

During the early postwar period, there were enormous quality problems. "Made in Japan" was a phrase of derision. Engineering research associations (ERAs) were seen as a way of providing the technology base that many industries lacked. The idea was borrowed from the British, but the Japanese ERAs were different in many respects. First, they had very few members, usually only a dozen or so, and were dominated by major companies. Second, they were set up with a specific objective and had only a limited life—typically 7 to 12 years. Finally, only a handful have established joint research facilities; the majority have operated by procuring R&D services from members and subcontractors. Over the years the format has been molded to suit changing experiences and circumstances, but the basic model remains an essential part of the Japanese R&D infrastructure.

One early success was in the use of integrated circuits in color television sets. Japanese companies were the first to introduce this technology, following a MITI-financed collaborative project begun in 1966.

The most successful of the Japanese collaborative programs is the Very Large Scale Integrated (VLSI) Circuits Project, which was conducted from 1976 to 1980. Its objective was to provide Japanese computer manufacturers with direct access to semiconductor technology capable of competing with IBM's. The success of the participating Japanese companies sent shock waves through the U.S. and European electronics industries. By the time the program was completed, its participants had applied for a thousand patents in VLSI process technology. By 1980, three of the five Japanese companies involved were among the world's top ten semiconductor producers—an industry hitherto dominated by U.S. manufacturers.

When the Japanese government announced its intention of using a similar program—the Fifth-Generation Computer Project—to help achieve a position of world leadership in computer systems technology, the reaction was a powerful one. A group of U.S. computer companies moved rapidly to set up the Micro-electronics and Computer Technology Corporation (MCC). The European Esprit initiative and several national programs soon followed.

The Role of MITI

The Japanese collaborative R&D programs are coordinated through MITI, the government's powerful Ministry of International Trade and Industry. MITI spent $1.6 billion on industrial technology in 1989, roughly 13 percent of the government's total science and technology budget. More than half of MITI's spending is on energy technology and related projects. This includes MITI's spending on its own laboratories; major projects in energy technology and conservation; R&D support for aerospace; and the Fifth-Generation project. In addition, there are two major programs covering a range of technologies regarded as having strategic importance to the nation. These are the Research and Development Project on Basic Technologies for Future Industries (JISEDAI Project) and the National Research and Development Program, popularly known as the Large-Scale Project. Each program consists of a portfolio of projects of seven to ten years' duration. The Fifth-Generation Computer and Superconductivity projects are organized outside these two programs, and the approach adopted is different.

Because there is so much misunderstanding of the role and organization of the Japanese R&D effort, we analyze these projects here in some depth. Studying the Japanese approach provides some important lessons for other collaborative programs.

The Large-Scale Project

The Large-Scale Project was first established in 1966. It is regarded as one of MITI's most successful undertakings in research and development. All of the research carried out under the auspices of the Large-Scale Project is 100-percent funded. To be selected for funding, a proposal must involve important and urgent R&D with potential benefit for Japanese industry and society. In general, technologies chosen are those that:

- Are urgently required for raising the standard of Japanese technology, improving living standards, or ensuring a stable supply of natural resources.
- Promise to play a significant role in the growth and creation of Japanese industries.
- Pose unusual problems such as higher risk or long development time.

CASE 7–1
High-Speed Computing System for Scientific
and Technological Users

The High-Speed Computer Project is typical of projects carried out under MITI's Large-Scale Project. It was set up in 1981 and projected to run until 1989, with a total budget of $150 million.

The object of the project is to conduct research on the use of alternatives to silicon devices in computers. The aim is to develop a system that will operate at more than 10 Giga FLOPS—that is about seven times faster than the current generation of supercomputers.

The project incorporates parallel programs of work on novel logic devices, computer architectures and software development, and systems integration. Three technologies are being evaluated: superconducting devices that use the Josephson junction effect, gallium-arsenide devices, and the high electron mobility transistor (HEMT).

The project is managed by the Scientific Computer Research Association, which has six members:

- Oki Electric Industry Co., Ltd.
- Toshiba Corporation
- NEC Corporation
- Hitachi Limited
- Fujitsu Limited
- Mitsubishi Electric Corporation

This is a powerful consortium of companies, with total sales in 1987 of some ¥16,000 billion (about $115 billion). All are fierce competitors in the computer market.

- Have specific targets and clear, well-thought-out prospects for accomplishment.
- Are suitable for joint R&D among industries, national laboratories, and universities.

In 1989, nine R&D projects were under way, and 16 more have been completed (see Exhibit 7–2).

Ideas for research can originate in the private sector, government laboratories, or MITI, and there is a good deal of discussion before plans become final. The general aim of projects is to produce a prototype product that demonstrates the technical feasibility of a concept, but that is not ready for commercialization.

MITI's Science and Technology Agency (AIST) is responsible for managing these programs. Once the decision to set up a new project has

EXHIBIT 7-2

Japanese Research and Development Collaborations Under the Large-Scale Project (chronological)

Project	Total Expenditure ($ million)
Super-high performance electronic computer	28
Desulfurization process	7
Production of olefins by direct cracking of crude oil	3
Remotely controlled undersea oil drilling rigs	13
Sea water desalination and by-product recovery	20
Electric car	16
Comprehensive automobile control technology	27
Pattern information processing system	64
Direct steelmaking process using high temperature reducing gas	52
Olefin production from heavy oil as raw material	48
Large scale turbofan jet engines for commercial aircrafts	57
Urban waste disposal based on resource recycling	46
Flexible laser based manufacturing systems	50
Subsea oil production system	82
Optical measurement and control systems	72
Chemicals production from alternative carbon sources	46
Manganese nodule mining system	91
High speed computing system for scientific and technological uses	105
Automated sewing system	40
Advanced robot technology	84
Observation system for earth resources satellite-1	97
New water treatment system	50
Interoperable database system	63
Advanced material processing and machining system	89

been made, the AIST selects the companies to be involved. The basic criteria are technical ability and the capability to commercialize the results. Government laboratories may also be involved, usually to carry out more basic R&D.

The participating organizations then establish what is known as a Research Association, with a small secretariat responsible for detailed project management. The Scientific Computer Research Association, for example, has a staff of about 10. Detailed replanning is carried out each year as the project evolves.

Programs under the Large-Scale Project operate largely by procuring R&D from the research association's members. It is the careful division of research responsibilities that makes it possible for competitors to work together. In general, the current large-scale projects do not establish central laboratories, and there is very little exchange of staff between participating companies or between companies and the government research laboratories involved. There is, however, active sharing of results through regular meetings and seminars.

One of the problems with collaborative R&D is the treatment of intellectual property rights (IPRs). In the case of the Large-Scale Project and other AIST projects, all IPRs belong to the Japanese government. They are licensed for commercial use through the Japan Industrial Technology Association (JITA). In principle, all Japanese and overseas companies can apply for licenses. In practice, JITA is likely to favor the company that created the subject of the IPR. It may also try to regulate competition by limiting the number of licenses granted.

Basic Technologies for Future Industries

The JISEDAI Project was established in 1981, following a major MITI report on the future of Japanese industry. MITI regards advanced technology as the key to Japan's economic development. Despite the nation's progress as a manufacturing power, it was seen as still being five to ten years behind the United States and Europe in its ability to create innovative technologies. The objective of the JISEDAI program was to close this gap by developing the "enabling" technologies of the future—technologies with wide application across many industries.

The program concentrates on new materials, biotechnology, and new electronic devices. It is much smaller than the Large-Scale Project, with a 1989 budget of about $50 million. Like those of the Large-Scale Project, JISEDAI projects typically last 7 to 11 years and involve small consortia of companies and national laboratories. Direct participation by universities is limited, although they do frequently act as subcontractors. AIST funding covers 100 percent of direct staff costs, plus the costs of special equipment and materials and of participation in meetings and conferences.

The AIST tries to focus on specific areas within its broad mandate. It invites proposals within these areas from the national laboratories, individual companies, or consortia. Where there are two or three similar proposals, the AIST may encourage the organizations to work jointly. Sometimes a project has several subthemes, and more organizations can be involved. As in the Large-Scale project, once the participants are identi-

CASE 7–2

The High-Performance Ceramics Project

The High-Performance Ceramics Project is one of the largest of the JISEDAI projects. It involves some 15 companies and 4 national laboratories.

The goal of the project is to develop new third-generation ceramics that are highly reliable and very tough, and to establish an integrated technology system supported by performance estimation, simulation, and design technology. The project aims to replace some of the main components of large gas turbines with ceramic parts—a practical and demanding testing ground for the new technology. There are two parallel streams of research, one developing silicon-carbide ceramics, the other using silicon nitride.

The setting of difficult research targets within the context of a clear, practical application is an important part of the overall AIST approach. In this instance, one of the main measures is the Weilbull modulus, which measures strength reliability. The project has adopted a target of 20 to 20, compared with 6 to 10 for conventional ceramics and 15 for a comparable project in the United States.

Detailed project management is handled by the Engineering Research Association for High-Performance Ceramics. The Association has a full-time secretariat of three, of whom two are retired technical managers from the companies involved.

The project is a good example of vertical collaboration. To achieve the ultimate technical goal, success must be achieved at the powder, forming, and component-assembly stages. This requires the collaboration of three different types of companies—chemical companies (Showa Denko and Toshiba Ceramics), component manufacturers (Kyocera and Asahi Glass), and the ultimate engineering companies (Ishikawajima-Harima Heavy Industries), which will try to use these parts in engineering assemblies.

The project is divided into three phases. Phase I (1981–83) focused on powder-synthesizing techniques. Phase 2 (1984–87) focused on the relationship between powder technology and the forming and machining properties of downstream materials. The final phase (1988–91) combines all the developed technologies into an integrated technology for use in large-scale ceramic gas turbines.

As in the other JISEDAI projects, no special laboratory has been established, and there are no transfers of personnel from one company to another. The Research Association encourages communication between participants, however, and it organizes two internal seminars a year to discuss progress. Another major, annual conference is open to outsiders.

The first phase of the research produced powders with properties far exceeding the original target. As a result, even higher performance targets have been established, and the project has been extended.

fied, they usually establish a Research Association to promote communication among members and carry out detailed project management.

The teams that manage JISEDAI projects consist of:

- Officials of the AIST Planning Office of Basic Technologies for Future Industries.
- A promotion committee (consisting of senior officers from the AIST, representatives of the participating organizations and leading academics) to move the project along at the top level.
- An independent evaluation committee of outside academics and people from the national laboratories to assess whether the project has achieved its technical targets.

The JISEDAI projects use both parallel and collaborative programs to achieve their objectives. For example, the early stages of a project might involve three companies working on different approaches to a particular problem. Only the most successful is carried forward to the next stage. This approach helps to reduce overall development time.

The JISEDAI handles IPRs in essentially the same way as the Large-Scale Project. Of course, many of the companies involved will have been carrying out R&D in related areas for some years, giving considerable scope for conflict over origination and ownership. To provide a way of resolving conflicts, companies are invited to submit to MITI, at the beginning of a project, a sealed box containing documents and sample materials that define the current state of their research. These boxes can be opened later if a dispute arises. In fact, major disputes rarely arise in Japanese commercial life, and companies are eager to avoid problems with MITI. In any case, the element of ''black art'' in many of the projects is considerable. Much of the most valuable technical expertise will remain with the scientists and engineers directly involved, and the practice of lifetime em-

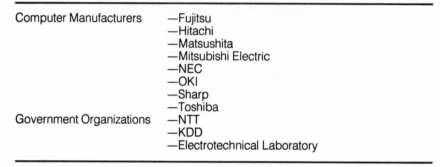

EXHIBIT 7–3
Participants in Japan's Fifth-Generation Computer Project

Computer Manufacturers	—Fujitsu
	—Hitachi
	—Matsushita
	—Mitsubishi Electric
	—NEC
	—OKI
	—Sharp
	—Toshiba
Government Organizations	—NTT
	—KDD
	—Electrotechnical Laboratory

ployment in Japanese companies means that this know-how is much less vulnerable to competitors than it would be in the West.

The Fifth-Generation Computer Project (ICOT or 5G)

ICOT, or 5G, is MITI's flagship research program for information technology.

Conventional computing technology is based on concepts of memory, numerical calculation, and comparison. The objective of the 5G project is to provide the basis of a very different approach to computing, which will be much closer to human intelligence. This new approach is characterized by mechanisms for decision making, inference, recognition, understanding, and learning.

The decision to establish the 5G project was made in 1982, following three years of preliminary research by a Study Committee set up by MITI. The 5G project differs from the other programs we have discussed in two important ways. It has established a central laboratory, the Institute for New-Generation Computer Technology (ICOT), to undertake much of the research, funded jointly by government and industry. Government funding over the 10-year life of the project is likely to amount to about $400 million, of total spending expected to reach about $600 million.

Eight companies are involved in the 5G project, together with NIT, Japan's telecommunications agency (now a private company), and the government's Electrotechnical Laboratory (ETL). ICOT itself has a staff of about 80 researchers and 20 planning and administrative staff members.

Its director was appointed from the Electrotechnical Laboratory and is therefore neutral with regard to the commercial companies involved.

Each of the participating companies is represented on a Steering Committee, which in turn has two subcommittees to handle management and technology issues. ICOT's director is responsible for preparing the annual research plan, advised by a series of technical working groups drawn from universities and research institutes and coordinated by the Project Promotion Committee. An internal advisory committee within MITI has responsibility for overall policy.

Because of the practice of lifetime employment, the exchange of personnel is difficult in Japan, and the ICOT's staffing problem has been increased by the scarcity of suitable computer scientists. This caused some difficulties at first, but the main problems seem to be solved. Staff members are transferred on loan from the parent organizations or recruited directly from universities into the participating companies.

Most researchers stay with ICOT for two or three years before moving back to their home companies, with which they maintain close contact. Many return weekly for discussions, a process facilitated by the strong social bonds among employees of Japanese corporations.

Besides work undertaken within the ICOT laboratory itself, much detailed development work is subcontracted to the participating companies. In addition to ICOT's 80-odd researchers, there are probably three or four times as many working as subcontractors within their parent corporations on ICOT-funded development projects.

The 5G project involves development of both hardware and software. It is a long-term program, tackling some difficult and complex problems. As in the other MITI programs, the ultimate goal is a total system, capable of executing specific demonstration tasks in areas such as image recognition and language translation. The project is nearing completion, but commercial spin-off products had already begun to appear about halfway through it.

An important feature of the project is the development of a novel computer architecture and the production of test machines for use by the 5G researchers. This was carried out under contract by Mitsubishi Electric, which has now produced some 200 PSI machines. Mitsubishi offers the PSI commercially, and it has gone on to develop a more powerful and cost-efficient version, the PSI II. A second machine, the CHI, has since been developed for ICOT by NEC.

In addition to this work, there is a good deal of parallel R&D in the participating companies, financed either through other MITI programs such as the Sigma Software Project (which has a MITI budget roughly equivalent to that of the 5G project), or by the companies themselves.

Foreign Participation

The Japanese collaborative projects involve only Japanese companies.* Technical reports are widely available in English, however, and there are increasing efforts to attract scientists from abroad. Both the United States and France have signed agreements that will enable researchers to be loaned to ICOT.

International cooperation has been given particular emphasis in the important new Human Frontier Research Program, announced in 1986. Preparatory planning for this project is under way. In addition, MITI has established a special charitable trust and fund, managed by the Japan Key Technology Center, to invite foreign researchers in key technologies to Japan.

THE UNITED STATES

> The use of basic knowledge by one party should never preclude its use by another. For every corporation to rediscover what others have already learned represents waste of the most pernicious sort, not only to each of them, but also to society.
> —William C. Norris, Chairman, Control Data Corporation
>
> (Remarks at a meeting in Orlando, Florida, February 19, 1982, which led to the creation of the Micro-electronics and Computer Technology Corporation.)

Industrial R&D cooperation is not a new idea in the United States. A number of traditional industry associations were formed in the early part of the 20th century. Their primary role was to share the cost of noncompetitive R&D by developing standards, increasing technical and scientific education, and filling technological gaps.

Three large collective organizations have also been in existence for many years: Bell Communications Research (Bellcore), the Electric Power Research Institute, and the Gas Research Institute. Each provides a

---

*In practice, this is also largely the case in U.S. and European collaborations.

CASE 7-3
Microelectronics and Computer Technology Corporation (MCC)

MCC is the joint research laboratory established in 1983 by a group of leading U.S. computer and semiconductor companies. It was founded as a direct response to the threat to U.S. computer supremacy posed by the Japanese Fifth-Generation Computer Project.

The idea for MCC originated with William Norris, Chairman of Control Data Corporation. The initial meeting to discuss the proposal was held in Orlando, Florida, on February 19, 1982, and was attended by 16 U.S. semiconductor and computer companies.

A series of working groups was set up to examine project feasibility, and a team of five managers was gathered from interested companies to move the initiative along from August 1982 toward an Interim Board. By December, 10 companies had signed a memorandum of understanding. Three more companies joined later, giving MCC its initial membership: Advanced Micro Devices, Allied Signal Corporation, Control Data Corporation, Digital, Harris Corporation, Honeywell, Martin Marietta, Motorola, Mostek, National Semiconductor, RCA, NCR, and Sperry. By 1986, membership had doubled. The most significant nonmembers were IBM and Texas Instruments, world leaders in computers and semiconductors, respectively, throughout the 1960s and 1970s.

MCC's first CEO was Admiral Inman, appointed in January 1983. Inman was a highly capable manager, offering the combination of independence and political contacts necessary to get the project off the ground. As a condition of accepting the post, he insisted that he become both Chairman and CEO, with total authority over MCC staffing. This was essential to give him the authority needed to manage the competing interests of the many companies.

Each company owns a single share in MCC. Shares initially cost $150,000, but the price was increased for new members. (Bellcore's membership cost $500,000 in 1985.) Foreign companies, including wholly owned U.S. subsidiaries, are excluded from participation.

From the start, it was decided that MCC should operate in a central laboratory, pooling the talents of researchers in participating companies. The search for a suitable site proved time-consuming but rewarding. Fifty-seven cities approached the Interim Board with proposals. It finally chose Austin, Texas, after the state government agreed to build a $23-million headquarters, for which MCC paid only a token rent of $5 a year.

MCC's research objective is to develop generic technology and development tools and transfer the results to its shareholders.

The research program is divided into four areas—software technology, VLSI/CAD, packaging/interconnect, and advanced computer architecture. Each program is headed by a Vice President. Member firms contribute financially only to those programs in which they wish to participate. Patents on technology developed in the laboratory are held by MCC, and program participants have a three-year royalty-free exploitation license.

The first two years were mostly taken with startup activities such as project definition and staff recruitment. Despite this, by 1987 MCC was beginning to come in for some criticism for not producing enough deliverables, and there was pressure from some companies for a more short-term focus. Nevertheless, by 1987 commercial products were beginning to appear. One of the earliest examples was a semicustom chip, Design Advisor, marketed by NCR.

MCC is controlled by a board made up of one representative from each member. Voting is by qualified majorities. There are three permanent subcommittees, and a Technical Advisory Board reports directly to the CEO. Each of the four programs has a Program Advisory Council, involving line managers from sponsoring companies to review operational issues. Each reports to the Vice President of the appropriate research group.

Considerable efforts have been put into establishing an effective mechanism for transferring technology from MCC to participating firms. This was high on the agenda from the early planning stage. A variety of channels for technology transfer are used, including seminars, publication of papers, video reports, and satellite-link conferences. The members of the Project Advisory Councils (PACs) and the liaison staff drawn from member companies play a particularly important role in this respect.

base of technical support for regulated industries, serving large companies in noncompetitive situations. A further important precursor of the new form of industrial R&D collaboration is the Semiconductor Research Corporation, an organization funded by 36 semiconductor, computer, and materials manufacturers, which supports research in U.S. universities.

Japan's success with the VLSI initiative coincided with the launch of the Fifth-Generation Computer Program. Modeled on the same pattern of collaboration, ICOT promised to make an equivalent transformation in the computer industry. The announcement stimulated an almost immediate reaction in the United States. Led by William Norris, Chairman and CEO of

Control Data Corporation, representatives of 16 of the United States' most important computer and semiconductor companies met in Orlando, Florida, on February 19, 1982, to discuss the establishment of a joint research laboratory to respond to the Japanese threat.

Norris's initial proposals encountered some reservations. As H. Glen Haney, Planning Vice President at Sperry Univac, put it: "The very essence of our business technology is the chips and micro-electronics. To willingly put the core of your R&D thrust outside your control and share it with competitors is basically unattractive.[1] But the Orlando meeting moved forward, and the Micro-electronics and Computer Technology Corporation (MCC) was formed six months later. By 1986, it employed 340 and had an annual budget of around $65 million.

The establishment of MCC was a radical departure from the more traditional U.S. approaches to collaboration. The reluctance of U.S. firms to participate was in part a result of the fierce competition between domestic companies, and in part a reflection of the antitrust laws. The Justice Department's attitude to collaborative R&D had at best been equivocal. As an illustration of the tough line taken, in 1969 Ford, Chrysler, and General Motors were forced to sign a Justice consent decree agreeing not to enter into any joint efforts with other car makers commanding more than 2 percent of world car sales. Even collaboration on emission control required special Justice Department approval.

The sanctions that can be imposed on companies breaking the antitrust laws are heavy—treble damages and criminal action in some cases. The creation of MCC, a collaboration of 13 clear competitors to produce commercial technology that all might use, broke new legal ground. Its successful formation owes much to the political ability of Admiral Inman, MCC's first Chairman and Chief Executive Officer. Even so, IBM, which had just come to the end of a 10-year antitrust law suit, decided that participation would be too dangerous.*

The laws inhibiting collaborative R&D were subsequently modified by the National Cooperative Research Act of 1984, protecting R&D ventures from the treble-damages provision, and subjecting them to a rule of reason. The act covers research collaborations up to the prototype stage. J. Paul Mc-

---

*A perverse result of the tough U.S. antitrust line was to encourage collaboration with international competitors at the expense of domestic ones. For example, Pratt and Whitney's participation in the International Aeroengines consortium arguably received less scrutiny than if it had been a purely U.S. partnership.

Grath, head of the Justice Department's Antitrust Division, expressed the change in attitude when he called joint ventures the preferred means of "creating efficiencies and bringing forth new products and technologies."[2]

In the first three years after it became law, some 70 projects were registered under the Act. The industries represented vary widely, from steel to pesticides.[3] Some are joint-equity ventures, some just loose collaboration agreements. A number have partners from different countries—for example, the collaboration between Bellcore and Hitachi Ltd. on optical transmission for telecommunications, and International Partners in Glass Research, a consortium of companies from six countries that funds university research to find ways to meet competition from nonglass bottling technologies.

The most significant instances of U.S. precompetitive collaborative R&D are MCC and the even more ambitious Sematech, a $1.3-billion, six-year research project to develop new-generation semiconductor manufacturing technology. Sematech was the idea of Charles Sporck, President of National Semiconductor. Its object is to regain U.S. leadership in semiconductor technology, focusing initially on memory chips, the market segment in which the United States has lost most heavily to Japanese technology.

Sematech's funding is split 50–50 between participating companies and the government. The Defense Department provided a $100-million grant for 1988. Member companies are required to contribute 1 percent of their semiconductor revenues to the project—roughly a tenth of their total R&D spending. By September 1987, 13 had signed up, including AT&T, Hewlett Packard, IBM, Motorola, National Semiconductor, and Texas Instruments. Like VLSI before it, Sematech will develop the next generation of semiconductor production processes, materials, tools and test equipment, with its own pilot production processes. A more radical plan involving large-scale manufacture was rejected.

EUROPE

> My experience tells me that you cooperate with true confidence only with people you have worked with in your young years. It will take 25 years for the benefits of European collaboration to work through.
> —Dr. A. C. Pannenborg, former director of R&D at Philips

Cross-border, government-sponsored collaborative research has a long history in Europe, especially in very expensive projects with slim prospects for early commercialization. Examples include Euratom, an imaginative but largely unsuccessful attempt to coordinate European research into nuclear power, which ran from 1958 to 1967, and the much more successful European Space Agency, founded in 1975.[4]

As in the United States, the unveiling of Japan's Fifth-Generation Computer Project triggered the growth of a new form of R&D collaboration in which industry clearly took the lead. The political architect of this collaboration was Viscount Davignon, European Industry Commissioner from 1979 to 1984. Until Davignon's appointment, industry had always been the poor relation in European Community politics. Agricultural support drew the big budgets, and EEC member governments were reluctant to relinquish control. The Japanese threat to Europe's fragmented and weak computer industry provided the opportunity to change this situation.

Davignon decided to press for a new policy to encourage cross-border cooperation, the priorities to be worked out directly with industry. In attempting to shift the barriers that had hampered previous attempts at collaboration, he dealt directly with the heads of Europe's 12 leading electronics and IT companies, inviting them to a series of roundtable discussions in 1979 and 1980.[5] The first meeting will, by all accounts, be long remembered by all who took part. The idea of collaborating with competitors was extremely hard for company executives to accept, and, in fact, it was not until 1984 that the main phase of ESPRIT I got under way.* Its success has stimulated similar programs in other industries under the EEC's Framework Program and a quite separate initiative, EUREKA.

A New Model for European Collaboration

The structure for ESPRIT I was worked out by the EEC Commission in conjunction with the roundtable of European IT companies: Bull, CGE, Thomson, AEG, Nixdorf, Siemens, ICL, Plessey, GEC, Olivetti, STET, and Philips. Each was represented by either its research or its strategic-planning director. Discussion first focused on measures for creating business alli-

---

*The European Commission's overall strategy for information technology has three main thrusts: (*a*) mounting a technology push through cooperative IT research, (*b*) development market pull for European IT products and systems, and (*c*) improving the infrastructure to make the common market a reality. ESPRIT is a key element in the technology-push aspect of Community policy. The overall commercial impact will also be closely linked with the impact of the 1992 move to eliminate barriers to trade.

ances between companies. Not surprisingly, this was not a topic that lent itself to roundtable deliberation, and attention shifted to R&D. After a short pilot phase in 1983, the main ESPRIT program was begun in 1984.

ESPRIT was designed as a 10-year program. The first phase, ESPRIT I, lasted until 1988. The initial budget was 1.5 billion ECUs—about $1.3 billion. Funding was provided half by the EEC and half by participating organizations. The technical focus encompassed key enabling technologies (microelectronics, information processing, and software technology) and important applications areas (office automation and computer-integrated manufacturing as well).*

After a long argument over financing, ESPRIT II, with an overall budget of 3.2 billion ECUs (about $2.7 billion), was finally approved in December 1987. It continues the focus of ESPRIT I on precompetitive collaborative R&D, but places greater emphasis on the industrial nature of the program. Particular aims are to:

- Provide a sustainable European capability in advanced components, especially application-specific integrated circuits.
- Provide the technologies needed for the next generation of information processing systems.
- Enhance the capability of European industry to integrate IT into complete applications systems in a broader range of environments.[6]

An important new refinement of ESPRIT II is a limited number of technology integration projects. Aimed at well-defined industrial targets and requiring much closer integration and tighter project management by partners, they take the ESPRIT model of collaboration much closer to that of Japan.

ESPRIT II also opened participation to European countries outside the Community, and its geographic scope is much the same as that of EUREKA, discussed later in this chapter. Unlike the Japanese collaborative programs and the two major U.S. initiatives, ESPRIT operates by providing a framework for research within which applications for support can be made. To meet ESPRIT's criteria, proposals must involve at least two independent industrial partners from different member countries, and the transfer of technology across at least one national frontier. Projects are also required to:

---

*A number of purely national collaborative IT programs were also established at about this time, most notably the United Kingdom's $800-million Alvey project.

- Promise significant industrial impact.
- Show potential for exploitation of results.
- Specify, as far as possible in quantitative terms, what improvement over existing technology will be achieved.
- Lead, preferably, to demonstrable results or prototypes.
- Contain clear review points and quantitative specifications for assessment of progress.

Organization and Management

Day-to-day management is the province of the Commission's Task Force for Information Technology and Telecommunications, which reports directly to the member of the Commission responsible for industrial affairs. To assist the Task Force, authorization has been given for the recruitment of temporary staff from companies and research organizations for the duration of the program.

Projects are selected from replies by panels drawn from some 300 independent technical experts. After consultation with the Esprit Management Committee (the international steering group) and the European Advisory Board (the main technical committee), the European Commission awards contracts and supervises their execution. Each contract is monitored by a project officer, who is normally responsible for 10 to 12 projects altogether. ESPRIT's projects include both well-defined programs with clear performance targets and more speculative work. At least one sixth are concerned with standards. Projects typically last for five years.

In ESPRIT, all principal parties have equal access to all results. Intellectual property rights are subdivided into foreground and background IPRs. Foreground IPRs are the property of all participants; access to background IPRs can be limited. Subcontractors own IPRs arising from their own work, but they do not have the right to the full results of projects.

An important component of a genuine European R&D community is communication. A special database system—the ESPRIT Information Exchange System—has been created to help individual project teams keep in touch with the overall program and share results. ESPRIT also organizes an annual technical conference at which participants can exchange views and information face to face. Workshops on each research topic provide a detailed review of problems and progress, which serves as the basis for decisions that define the work plan for the following year.

By the end of 1987, 227 ESPRIT projects had been established, representing roughly 20 percent of all proposals. Altogether, 536 organizations were directly involved in the program.

Unlike ICOT and MCC, ESPRIT has no central laboratory. It finances projects carried out jointly in the laboratories of companies and academic institutions. It also has a rather less centralized apparatus for project specification that is typical in Japanese programs. While this framework offers flexibility, it probably also results in projects that are less focused and less demanding from an industrial standpoint. The geographic spread of participants obviously adds to the cost.

ESPRIT has been criticized for concentrating its focus too heavily on the 12 leading companies. The opposite criticism could as easily be made. Whereas part of the success of Japanese projects results from the selection of a small number of companies with the capability to exploit results aggressively in world markets, there is political pressure to spread ESPRIT contractors more widely. Nearly 60 percent of projects involve companies with fewer than 500 employees. As a result, some funds inevitably end up with organizations that are ill equipped to exploit the results commercially, at least on a global basis.

Results—A Step in the Right Direction

The creation of ESPRIT has done much to create a pan-European technological community in the IT industry, and the progress achieved to date is encouraging. By December 1987, the Commission had identified 143 results of industrial significance originating from 108 of the 227 projects undertaken. These include 27 products currently on the market and 44 under development.[7] ESPRIT I is generally regarded as more successful than the United Kingdom's Alvey project, which ran at roughly the same time.

ESPRIT's real success, however, must be measured in political and commercial terms. The contacts forged between European companies at the technical level are already having a major impact at the commercial level. Before the start of ESPRIT, there were relatively few pan-European alliances. European IT companies found U.S. partners far more desirable. Between 1983 and 1986, the number of European cross-border agreements (excluding precompetitive R&D) increased seven times, bringing it to the same level as that of U.S.–European partnerships).* As Dr. A. E.

---

*Before ESPRIT, the dominance of the United States in computer science meant that in Europe there was no forum with sufficient prestige to attract the presentation of research results.

Pannenborg, previously Philips' R&D Director, put it: "For ESPRIT I, the main benefit for the European community is as an agent of European cooperation. People lost their shyness to telephone to Italy, even if the operator could not understand them."

At the same time, resistance to commercial cooperation remains strong. Some industrialists believe that the greatest weakness of the European IT industry is its reliance on OEMs from Japan and the United States and its inability to establish its own OEM market. "This can, in part, be attributed to its inability to collaborate beyond the precompetitive stage. Precompetitive research between European companies is reasonably easy," said one. "Cooperation in the marketplace is much more difficult; it is easier to collaborate with the Americans or Japanese."

The Framework Program

ESPRIT I's success has inspired an extension of precompetitive collaboration to other areas. The budget for the Framework Program for European R&D is 5.4 million ECUs for 1987–91. Key industrial components of the program include ESPRIT II; RACE (Research and Development in Advanced Communications Technologies in Europe), a program to establish a strong European capability in integrated broadband communications; and BRITE (Basic Research in Industrial Technologies for Europe).

Both RACE and BRITE were started in 1985. The initial RACE program focused on project definition and standards. By 1987, BRITE had funded a total of 112 projects in a variety of industrial technologies, including:

- Laser technology and powder metallurgy.
- Joining techniques.
- Testing methods.
- CAD/CAM.
- New materials.
- Membrane science.
- Catalysis and particle technology.
- New production technologies for flexible materials.

Each project was 50-percent funded by the European Commission and involved an average of four to five companies.

EXHIBIT 7–4
Participation in Esprit Program

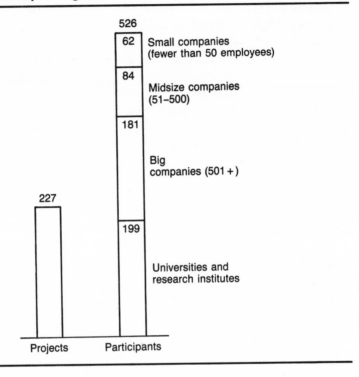

EUREKA

EUREKA began in 1985 as a political response by the French government to the U.S. Strategic Defense Initiative ("Star Wars") announced by President Reagan in 1983. The primary purpose of the EUREKA initiative is to act as a clearinghouse for projects that would benefit from European collaboration and to give the important ones a political stamp of approval.

EUREKA had initial support from 18 governments, including the then-10 EEC members and Austria, Finland, Norway, Portugal, Sweden, Switzerland, Spain, and Turkey. It now involves 21 countries, with the European Commission as an additional partner. There is no central funding; consortia members must apply for funds individually to their own national coordinating bodies. Some projects have gone ahead without receiving financial support from national governments. National criteria for support and funding levels

CASE 7–4
EUREKA Project EU83–1: 25-kw Laser Cell

EU83–1 is one of a number of projects under the Eurolaser umbrella program for laser development within the EUREKA initiative. The yearly world market for lasers is about $5 billion and is growing at about 20 percent each year. High-powered lasers and materials-processing applications account for the largest segment of the market.

Lasers were one of the technologies specifically identified when EUREKA was announced, and a number of proposals were promptly submitted. The EU83–1 project involves developing a 25-kw CO_2 laser for use in a variety of advanced manufacturing processes. It was the first U.K.–led EUREKA project to receive full approval.

The initial idea came from the Welding Institute, the largest research institution of its kind outside the Soviet bloc, with a staff of about 400 and corporate members from all over the world. The Institute was largely responsible for assembling the consortium to undertake the project and negotiating for government financial support. It is also responsible for overall project management. Discussions with partners and government agencies began in January 1986, and an international Eurolaser group was established to coordinate the various EUREKA proposals. However, it was not until December that the detailed proposal for the definition stage of the project was accepted. By this point, the Belgian, Spanish, and Italian governments had decided to support parallel projects, each focusing on lasers of different power.

The definition stage of the project cost some $2.4 million and was completed in October 1987. Final approval for the main phase of the work was given in May 1988, and it was agreed at this point that the team would also collaborate on *precompetitive* research with organizations from West Germany working on a parallel project, EU83–2. The Fraunhofer Institut for Lasertechnik is a full member of both consortia.

EU83–1 involves 11 companies and research organizations from the United Kingdom, Denmark, West Germany, and Spain. The lead industrial contractor is Ferranti; other participants include potential users such as Imperial Chemical Industries and Northern Engineering Industries. The total cost of the project will be $29 million, spread over five years. It will result in the construction of a prototype machine, to be built in the United Kingdom. They are expected to be five times more powerful than lasers currently used in manufacturing

EU83–1—Collaborating Organizations	EU83–2—Collaborating Organizations

United Kingdom:
  Ferranti Industrial Electronics Ltd.
  Imperial Chemical Industries plc
  International Transformers
  Northern Engineering Industries plc
  OCLI Ltd.
  Opto-Electronics Holdings Ltd.
    (Integrated Laser Systems)
  R Applications Ltd.
  The Welding Institute
  United Kingdom Atomic Energy
    Authority, Culham Laboratory
 	
  Subcontractor: Liverpool University
 	
Denmark:
  The Danish Welding Institute
    (Svejsecentralen)
 	
  Subcontractor: Andrex SA
	Federal Republic of Germany:
	  Fraunhofer Institut fur
	    Lasertechnik
	  ISF Aachen
	
	Finland:
	  Valmet Paper
	    Machinery Inc.
	
	Spain:
	  International Electronics
	    SA
	  M Torres Disenos
	    Industriales SA

and capable of welding 40-mm steel in a single pass. The prototype machines will be used for preproduction trials and small-batch processing.

The final stage in the project will involve evaluating the laser cell (source, manipulation system, and computerized control system) in a variety of industrial applications.

vary substantially—from 25 percent or less for certain types of project in the United Kingdom to 60 percent in West Germany.

EUREKA provides a framework for collaboration in a wide range of technologies, including information technology, telecommunications, robotics, materials, advanced manufacturing techniques, biotechnology, marine technology, lasers, environmental protection, and transport. A project must involve participants from at least two member countries, and the typical one involves five organizations from three countries, with one country taking the lead. The first 10 projects were approved at a ministerial meeting in Hanover in November 1985. By June 1988, 214 projects had been approved, involving a total projected expenditure of some 3.8 billion ECUs (about $3.2 billion).

EUREKA has a limited organization consisting of a small secretariat based in Brussels, which operates predominantly through national governments. Details of proposals are incorporated in the secretariat's computer database, providing a sort of marriage brokerage for potential participants. As with ESPRIT, the wide circulation of proposals in this way helps to eliminate wasteful duplication of research effort across Europe, though it also means that consortia tend to be quite large, which can lead to inefficiencies and dissipation of research effort.

Even more than ESPRIT, EUREKA provides a bottom-up approach, relying on proposals from individual organizations and consortia to define its direction. At the same time, a degree of coordination has been imposed by the creation of umbrella projects to coordinate the definitional stages of related proposals.

Participants are large and small companies, universities, and public-sector research organizations. Links are also being built with venture capitalists through the European Venture Capital Association. Collaborations tend to be more commercially oriented than those under ESPRIT, with a strong emphasis on production, as opposed to product technologies. Like ESPRIT, the creation of European standards is an important theme running through the overall initiative.

It is still too early to assess the impact of EUREKA, as no project has yet been completed, but despite the lack of planning in its establishment, it is likely to be an important long-term force for European integration. As one senior European R&D figure put it: "Policy was a complete void; it was a miracle that EUREKA started to happen."

In essence, EUREKA complements the EEC-financed Framework Program. Together, they are ensuring that a significant proportion of government-funded industrial R&D programs is carried out on a pan-European basis.

Private-Sector Collaboration

Most collaborative research in Europe falls within one of the government-controlled programs, but there are also some purely private-sector collaborations. Two of the most significant are Megaproject, Phillips' and Siemens' $1-billion project to develop the next generation of semiconduc-

CASE 7–5
European Computer Industry Research Center (ECRC)

The ECRC was set up in January 1984 to undertake research on fifth-generation computing. It was established under German law as an independent company with three shareholders, Siemens, one of the world's largest diversified electronics companies, with more than 330,000 employees, and two of Europe's main computer companies; Groupe Bull of France, with 26,000 people, and ICL of the United Kingdom, with 21,000 people. Each company has one third of the ECRC's equity and provides one third of its annual operating budget. The ECRC's laboratory is located in Munich, close to Siemens' R&D facilities, and it has a staff of about 50 people of 16 different nationalities. Each parent sponsors one third of the total complement, combining loaned employees and recruits from outside.

Like ESPRIT and MCC, the ECRC was conceived in part as a response to the Japanese Fifth-Generation Program. Its architects within the parent companies already knew one another as a result of the Unidata negotiations five years earlier. The ECRC, however, is an industrial research center, not a development center. The ECRC's main focus is on machine-assisted decision making. Its goal is mid–1990s—a time frame much longer than those for ESPRIT projects. Despite this medium- to long-term focus, significant spin-off benefits are expected. Any intellectual property produced belongs to the ECRC; the partners have free exploitation licenses.

An independent Managing Director directs the ECRC's activities, reporting to a Shareholders Assembly of six people, two from each partner, with a rotating chairman. A separate Scientific Committee advises on future research policy and technology transfer, although the director is primarily responsible for recommending future research programs. There is also a Financial Committee to audit the ECRC's accounts.

The ECRC is established in perpetuity, although there is a provision in the agreement for renegotiation if ownership of one of the partners changes. Despite the acquisition of ICL by STC and the merging of Bull into a new company with Honeywell and NEC as additional shareholders, this right has not been exercised.

The ECRC operates very much as an independent center of excellence, with a culture quite different from those of any of the parents. As such, it is highly valued by its sponsors.

In addition to the permanent (or semipermanent) staff, there is a regular flow of loaned employees for one or two months to aid transfer of technology back to the parents. Other technology-transfer mechanisms include annual seminars and regular contact with parent operations for demonstrations and the exchange of information.

tors, and the European Computer Industry Research Center (ECRC), a joint laboratory set up by ICL, Groupe Bull, and Siemens.

The organization and rationale for the two projects are quite different. The Megaproject was a very loose collaboration, involving parallel programs by the two companies. The project extends to manufacturing and commercialization and is not, strictly speaking, precompetitive in nature. This and its size would rule out collaboration within ESPRIT. In the case of ECRC, the research is rather longer term in its objectives, and the approach has been to create a center of excellence in a jointly funded research laboratory.

MAKING SENSE OF THE PATTERN

There are many variants of this new form of collaborative R&D, ranging from the tightly controlled, 100-percent-funded procurement approach of many Japanese projects, to central laboratories like those of MCC, ECRC, and ICOT, and to looser forms of collaboration such as some of the ESPRIT projects and Megaproject. In the West, none of these projects has been operational for very long. Managers are only just beginning to come to grips with the problem of managing them and generating commercial results. The new forms of collaboration can be divided into three main categories: vertical collaboration, collaboration on standards, and horizontal collaboration.

Vertical Collaboration

Vertical collaboration takes place when new technology can be developed only by the cooperation of suppliers and customers, and collaborative research between supplier and user is essential to rapid progress. Informal collaborations along these lines have been relatively common, typically initiated by the supplier. Customer involvement has often been an essential part of the supplier's product development and market research program.

But the complexity of technological change and its increasingly strategic impact now make such collaborations essential for many industries.

For example, semiconductor companies can compete only if they have the best design, manufacturing, and testing technology; high-performance lasers are produced by a wide variety of optical, electronic, and engineering skills that cannot all be found in one supplier; and the development of advanced ceramics requires input from at least three links in the production chain—at the powder stage, from component manufacturers, and from end users.

While competitive product positioning is the primary motive for collaboration, significant benefits accrue to all companies in the supply chain. For instance, the impact on downstream suppliers is an important, little-recognized feature of the VLSI program's success. Although the objective was to improve the competitive position of Japan's computer manufacturers by giving them leading-edge semiconductor technology, many benefits accrued to the equipment manufacturers and silicon vendors further down the supply chain (see Exhibit 7–4). In the mid–1970s, Japan imported about 80 percent of its semiconductor process equipment from the United States. By 1984, it was buying virtually all of its equipment (worth about $2.5 billion per year) from domestic suppliers.[8]

Government involvement has an important role to play in accelerating the formation of partnerships of this kind, both in identifying promising areas for development and in funding. Without this encouragement, linkages in the supply-research chain would often be slower to form. As the speed of innovation becomes more important in the overall competitive battle, government's role will increase in importance.

Collaboration on Standards

As technology becomes more complex, standards have a more crucial bearing on the ability to compete. IBM provides an obvious example. Its dominance of the world computer market has enabled it to impose standards across many different types of equipment. This provides opportunities for some companies, including Fujitsu in mainframes and Compaq and Olivetti in micros, to follow in IBM's wake, but it is difficult for companies with their own standards to retain their position. In VCRs, the alliance of JVC, Matsushita, Thorn–EMI, and Thomson was critical in establishing the VHS standard over rivals such as Betamax.

EXHIBIT 7–5
Development of Linkages within the VLSI Industrial System

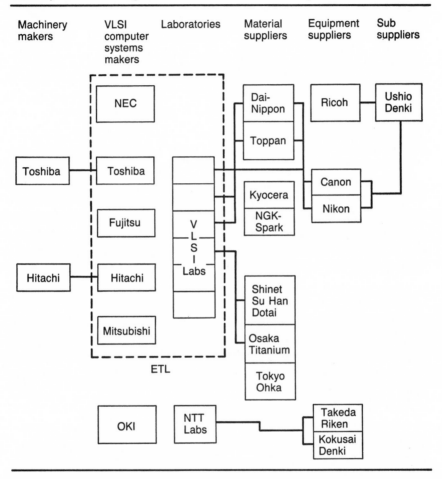

Standards wars have been fought out in the market. Now, companies are collaborating in an attempt to settle the problem at the development stage. Philips enlisted Sony's support to complete development of the compact disc so that a consistent standard could be adopted for launching product in the Japanese, European, and U.S. markets. Many ESPRIT and EUREKA projects are concerned with standards, although the extent to which this purely European approach helps companies compete *globally* is yet to be established.*

Horizontal Collaboration

Collaboration on standards and vertical collaborations are relatively safe from the point of view of the participants. The dangers of horizontal collaboration—working with competitors—are much greater.

Dangers

Participants have numerous and justified fears. One partner might give away technological leadership without realizing the extent of its lead. Technological bleed-through might enable competitors to acquire proprietary technology outside the scope of the collaborative project itself. Partners might not act in good faith, using the collaboration only as a means of snooping into competitors' R&D programs. And they might put more effort into parallel in-house R&D. Other participants might be better placed to exploit the results of collaborative projects commercially. The strongest companies might even adopt diversionary tactics, deliberately encouraging competitors to collaborate in an area of little strategic importance.

The dangers are far greater in Europe and the United States than in Japan, where precompetitive collaborative R&D originated. Collaborating companies are more widely dispersed geographically, and the company loyalty and close personal relationship that exist within Japanese companies are less important parts of the business culture. This makes technology transfer, and therefore commercialization, more difficult when central laboratories are established. There is also much more job mobility in the West, making companies vulnerable to the poaching of their best staff by competitors. Employees may even set out to exploit on their own the expertise they have acquired.

---

*At the time of writing, two large alliances were competing within the computer industry for control of the UNIX operating system standard. Originally developed by Bell Laboratories, and widely licensed to other companies by AT&T, UNIX opens up the possibility of greatly reducing a user's dependence on a particular manufacturer. It offers a particular challenge to IBM's dominance of much of the industry. However, a proliferation of different UNIX versions has undermined this possibility, and AT&T's standard is being challenged by a version promoted by the Open Software Foundation, a powerful consortium led by IBM and including ICL, Unisys, DEC, Hewlett Packard, Apollo, Groupe Bull, Nixdorf, and Siemens.

Defenses

Horizontal collaborations must therefore be entered into with considerable care. A company must have a clear understanding of where its own technological strengths lie, retain core technologies in-house as much as possible, and be wary of collaborations in areas where it has a clear and sustainable lead. Management can help safeguard the company's position through five defensive actions.

Basic Research

One way to ensure that collaboration is strictly precompetitive is to limit it to basic research. This is, however, a difficult position to sustain. Once a team is set up, it makes sense to continue with it through to the early development stage. In addition, there is always pressure for delivery of an actual product, and unplanned spin-off developments can occur.

Minimum Competitive Potential

It may be possible to select a partner with whom competition is limited or to negotiate a *modus operandi* in which the rights to commercial exploitation will be split. The natural division of interests between Siemens and Philips is one reason they are able to collaborate on semiconductors. Their business focuses are rather different—Siemens' on industrial systems and electrical engineering, Philips' on office equipment and consumer electronics.

Commercial agreements on market splitting are, of course, strictly limited by law in most jurisdictions, so partner selection is critical. Where collaboration with a company in the same business is required, it is often simpler to team up with an overseas partner with whom the conflict is less direct.

Noncore technology

Another defense is to limit collaboration to noncore technology. Indeed, many critics of programs such as MCC and ESPRIT argue that they are biased toward the lowest common denominator—projects that are academically interesting but commercially unexciting. Partner and government contributions to EEC projects, for example, mean that each dollar a company spends on collaborative R&D gives it access to another three dollars. On this basis, the risk/reward ratio of investment in collaborative R&D begins to resemble that of corporate venturing (discussed in the next chapter). It enables a company to participate in the development of technology that is not currently applicable to its core business but that could be of significance later.

Division of Labor

A collaboration can be structured to minimize points of overlap and enable companies to develop and protect their own intellectual property. This can be achieved either by shaping the partnership into a more vertical form of collaboration or by clearly dividing research tasks between companies. Collaboration in semiconductor research is possible partly because the prime focus is not on semiconductor design but on semiconductor processing technology. A variety of upstream suppliers must be involved in developing new production processes, which the primary participants—the semiconductor manufacturers—will use to fight out their own competitive battles.

The extent of the efforts of the participants in VLSI to protect their proprietary positions is illustrated by the patent statistics. Only 16 percent of the resulting patents are held jointly by individuals from different companies. Three of VLSI's six laboratories were dominated by a single company, and there was a clear split between fundamental research carried out within the joint laboratories and the more-applied work undertaken with the companies themselves.[9]

Collaborative Exploitation

The final defense is to establish collaborative vehicles for exploitation. This approach is little used in Japan. After VLSI, in fact, each of the participating companies went its own way, competing aggressively at home and abroad. The number of participants in Sematech and MCC is likely to preclude joint exploitation, except in special circumstances.

This is not the situation in Europe, where the ultimate objectives of programs such as ESPRIT and EUREKA can be achieved only with some industry restructuring. The formation of commercial joint ventures to exploit the joint R&D work is a logical outcome of this process. Turning R&D collaborations into commercial ones takes time. The European Commission has so far given relatively little attention to how this progress should be encouraged.

PLANNING, SPECIFYING, AND MANAGING A PROGRAM

The planning phase of collaborative R&D programs is crucial. For the individual company, this means linking programs with the overall corporate

R&D plan and deciding which projects to keep in house and which to carry out in collaboration with others. The greatest difficulties lie in technology transfer and commercial exploitation. These aspects must be addressed from the start.

For government, planning includes selection of target areas and individual projects that will have the greatest impact on the long-term direction and performance of industry—funding development work that would not otherwise be undertaken so effectively or so quickly. Government programs to develop technology systems, which require input from various kinds of companies, are likely to have the greatest impact.

MITI has a sophisticated process for assessing future technological needs and opportunities, and it spends two or three years in identifying areas for research and formulating detailed program plans. R&D projects are chosen to provide a clear strategic direction for the development of industry. They are clearly concerned with core business developments, but are sufficiently long-term to be too risky for companies to undertake themselves. The 100-percent funding of most MITI projects reflects this long-term view. In the United States, the Department of Defense performs a similar role. In contrast, ESPRIT seems to be in danger of attracting projects without enough central significance to be of crucial commercial importance and too limited in duration to add anything really new or difficult. There is no vehicle for long-term funding in Europe comparable to those in Japan and the United States.

The starting point for the individual company embarking on a collaborative R&D project should always be a statement of objectives and an outlined project plan. This should indicate not just the research and development required, but also the manufacturing and marketing implications. The likely pattern of exploitation should be sketched out, even for long-term research programs. An important factor is the time over which the project is expected to deliver results—is it designed to lead to commercial output in five years or ten? The early planning stage should involve not just R&D people, but also corporate planners and, except for very long-term strategic projects, key business functions such as manufacturing and marketing.

When the outline of the plan is finished, partner selection criteria can be established. In many R&D collaborations, partners effectively choose themselves. In arrangements such as MCC and Sematech, and in standards collaborations in which wide industry support is required, there is no choice at all. In other forms of collaboration, projects often evolve from existing relationships. This is a common process, and the importance of mutual trust should never be underestimated. Nevertheless, prospective partners should always be screened by a more systematic selection procedure.

Strengths in complementary technology will always be high on the list, but equally important are factors that include commitment, culture, and financial stability. The precise requirements will depend on the type of project. Marketing strength is important in standards collaboration, where the object is rapid imposition of your own standards on world markets. It is also important for companies entering vertical partnerships with potential customers.

Marketing is not always an important element in horizontal collaborations. The ideal will usually be a partner with strong technology but an inability to market the results effectively in competition with you. The same argument applies to vertical collaborations with suppliers; the ideal is a supplier strongly dependent on you for marketing and unlikely to seek out competitive channels of distribution.

The very same planning process should be applied to proposals for collaboration received from other companies: to make sure that projects are consistent with overall strategy, to establish who will gain what from the arrangement, and to decide on an appropriate level of commitment.

Choosing the Form of Organization

R&D collaboration can take one of three main forms: a subcontracting approach, the creation of a central laboratory, and the pursuit of parallel R&D programs.

Subcontracting

Subcontracting is used where a single organization is given authority for project management and the procurement of specific R&D tasks from project partners. Project management can be handled either by a team specifically created for the duration of the project (as in most of the Japanese programs) or by a lead contractor (as in the case of many EUREKA projects).

The subcontracting approach is ideally suited to vertical collaborations and to collaborations involving the development of complex systems, where input is required from companies and research organizations with a variety of different skills. Tight project management is essential in this situation, and authority must be clearly vested in a single individual. The approach lends itself particularly to projects aimed at developing a prototype. It is also appropriate when a choice is to be made between competing technical approaches to a particular problem that have been developed by different companies.

Central Laboratory

Typically, a central R&D facility is staffed by a combination of partners' personnel and special recruits. It is most appropriate for research in a new area of technology in which skills are scarce or expensive equipment is required. Examples include VLSI, ICOT, MCC, and ECRC.

The primary difficulty with this approach is the transfer of technology back to the parent companies. This is achieved primarily by the nature of loaned personnel to the parents. In Europe and the United States, however, the creation of the kind of first-class research and living environment necessary to attract the best scientists also mitigates against their return. Then the continuing turnover of management in sponsoring companies means that within three or four years the personal relationships through which technology might have flowed may well have been severed. A second important disadvantage of the central laboratory is the unwillingness of companies to send their best staff, a problem encountered in both the United States and Japan.

As a result of these problems, there is a danger that the laboratory will turn into a basic research organization, sometime like a university department. Such centers have an important role to play in the development of commercial technology, and industrial companies need to tap into them, but this is not the objective of the new type of collaborative project.

It is, therefore, particularly important for companies involved in this form of R&D collaboration to set up clear internal sponsoring relationships, with teams carrying out parallel development in-house. A continuing program of short-term personnel transfers is necessary to prevent the two groups from drifting apart and to ensure that the technologies developed by the collaboration can be effectively applied within the sponsoring companies. As the collaborative R&D moves through to commercialization, the parallel team can be expanded to include production and marketing personnel, thus encouraging technology transfer and early, efficient exploitation.

Parallel Research Programs
Companies can also carry out work in the same or related areas on their own premises but agree to exchange information and coordinate planning. A prime example of this approach is the Mega project of Philips and Siemens. Each company can examine twice as many options and test twice as much equipment for the same cost, but without having to give up control of its own R&D program.

Parallel research is appropriate for horizontal collaborations where companies wish to retain their independence. It enables companies to use their best staff people for projects without risk, and it avoids the technology-transfer problems associated with a central laboratory. It also makes it easier for companies to control the extent of contact with competitors and reduces the danger of technology bleed-through in other areas.

Many ESPRIT and EUREKA projects involve a high degree of parallelism. This is inevitable, given the geographic context and fundamental objective of changing attitudes about collaboration. In some cases, however, it probably reduces the potential for gains in R&D efficiency. As one participant put it, "Project management in the ESPRIT context is quite an artistic feat."

Getting the Team to Work Together

The management of all strategic partnerships requires great subtlety, and collaborative R&D is no different. The style of management needed depends on the form of collaboration chosen and on the proximity of the project to marketability. Leading-edge research requires an atmosphere that encourages free thinking. Near-market developments require much tighter project management. Strong project management is also essential for vertical collaboration: The partners must agree to having one organization take the lead or appoint an independent project manager.

There are special problems where a central laboratory is established. It is usual to appoint an independent manager to balance the conflicting interests of partners. Handling the complex personnel issues that arise is at least as important a part of the manager's job as providing technical leadership and project direction.

Achieving real, long-term collaboration between competing teams is heavily dependent on establishing trust at all levels. The creation of a joint facility makes it much easier to nurture genuine cooperation—at least within the laboratory.

In addition to formal seminars, socializing is an important part of getting people to communicate and work together well. *Yomu atsumari* (drinking meetings) were an informal but effective way of discussing critical points in the VLSI project.[10]

In the best-managed collaborations, however, there will still be some conflict of interest between the project manager, who wants the participants to work as a single team, and the parent companies, which must of necessity be circumspect.

Success Factors

Japan has by far the greatest experience in managing precompetitive collaborative R&D, and the biggest success story is still VLSI. Several factors seem to underlie the more successful Japanese projects.

Planning
First, a great deal of time and effort goes into deciding the subject of the research and then into formulating objectives and preparing the climate for cooperation. Projects are typically designed to produce prototypes or demonstration applications and have a narrowly defined, quantitative performance target. When the VLSI project was conceived, very few potential partners thought the technological goal was attainable. A key element in the success of the project was mobilizing opinion and getting companies to participate.

Partner Selection
Second, it is important to choose the right partner. MITI chooses companies that can handle the technology and exploit projects commercially. There is no attempt to involve smaller companies that offer no unique contributions, and the number of participants is limited.

Separating Research from Development
In this more complex environment, it is essential to distinguish between the research and the development components of the R&D pipeline. A research-oriented collaboration requires powerful intellectual leadership and minimum attempts at direction by partners. In contrast, very clear direction and tight project management are required for the later development phases, almost certainly within a different organizational context.

Harnessing R&D programs commercially is always difficult. Not only is the process complex, but the natural stimulation of interacting with international colleagues can easily become a distraction from the commercial focus of the project. The process must be carefully managed to keep it on track and bring the program through to commercial exploitation.

Sponsor Support

Success also depends on maintaining the wholehearted support of sponsors. Major collaborations usually have a high political profile within sponsoring organizations but, in time, responsibility is likely to be passed to less-senior or less-committed managers. In one case we examined, this process was seen as resulting in sponsors' taking a shorter-term perspective. Project directors must therefore plan to produce at least some tangible evidence of progress within about three years, and an atmosphere of urgency must be created within the project team. An important feature of the VLSI project was the intensely demanding timetable that was forced on the team. A good deal of overnight work was required, and the entire project lasted only four years.

Safeguarding Proprietary Data

R&D alliances need be organized to minimize competitors' access to commercial information. Collaboration is a mechanism for creating new technological competences, not for giving your old ones away. Companies must structure the partnership to prevent others from acquiring the core skills on which either the current or a future business will be built.

Exploiting the Results

The ultimate test is in the market: press the new advantage aggressively. VLSI is counted a success not because of the quality of the research or even the number of patents it generated, but because of the competitive vigor of its participants in exploiting the technical lead it gave them. It is up to companies to use new tools and products to their greatest advantage.

CHAPTER 8

THE ROLE OF CORPORATE VENTURING: OPTIONS ON THE FUTURE

If it works, it's obsolete.

—Marshall McLuhan

As used in this book, the term *corporate venturing* refers to large corporations that take minority equity positions in young, unlisted companies that have substantial growth prospects. In other contexts the term may be used to describe a variety of business arrangements, ranging from subcontract design and manufacturing to outright acquisition. Corporate venturing should not be confused with the typical venture-capital investment; it does not aim primarily at direct financial return.

REASONS FOR CORPORATE VENTURES

Principal Objectives

Companies typically make venture-capital investments for two strategic reasons. The first is to provide advance warning of key technological and market developments that might affect their own businesses—an objective often described as gaining a window on emerging technologies. Direct involvement with small businesses gives a company's executives a much better understanding of what is going on in the entrepreneurial undergrowth than can be obtained from reading reports and attending conferences. This knowledge helps in identifying new strategic opportunities and provides a distinct competitive advantage when a company comes to planning its own market-entry strategy. Some regard this so-called "radaring" activity as the sole reason for corporate venturing; more tangible benefits are icing on the cake.

In this sense, the corporate-venturing process also plays a special role in the early stages of a major diversification program. It provides a means of prospecting for emerging growth sectors and companies and a mechanism for making a wide range of small early-stage investments as a prelude to a more substantial secondary investment program in a limited number of growth businesses.

The second reason for corporate ventures is to provide specific opportunities for commercial relationships with the companies invested in—through OEM deals, licensing, joint ventures, or research contracts. This can sometimes greatly shorten product development times and provide access to expertise the investor does not yet have. Backing this with an investment underpins the commercial relationship and enables the investing company to participate in the successes flowing from its support.

Corporate venturing can also provide a mechanism for the exploitation of in-house technology in partnership with smaller companies, including spin-offs. This is particularly appropriate for markets and technologies outside the core business. It provides a means of sharing costs and risks, creating a more entrepreneurial business environment, and of handling projects that would not otherwise fit naturally within a company's strategy.

Less Tangible Benefits

Close involvement with the venture-capital and small-business communities yields a number of other, less tangible benefits to the corporate venturer. One of the most important is access to the broader venture-capital deal flow. While the vast majority of the hundreds of investment propositions received every year may be unsuitable for venture-capital investment as such, some may provide other commercial opportunities—through contract R&D or technology licensing, for example.

Involvement with entrepreneurial businesses can also be valuable because of its influence on the investor's own culture: exposing management to new ways of running a business and helping to sharpen up internal innovation processes. It can also help to develop the management skills of the people involved.

Benefits and Drawbacks for Investees

The benefits of corporate venturing are by no means one-sided. A corporate partner offers the small company a variety of potential benefits. These include access to large-company management skills, marketing networks, technical expertise, and the credibility provided by the backing of a big company.

At the same time, being tied to a large company can restrict freedom of action. It may make it more difficult to obtain contracts with the corporate partner's competitors, for example, and it could restrict the options if the shareholders want to sell out at a later date. Entrepreneurs are frequently wary of being dominated by their industrial partners, and many large-small firm partnerships are dogged by cultural and strategic conflicts.[1] Moreover, it is often more difficult to tap into the large company's resources than was expected, and these resources frequently turn out to be of limited relevance to the investee's business. Relatively few large companies have learned how to manage partnerships with small businesses effectively. The excessive time that a small company must often spend in dealing with an organization that is both organizationally and politically complex may come to outweigh the benefits. As a result, some entrepreneurs prefer more-neutral investors.

CORPORATE VENTURING IN THE TRIAD

Corporate venturing has been used to achieve specific objectives for a long time. For instance, du Pont took a substantial equity position in General Motors just after World War I. By 1919, it owned more than 28 percent of the stock, hoping to secure GM's paint and varnish business. Fairchild Semiconductors started as a spin-off from Shockley Transistor, partly financed by Fairchild Camera.

For these companies, however, the deals were one-time opportunities, not early examples of long-range ventures. The rise of corporate venturing as a systematic part of the business-development armory did not really begin until the 1970s. Today, companies around the globe are setting up corporate venturing programs. It is possible to invest in new business virtually anywhere in the world. Few corporations, however, have a genuinely international program. In practice, the main hunting ground is the United States.

The United States

Corporate venturing is now a well-established and widely accepted tool of corporate strategy in the United States. By 1987, 86 venture-capital operations were backed by industrial companies, with nearly $2 billion under management and an average fund size of $22 million.[2] Typically, a venture employed a team of two or three professionals. Many more companies make investments on an occasional basis, and there are several hundred direct investments each year.

Despite the continuing growth of interest, many companies find it difficult to get the management formula right. A number of corporate programs have been discontinued, including that of General Electric. Others shifted from wholly owned activities to investment in independent funds.

Europe

Europe has been rather slower to recognize the potential of corporate venturing. Companies that are active include Siemens, Olivetti, Philips, and Elf Aquitaine. For many, the first priority has been to establish venture-capital funds across the Atlantic in order to watch trends and gain access to the wealth of developing technology in the United States. In other cases, attention has been focused on spin-offs.

A number of U.S. companies have also invested in European funds, starting in the United Kingdom, the first European country to develop a venture-capital industry of any size. Examples include Johnson and Johnson, Monsanto, du Pont, and 3M. There have also been some direct investments.

One of the most interesting European funds is Euroventures, founded in 1984 by the European Round Table of Industrialists. Its financial backers include Asea, Fiat, 3M, Olivetti, Saint Gobain, Robert Bosch, and Volvo. One of Euroventures' objectives is to encourage pan-European collaboration. To achieve this, it operated through a network of satellite funds throughout the European Community.

Japan

In Japan, the development of venture capital is still at a very early stage, and industry tends to be more institutionalized and averse to risk than in the United States. Starting a business from scratch is extremely difficult, and it is proving hard to attract good staff from the big corporations, which a U.S. start-up finds comparatively easy. In the event of failure, it would be extremely difficult for Japanese staff members to find new employment.

Despite the difficulties, there is a steady stream of new businesses each year, often formed through the creation of specialist subcontractors as sponsored spin-offs from larger companies. Those who express doubt of Japan's ability to create entrepreneurs must remember the short history of Japanese industry. You don't have to go back far to find an entrepreneur in most Japanese companies. Two of its most broadly international corporations, Honda and Sony, were founded by entrepreneurs after World War II. The number of new joint-stock companies formed in Japan each year, however, remains low—48,000, as compared with 560,000 in the United States—and only about one tenth as many companies go public each year.

The Japanese venture-capital industry received a significant boost in 1982, following key measures to liberalize Japanese financial markets. The number of funds quadrupled in three years. Foreign financial institutions played an important part in the industry's early growth, by 1984 providing 25 to 50 percent of all funds invested.[3] Overseas players included Paribas (Paris), Kleiner-Perkins-Caulfield & Byers (San Francisco), Citicorp Venture Capital (New York), and Schroeder (London). The investment climate in Japan is still a difficult one, however, and there are few really good investment prospects. The largest funds are affiliated with other financial institutions, and investment policy is predominantly conservative.

The largest of the 70 or so venture-capital organizations now in operation is Jafco (Japan Associated Finance Company), with $300 million invested in some 350 small and medium-size businesses. A number of Western companies have made investments in Jafco in order to gain access to Japanese technology.

Against this background, it is not surprising that the role of corporate venturing is not well understood by most Japanese executives. But there is increasing interest in investing in growing companies, particularly in the United States. The large trading companies have been active catalysts in this process. Both Mitsui & Co. and Mitsubishi Corporation have organized U.S. venture funds, backed by Japanese industrial companies interested in U.S. technology. Several Japanese funds are internationalizing their operations. For example, Jafco now has a presence in San Francisco, Hong Kong, and Singapore.

Japanese companies in general seem more interested in making direct investments. One of the most active is Canon, with minority stakes in Energy Conversion Devices, Rise Technology, and Zygo. Kyocera, Nippon Steel, and Kobe Steel are also beginning to experiment with corporate venturing.

APPROACHES TO CORPORATE VENTURING

The corporate-venturing activity can be organized in four main ways. Many companies use a combination of these approaches:

- An in-house new-ventures division.
- A self-managed, independent fund.
- Investment in externally managed funds.
- Ad hoc investments and coventuring.

In-House Ventures Division

A specialized in-house division can be set up to make investments and monitor their performance. The main objective is often to exploit in-house technology.

Many companies have found it difficult to make a purely internal approach to venturing work. Those that have tried and failed include Exxon and BOC. There are many practical problems. First, it is difficult to get the right kind of staff involved. Running a venture-capital portfolio requires a high level of general management skill, and it involves monitoring and decision-making processes that differ from those a company might use for a wholly owned subsidiary. Executives who have the right qualifications for this task are likely to have, or be in line for, larger responsibilities for operations with a more immediate commercial payoff. It is difficult to give venture capital the same allure as managing a major division. Running an operation in which success takes several years and early failures are to be expected is likely to appear a far less certain route to promotion.

Professional venture capitalists are insulated from these problems by the financial incentives that go with equity participation in portfolio companies and by performance incentive programs. Large companies find it difficult to provide a comparable incentive package for a handful of middle-ranking staff. Recruitment of skilled venture capitalists is therefore a problem.

Even if these problems are resolved, there is still likely to be an internal clash of cultures. Large-company management procedures are inappropriate for a venturing operation. Many in-house venture groups find themselves having to bid for investment funds on a case-by-case basis, without the machinery to make decisions quickly. Company boards are unused to dealing with the degree of risk involved, and fear of failure inhibits investment. Cultural conflicts often get worse after investments have been made. There are many instances of investors trying to dominate the companies they have backed and falling out with their managers as a result.

Perhaps the greatest danger is in expecting too much. It normally takes more than five years for even very successful new businesses to become of major importance to the large company. Patience is required, and so is continuity of commitment. Changes in corporate objectives and management or financial difficulties can torpedo a well-set-up venturing program. Because venture-capital decisions tend to be viewed in the same way as larger investments, they have a high profile within the company. In their desire to get internal support, promoters of corporate venturing deals often overplay the benefits and give insufficient emphasis to the risks. This is followed by overreaction of senior management as the inevitable delays and problems arise. The failure of a single company provides the ammunition for antagonists elsewhere in the company to snipe at the entire corporate-venturing initiative.

Self-Managed Fund

A self-managed fund is similar to an in-house division in that the investing company maintains ultimate control. However, finance is not drawn from the company's cash resources in competition with other projects, but from an identifiable amount of money set aside in a special fund. A separate venture-capital team is usually recruited to run the fund at arm's length from the parent company.

This approach is common in the United States, where there have been important government incentives for investment through small business investment corporations (SBICs). Some European companies have also set up funds to provide venture capital to U.S. businesses using the SBIC vehicle.

External Fund

Most venture-capital funds have a combination of corporate and institutional investors. A corporate investor is particularly attractive to the fund manager, as it offers access to a variety of technical and marketing skills with which to investigate and monitor investments. The search for opportunities and investment decisions remains the responsibility of . the fund manager, but having a corporate sponsor reduces the investment risk.

For the corporate investor, a professionally managed external fund offers an effective way of getting involved with venture capital for a modest commitment of finance and management time. It also offers a highly flexible investment tool. Companies can choose to invest in general funds or funds specializing in tightly focused sectors—defense or health care, for example. Some funds invest internationally; others are highly localized. Some specialize in early-stage investments, others in more-established companies.

Many fund managers will design new funds specifically to invest in technologies and markets of interest to the corporate investor, attracting institutional money to add to the corporation's investment. Some managers offer corporate investors the opportunity to establish a separate, 100-percent fund, alongside the main fund, to be drawn on only when appropriate investment opportunities arise.

Investment in venture-capital funds has some important advantages over the approaches already discussed. First, it provides a ready mechanism for making and managing long-term, high-risk investments, removing many of the cultural and organizational problems associated with an in-house or wholly owned operation. Further, it enables the corporate investment to be leveraged with institutional money (perhaps by a factor of several times). This helps spread the risk and increase the number of companies with which the investor can become involved. In addition, it provides much better access to the deal flow that passes through the venture-capital community. As we have seen, access to the wider flow of potential investment opportunities is one of the most important side benefits of corporate venturing. Participating fully in the venture-capital community gives companies the opportunity to see many more deals than if they invested alone.

Investing through an independent financial intermediary can also allay the fear of domination that is common among entrepreneurs, and it can make possible investments that would be out of the question on a direct basis. Most active corporate ventures therefore invest in venture-capital funds, even if they are primarily interested in direct investment.

Ad Hoc Investments and Co-venturing

Co-venturing is the process of a corporate investor's making a direct capital investment together with other venture capitalists or corporate investors. Some companies with no corporate-venturing staff use this approach to make occasional investments in companies of interest to them, relying on divisional managers and others to bring them projects of interest.

Co-venturing on its own, however, is not an entirely satisfactory policy, because it does not provide good access to the venture capital community's wider deal flow. Corporations with investment funds are more likely to get the first crack at the best investments, and companies find it difficult to develop either the decision-making or the management apparatus necessary for occasional investments. The result can be a poor reputation in the venture capital community and a reluctance to offer further investment opportunities.

In addition, the number of investments made by this process is usually small. This means that both the executives involved and the overall policy are heavily exposed to the risk of failure.

ESTABLISHING A PROGRAM

A well-managed corporate-venturing program can provide a valuable part of any technology-based company's competitive arsenal. It is a feasible tool that can be organized in many ways—as long as a clear strategic vision, operating flexibility, and realistic expectations are all in place.

The first step in drawing up a venturing strategy is to establish a clear understanding of what you want to achieve and what you are willing to invest. These elements should be spelled out clearly:

- Specific objectives and overall benefits targets.
- Target sectors.
- Geographic coverage.
- Extent to which the focus is on start ups or more advanced investment opportunities.
- Degree of influence sought in investee companies.
- Downstream commercial benefits sought.
- Relationship with other business-development strategies.

CASE 8–1

The Olivetti Approach to Corporate Venturing

Olivetti is Europe's largest indigenous information-technology company, with revenues in 1987 of more than $6 billion. Its business has been transformed by strategic alliances over the last 10 years, and corporate venturing represents an important component of its strategy for acquiring innovative new technologies and products. The most important source is the United States.

The U.S. venture-capital operation is handled through a specially formed $40-million fund, Olivetti Partners, funded half by Olivetti and half by various financial institutions. Olivetti Partners is operated by a small team of Olivetti staff members who report to Elserino Piol, Olivetti's Vice President of Strategy and Development; he is ultimately responsible for all investment decisions.

Olivetti has also made smaller investments in a number of other funds around the world, primarily to provide access to the international deal flow and gain a window on emerging technological and market trends. This includes an 8 percent stake in Euroventures and a number of smaller investments in specialized funds based in Boston, San Francisco, Japan, and elsewhere.

Olivetti has also made many direct investments. Some of these date from before the formation of Olivetti Partners, and the parent company continues to make direct investments where a close and longer-term relationship is sought. They are wide ranging in terms of both product and geography and include a 7-percent stake in European Silicon Structures; a 40-percent investment in Olicom, a Danish start-up company; a 25-percent stake in Torus Systems in Cambridge, England; and a 9-percent stake in Dixi Corporation, a Yokohama company formed to develop flat plasma displays.

Over the years, the company has established a clear philosophy with regard to venture capital. The objective is to acquire innovative technology; Olivetti never looks on investment as a first step toward acquisition. Indeed, as companies in which it has invested expand, their role as leading-edge innovators is likely to diminish. They become more like Olivetti itself and therefore less interesting. As Piol explains, the approach "gives Olivetti the chance to become a player in very early growth markets."

Any venture-capital investment is high in risk, and there are many that fail to achieve their business objectives. Olivetti's portfolio reflects this pattern. However, some of the company's investments have led to useful OEM marketing agreements. Olivetti's first word processor was provided by Syntrex. It markets fault-tolerant computers produced by Boston-based Stratus and optical storage systems made by FileNet in California. Both Stratus and FileNet provide products with significant leverage for the sale of other Olivetti products as part of total systems packages, with products like Stratus' AX 2000 computer at the center of a network for Olivetti work stations.

Selecting the Investment Vehicle

It is important that any investment program be clearly set within the context of the company's overall strategic objectives and business-development program. Venture capital is a highly flexible investment tool, and it is possible to create an investment vehicle that is molded closely to the investor's interests. The size of the investment will depend on the company's objectives, the financial resources it can make available, and the relationship with other business-development strategies.

Investment in venture-capital funds should always form part of the corporate-venturing strategy. It brings a company into contact with the industry's mode of operation and provides access to the venture-capital deal flow. The cost of entry is low. An investment of $1 million or less provides involvement with a fund over a period of perhaps five years.

An investment of this size will provide only a modest degree of influence over the fund's policies; there may be another dozen investors. For a rather larger sum, it is possible to construct a tailor-made fund that will focus much more closely on areas of specific interest. The commitment of a major industrial investor can then be used to attract participation by more-passive institutional investors. A relationship of this kind will offer better access to portfolio companies as well as to the broader venture-capital deal flow, and the investing company can expect full participation on the fund's management board, together with regular discussion of investment prospects.

Whatever the approach adopted, a systematic search should be made for professional fund managers. The capabilities of venture-capital fund managers vary considerably. Prospective investors should use their wide network of managers, associates, and advisers to evaluate those with whom they expect to deal. The final selection should rest on three factors: expertise in target industries and markets, track record, and a willingness to meet the corporate investor's requirements and cooperate with its management.

CASE 8–2
Corporate Venturing at Monsanto

Monsanto was set up in 1901 by John Francis Queeny, the purchasing agent for a St. Louis wholesale drug company. After failing to persuade his employer to manufacture saccharin instead of importing it, he decided to make it himself, naming the company Monsanto after his wife's maiden name. The company grew to become one of America's top five chemical producers, with a broad product line of chemicals, plastics, and fibers.

By the early 1970s, it was becoming increasingly difficult for Monsanto to make good margins on many of its products, which were predominantly petrochemical commodities. The search for new lines of business had already begun.

Monsanto made its first venture-capital investment in 1972, when it formed InnoVen with another St. Louis company, Emerson Electric. Each contributed about $5 million, with another $2 million coming from institutional sources. InnoVen invested in a wide range of high-technology companies. Monsanto's objective at that time was to obtain superior financial returns and a window on new technology. In the end, it achieved both, and it was venture capital that accelerated Monsanto's entry into biotechnology—by as much as two or three years. However, it was Monsanto that first pointed InnoVen in the direction of biotechnology, an area in which the former did not itself have an in-house research program.

InnoVen's first biotech investment was a minor stake in Genentech, a company founded in 1976 to develop commercial applications of recombinant-DNA technology, and it later went on to play a key role in organizing Genex. Founded in 1977, Genex concentrated on specialty chemicals and enzyme technology, as opposed to health care applications, and carried out contract R&D for a number of other companies.

In 1982, Monsanto expanded its venture capital activities internationally, through the overseas network of the Boston venture-capital firm, T.A. Associates. The largest overseas investment was in Advent Eurofund, based in London. Monsanto had a 50-percent interest. Besides various institutional investors, the fund included investments by the United Kingdom's premier research universities—Oxford, Cambridge, and Imperial College. Advent's areas of interest include electronics, robotics, medical instrumentation and health care, energy and environmental management, nutrition, and advanced agricultural products. Other funds covered Japan and Southeast Asia.

As Monsanto's experience of corporate venturing has increased, it has refocused its strategy, concentrating on portfolio companies that are directly relevant to Monsanto's current and future strategic direction, and using venture capital as a vehicle for the exploitation of in-house technology through spin-offs. A special fund, Alafi Capital, was set up to make portfolio investments, although much of its effort has been directed at financing a single spinoff company, Invitron Corporation, set up to commercialize large-scale-mammalian cell culture technology developed within the company.

Monsanto takes an arm's-length management approach to its fund investment, leaving decision making to fund managers. A senior Monsanto executive generally sits on the board of each fund, supported by a manager who maintains close contact with fund managers. They make regular visits to portfolio companies to assess their potential value to Monsanto. In addition to this primary coordination network, managers in each of Monsanto's divisions are responsible for providing needed technical and commercial support. At the corporate level, the total venture-capital program is managed by a small operating board in St. Louis, which makes decisions on investments in new funds and determines the strategic direction of the program.

Monsanto has followed through by more direct involvement with small companies. Initially, R&D work on the BST animal growth hormone was subcontracted to Genentech. A technology for growing bone tissue, developed by Monsanto-funded researchers at Harvard Medical School, was seeded into Collagen, a company in which Monsanto took a substantial direct equity stake. And venture capital has been used to finance Invitron.

The most important contribution that venture capital has made to Monsanto has been to ease its entry into biotechnology, providing early experience of the opportunities, the players, and the problems. Direct ownership of technology and distribution is now more important. Monsanto has established its own substantial in-house biotechnology capability and has acquired a major pharmaceuticals company, Searle. In-house R&D, licensing and collaboration with universities are likely to be more important than venture-capital investments per se. An important milestone in the development of the company came in 1986 with the change from a capital-intensive to a research-intensive company. R&D now represents some 7 percent of sales, up from 3 percent in 1981, and 40 percent of this money is directed to biotechnology and the associated life sciences. Evolving from a peripheral exploratory activity, it is now set to be the core of the business in the 1990s.

Once the fund investment is in place, the corporation is in a better position to make direct investments to secure a larger interest in desirable individual companies. The venture-fund management team can be used to give a professional opinion on investment possibilities and compare the merits of apparently similar companies.

Investing in professional funds enables a company to build up a portfolio of interests in a wide range of companies quickly, without getting involved in complex internal discussions on a case-by-case basis. The number of investments protects the program from many of the risks to which corporate initiatives are subject, and at least some of the portfolio companies can be expected to perform extremely well.

The real danger to the venture-capital team lies in direct investments. These will inevitably be subject to more intense scrutiny. There will usually be conservative executives in a company who will be hard to convince of the merits of a venturing approach and quick to pounce on investment failures. One way of avoiding this danger is to focus the initial direct investments on second- or third-stage financing deals, where the technology or product is well advanced, and where the strategic benefits to existing core businesses are likely to be realized more quickly. This is the approach adopted by Raytheon Ventures in the United States. In fact, some 25 percent of Raytheon's investments are first identified by line managers.[4]

Managing the Program

One of the purposes of corporate venturing is to make investment decisions in a different way—in a number of small-scale, high-risk ventures to which normal corporate procedures are ill suited. It is important to provide the mechanism to make this possible. Clear individual responsibilities must be assigned. It is not possible to mix venturing with operational roles. Apart from very small programs, managing the venture-capital operation should be the sole responsibility of one person, usually supported by a small full-time team.

Handpicked Executives

Managing the activity demands entrepreneurial flair and the ability to work with different kinds of personalities without trying to dominate them. Managers must be excellent at networking—internally and externally. While they must be able to assess the relevance of technologies to the company's business, their perspective ought to be fundamentally commercial. Running a successful program also requires a clear strategic vision of what corporate venturing can and cannot be expected to do for the company. Achieving this subtle blend of skills is difficult, and careful personnel selection is essential.

Top-Level Support

Top-management support is vital for any corporate-venturing program. CEOs must be prepared to maintain a continuing parental interest. They must make sure that the complex web of operational and political interests that exists in any large corporation does not undermine the initial strategy before it has had a chance to bear fruit.

It is sometimes tempting for the chief executive officer to try to retain the same degree of control over venture-capital decisions as over major acquisitions. This is a recipe for failure. Once the commitment to the program has been made, operational responsibility should be handed over to the corporate-venturing team. Financial resources must be clearly segregated for investments, ideally over a five-year period, and all but very large ones should be the responsibility of the corporate-venturing team so decisions can be made quickly.

Managing the Interface

The success of a corporate-venturing program is measured by the impact it makes on the corporation's business, and this depends on how the interface with portfolio companies is managed. Realizing the potential synergies requires close involvement of managers at different levels and in different parts of the corporation—with R&D staff to evaluate technology and set up joint development projects, and with commercial managers to ensure effective exploitation. These four steps are helpful in creating the necessary connections:

1. Work out the organizational responsibilities early in the program, and gain the commitment of senior-level opinion shapers and decision makers.
2. Make regular visits to portfolio companies. Watch progress and discuss possible areas of cooperation, without exerting excessive influence. Establishing a single point of contact within the corporation for day-to-day exchanges is important for smooth relations. This does not need to be the same executive who represents the corporation on the board, if indeed a board seat has been negotiated.
3. Bring commercial managers on board quickly. Translating a technical interest in collaboration into commercial reality is one of the

hardest aspects of venturing. While the scientists in the two companies may get on well together, it is often difficult to get the investor's business managers really committed. It is the task of the corporate-venturing team to facilitate this transfer by getting commercial departments involved early and, if necessary, directly sponsoring the R&D work required to create these linkages. Good personal relationships between a few key individuals are instrumental in getting effective commercial collaboration. Managing the vertical supply relationships that many corporate investments are designed to facilitate is discussed in more detail in Chapter 11.

Managing the interface is even more difficult where overseas investments are involved. Language barriers and long flights make this much more difficult (though Fax machines are making it easier). One of the small European companies we spoke to still had not made direct contact with its U.S. corporate partner 18 months after the investment was made.

4. Empower local managers to act as liaison with overseas investees. Systematic international venturing is really practicable only for companies that have a business presence in other countries and that can exploit R&D opportunities locally and pass information to other parts of the corporation. Many multinationals fail to take advantage of international venturing opportunities because they do not have the right people on the scene or do not assign them responsibility to search for such opportunities.

Managing Expectations

The path of the corporate venturer is riddled with pitfalls. To avoid these, investments must be monitored carefully, and the support of the CEO and fellow executives must be sustained.

One of the greatest dangers common to these programs is failure to meet overly high expectations. Much as with a company's R&D program, only a small proportion of investments will deliver clear, tangible benefits, and these may take several years to come through. Messy situations are intrinsic to venture-capital business. A continuing internal propaganda battle may be required to explain the role of the program and relate it to the rest of the business-development effort.

There are also some specific risks. Getting too closely involved with poor or fraudulent investments can reflect adversely on the investing company. Fund managers must be selected with care, and companies must make use of their international finance networks to check out direct investments thoroughly.

Corporate venturing is an increasingly important part of the multinational's armory, providing a powerful adjunct to in-house R&D programs. As Al Heininger, Vice President of Corporate Strategy at Monsanto, puts it, ''The job of the R&D function is no longer that of creating technology, but of finding it.''

CASE 8–3
Exxon's New Ventures Program

One of the most publicized failures in corporate venturing is Exxon Enterprises, launched in 1970, which tried to combine internal venturing and investment in venture-capital-backed companies. Between 1970 and 1980 it made a total of 37 investments—19 internal start-ups and 18 investments in external companies. Exxon later acquired six of these. While the venture-capital program was successful, Exxon's internal ventures and acquisitions program was largely disappointing, and it was wound down in 1981.

Writing in the *Harvard Business Review*, Hollister B. Sykes, the manager responsible for the program, made the following observations on the reasons why Exxon's program failed to meet expectations:[5]

1. The managers of the internal ventures program were usually technical people, with limited management experience. This was in stark contrast to the venture-capital-backed companies.

2. Exxon's successful new ventures tended to focus on a single product. There was great difficulty in managing the rapid growth that comes with success and making the transition to a multiproduct company; two of the most successful ventures, the Vydec word processor and Zilog Z80 microprocessor, both failed to maintain their initial technical lead in the face of accelerating competitive pressure and a new generation of products.

3. As ventures grew and increased corporate investment was required, Exxon tried to impose more and more large-company management controls, undermining the motivation of key people, making it difficult to award appropriate salaries, slowing decision making, and adding to the venture managers' work load.

4. The venture program team was forced to bow to political pressure to amalgamate ventures in related areas too early in their

development, before any single venture was strong enough to command the respect of the other's management.

5. The ready availability of corporate funds cushioned venture managers from commercial realities.

6. An inability to offer equity participation in internal ventures until late in the program made it impossible to attract experienced managers.

7. The lack of synergy between ventures and Exxon's core business meant that Exxon could provide only limited functional support.

CHAPTER 9

USING EQUITY JOINT VENTURES TO CREATE NEW COMMERCIAL OPERATIONS

The term *joint venture* covers a variety of business relationships, from OEM supply agreements to the merger of major operating units. In this chapter, we are concerned with one type only—equity partnerships involving the creation of a totally new organization.

New joint ventures are undertaken for many reasons: to gain access to new geographic markets or customer bases; to get around import restrictions; to accelerate entry into a new product market requiring skills that neither partner can provide alone; to share costs and financial risks. Many joint ventures also provide an opportunity for partners to learn skills from one another that are advantageous to their broader business portfolios.

Whatever the nature of the joint venture, the partners involved always have different starting positions and different objectives. Tensions are inevitable, and there are always, at least in theory, other ways of achieving objectives. The primary advantage of joint ventures is that they allow companies to acquire resources that are not for sale or that cannot be bought, such as management skills or access to a distribution network.

Any company considering creating a joint venture must weigh the options carefully. It must make a thorough assessment of the resources it needs for the commercial operation, and it must evaluate the other means of obtaining them. Above all, it must be sure that it can establish a *modus vivendi* with its partner in which the potential for conflict is minimized.

This is true of all alliances, of course. The difference between an equity joint venture and other forms of alliance is in the extent of the power shared. Once the agreement is signed, management is handed over to an executive team, which may be able to exert a high degree of autonomy. It must both make the venture a success as an entity in its own right and ensure that the interests of the shareholders are fairly served. But inevitably, circumstances and objectives change. The chances of any one partner being fully satisfied diminish as time passes.

Equity joint ventures are therefore inherently unstable, and the anticipated benefits all too often turn out to be elusive. A thorough analysis of the strategic and commercial context is essential before negotiations with potential partners are started. This must cover five important questions:

- What are the strategic objectives and options of the partners?
- What will be the commercial and financial relationships between the parents and the joint venture?
- How is the joint venture likely to develop?
- What will be the impact on the parents?
- What are the main management issues?

Many companies do not undertake the necessary analysis in advance. As a result, they may fail to exploit their joint ventures effectively, be outmaneuvered by a stronger partner, or see the venture fail to survive a change in circumstances.

We therefore look first at the nature of the strategic and commercial context in which joint ventures are established and at the financial relationships between the venture and its parents. We then turn to consider the mechanics of each stage of a joint venture: Pre-venture planning and partner selection, the negotiations, and start-up. The chapter closes with a discussion of success factors and limitations.

UNDERSTANDING THE STRATEGIC CONTEXT

In many cases, the objectives of the joint-venture partners are different. The parents will be continually developing their own strategies. Each, therefore, must understand how the relationship between the joint venture and its own business is likely to evolve. The venture may gradually become more or less important to its core business. Later, it may wish to increase control or acquire the joint venture completely. Or it may see the ultimate goal as the realization of a good financial return by the sale of its stake.

Technological developments will create new opportunities, perhaps rendering the joint venture's business irrelevant. For example, many of the functions now fulfilled by complex electronic systems will within the next 10 years be carried out by simple devices or even single components; optical storage technology will take over from magnetic storage; and the computer manufacturers of tomorrow are likely to lean heavily on the skills of the consumer electronics companies of today. Parents have the choice of exploiting these opportunities either directly or in collaboration through joint ventures. The balance of power between the partners will change, depending on which has the strongest technology and which is best financed and organized to exploit it.

It is essential to try to understand the aspirations of each partner, particularly when it is an actual or potential competitor. All possible scenarios must be considered. What are the partner's plans for growth and diversification? How is the joint venture likely to relate to them? Is it likely to use the joint venture to learn technological skills so that it can develop its own products? What is the relationship with its in-house R&D programs? Is the joint venture strong enough to meet all the partner's ambitions, or might it eventually seek a competing alliance with a more powerful company? Can it use the joint venture to gain direct access to your own customer base? Is the partner getting a fair share of benefits of the joint venture? Will it try to increase that share? Can long-term commitment to the venture be guaranteed? For example, are the financial demands of your partner's other businesses likely to prevent it from further investments in the joint venture? Is the sponsoring business unit likely to be sold, or is a takeover likely? Would a purchaser have the same interest in the joint venture's success?

Each joint-venture opportunity raises a whole series of such questions. These must be tackled at the outset, when the possibility of a joint venture is being considered and potential partners are being evaluated. The answers should influence not just the selection of partners but also how the agreement is drawn up and, indeed, whether a joint venture is the appropriate vehicle at all.

Ultimately, one of the most important factors in successful joint ventures is trust, and trust can easily be destroyed by surprises. A clear understanding of these strategic issues and the partners' objectives is fundamental. It provides the background to the detailed operational planning.

There are four important reasons for embarking on a joint venture.

CASE 9–1
BT&D Ltd.—The Classic Joint Venture

BT&D was set up in 1986 to exploit the fast-growing market for op-toelectronic components. It is owned equally by British Telecom and du Pont.

British Telecom is the United Kingdom's principal public-telephone operator, with annual revenues of $17.6 billion. Privatized in 1984, it was until then the monopoly service supplier in the United Kingdom.

Maintaining and improving public switching networks requires major long-term investment. To be able to specify and select the ap-propriate technologies for the future, British Telecom needs a strong R&D capability, and its substantial R&D operation was internation-ally respected. However, British Telecom does not manufacture. While it cooperates closely with its suppliers on design, the manufac-turing of equipment for the telephone system has been left to British companies such as Plessey and GEC.

One of the most important new technologies in telecommunica-tions is optoelectronics. British Telecom spends more than 20 per-cent of its R&D budget in this area and had developed a proprietary manufacturing technology based on metal organic vapor phase epi-taxy. However, because of its lack of manufacturing and interna-tional marketing experience, it was, on its own, incapable of taking advantage of the commercial potential offered by its lead.

Du Pont, the other partner in BT&D, has a very different back-ground. A $30-billion U.S. chemical company, it had suffered from competition in the commodity chemical markets, which made up much of its business in the 1970s, and was anxious to diversify. As a part of its search for opportunities, du Pont formed a working group to examine the potential of optoelectronics. It sounded out a number of potential partners and first approached British Telecom at its Martlesham Laboratories during an open house in 1984. Du Pont could offer many of the skills that BT lacked—manufacturing compe-tence, the experience of setting up international marketing net-works, and strong international management. Its own optoelec-tronics R&D group had complementary technical skills and was involved in related areas such as high-performance connection sys-tems and optical storage media.

BT&D, formally established in 1986, involves a significant in-vestment of money by each partner. Each company is expected to invest well over $60 million in the venture before it moves into profitability in the early 1990s. The CEO, Howard Claussen, was previously Managing Director of du Pont's U.K. subsidiary. A new 90,000-square-foot manufacturing complex has been built close to British Telecom's research facilities, and the company has invested heavily in automation in anticipation of rapidly falling prices as the market grows.

Scale is an important part of BT&D's strategy; its factory is the largest custom-built optoelectronic plant outside Japan. Marketing was led initially from the United States, which accounted for roughly 70 percent of the world market, which is expected to grow by 30 percent per year, reaching $4 billion by the mid-1990s.

Du Pont entered a second important joint venture in 1986 to develop and market optical-storage technology. Like BT&D, Philips–du Pont Optical is aiming at a sizable global market—expected to be $4 billion by 1990. Each company is investing $150 million.

Exploitation of a New Product-Market Opportunity

Companies with a strong R&D base frequently develop technology that gives them the opportunity to enter a new area of business for which they lack appropriate skills and resources. This is becoming more and more common as the interconnections between technologies become more complex. Examples include BT&D Ltd., created to exploit British Telecom's optoelectronics technology; Siecor, established to exploit Corning's fiberoptics technology; and Japan New Media System Inc., a 50/50 joint venture between Philips and Kyocera to develop products in home banking and similar areas.

In this kind of situation, there are four main options for commercial exploitation:

* Joint venture.
* An in-house business developed by recruiting and buying in key skills.
* Acquisition of a company (or companies) with the missing skills.
* Licensing the technology to other companies for commercial exploitation.

Licensing is the simplest route, but it is suitable only where proprietary technology has been created that will not be rapidly superseded. This tends to limit it to areas like pharmaceuticals and chemicals, where patent protection is strong. Further, since the originator does not build a genuine *business* around the technology, it is unable to profit from the value added that can be derived from selling the technology into different applications markets.

In-house development offers the greatest degree of control. It is also rather slow, however, and there are usually problems for a large business in allowing the independence that a new business needs. A partial spin-off in which outside equity is introduced can sometimes contribute to a more entrepreneurial culture, but it is really appropriate only if the opportunity is unlikely to constitute an important part of the future core business.

Acquisition is, in principle, attractive as a means of obtaining the resources required to enter new markets. However, the cost is often high (especially if the missing resource is an effective global marketing network), and absorption is usually more difficult than expected. Furthermore, a suitable candidate may not be available.

Joint ventures frequently provide the quickest and most cost-effective means of market entry. They can help companies with technology to acquire adequate manufacturing or marketing skills; they can help companies to combine technologies to enter new applications markets; and they can help companies with little or no relevant technology diversify into new markets. In some cases, the venture is a carefully planned move to change the core business portfolio; in others, it is an opportunistic move to exploit a technological competence that would otherwise lie fallow.

Exploitation of an Overseas Market

Companies can usually sell into export markets in one or more of the following ways:

- Exporting from the home market base, either directly or through OEM contracts organized through a local company marketing subsidiary.
- Establishing a wholly owned facility to market and possibly to assemble or even manufacture products locally.
- Joint venture with a local company.
- Acquisition of all or a majority of a local company.

A further option is manufacture under license by a local company. Income would be derived from royalties and possibly the sale of components.

Usually, an ideal solution provides 100-percent control. Different national markets have widely different characteristics, however, and in most cases local management is required. This can make the creation of a new overseas subsidiary from scratch difficult and time consuming. A joint venture provides a means of accelerating market entry and reducing entry costs. This is often viewed as a merely temporary strategy—a prelude to outright acquisition or the establishment of a separate, wholly owned operation.

Overseas marketing is particularly difficult where the selling of systems is involved, requiring substantial local engineering input to meet individual customer requirements and strong aftersale service. Building up this capability through investment in a greenfield site is usually out of the question. A local partner with some knowledge of the market, and able to recruit the needed staff, is required. Setting up the operation through an equity joint venture (as opposed to a straight distribution relationship) provides a way in which the supplying company can participate in the locally generated added value.

The decision to manufacture locally should in principle be treated separately from that as to the business vehicle. Theoretically, the main determinants are cost and marketing factors. In practice, political considerations are often more important. As companies come more and more to wield competitive advantages on a global basis rather than nationally, the winners and losers in different industries are becoming more clearly identified. High levels of import penetration are more and more common in unprotected markets. For the United States and Europe, this is a relatively new experience, at least as far as more-advanced manufactured goods are concerned. There is often strong pressure for major importers to locate production locally, and this is likely to continue. In Japan, on the other hand, the pressure is diminishing.

One of the main reasons companies use joint ventures to set up assembly or production in major overseas markets, as opposed to 100-percent-owned operations, is to defuse local political pressure. In the developing countries there is often a legal requirement for local participation, and more subtle forms of commercial and political pressure can also be brought to bear.

Gaining a Share of Local Manufacturing Profits

This is the inverse of the preceding objective, with the prospective local partner looking to boost its share of local manufacturing. A local company usually teams up with an overseas supplier in one of four ways:

- As a straightforward distributor.
- By selling imported products under its own name as an OEM customer.
- By forming an equity joint venture.
- By manufacturing and marketing under license.

The share of value that accrues to the local company increases with its degree of involvement. A company with a strong local brand or distribution network is an ideal OEM customer for the overseas supplier. The established customer may then be able to negotiate greater participation through a local manufacturing joint venture, especially if it has government backing.

The J2T joint venture is a good example. When Thorn EMI and Thomson agreed to act as OEM customers for JVC's VHS video recorders in Europe, they agreed that a European manufacturing joint venture would be created if sales reached a certain level. The venture gave them the opportunity to participate in some of the manufacturing profits as well as the marketing profits from VCRs.

Acquiring Knowledge or Technology
For the Core Business

Every strategic partnership provides an opportunity for partners to learn from one another. Equity joint ventures are of particular value, as they provide direct access to technologies that are at, or close to, commercialization. They usually provide access not just to the hard technology of the product, but also to the product-planning and design skills that go with it, the manufacturing skills that enable it to be made efficiently, and the management skills involved in setting up a new business operation.

Once learned, these skills and technologies can be applied in other businesses outside the joint venture. They may eventually provide the means by which one partner can strike out on its own, developing superior products to be sold independently. The Japanese manufacturing industry has been built on the back of Western technology, often acquired through licensing and joint ventures. The newly industrialized countries are currently going through the same process.

A good example of a change in fortunes derived from technology transfer is NEC's relationship with Honeywell. In 1982, NEC signed a 10-year licensing agreement to produce mainframe computers using Honeywell technology. This arrangement was later renewed. In 1984, the position was reversed, with Honeywell manufacturing the NEC System 1000 under license. As a result of experiences like these, companies are less and less willing to license advanced technology. An equity joint venture provides a means of participating in the business they have helped establish.

Western executives sometimes regard the use of a partnership as a learning experience as unfair in some ways, and the not-invented-here prejudice prevalent in the West impedes technology transfer in the opposite direction. Imitation, however, is usually the only way open to a NIC company for breaking into a new market. "We do a lot of reverse engineering," admitted one Korean executive. Joint ventures provide the ideal training ground.

Technology transfer is an important objective in many joint ventures, though generally it is a long-term goal that sits somewhat apart from the shorter-term financial and marketing objectives. Joint ventures are increasingly being created to transfer know-how from East to West—in industries such as consumer electronics and semiconductors in which Japanese companies have obtained supremacy. NUMMI is a good example of a two-way flow, providing Toyota with the experience of operating in the United States and General Motors with the opportunity to learn Japanese manufacturing methods. Besides experience with Toyota's management approach, the venture also provides access to new process technology. One of the start-up team's first tasks was to install a $30-million metal stamping facility based on Toyota's design.

COMMERCIAL AND FINANCIAL RELATIONSHIPS
WITH PARENTS

Two types of benefits flow from joint ventures—strategic and financial. Strategic benefits come from access to new technologies or skills, from the impact on sales volume with its resulting ability to support higher levels of R&D, and from the reduction of financial or political risk. Such benefits are difficult to measure, though they must not be ignored. Whatever the strategic context of the venture, the direct financial impact on the parent is a key yardstick of the joint venture's performance. The question "Will it be a good investment?" is fundamental.

The commercial and financial relationships involved in joint ventures are complex and varied. Different partners usually benefit in different ways, with a resulting conflict of interests. Financial benefits can flow directly from the joint venture to its parents through:

- Dividends on the venture's profits.
- License royalties from designs or technologies developed by the parents.
- Purchases of raw materials, components, or assemblies from the parents.
- Consultancy or management fees.
- Sharing in the growth in the capital value of the joint venture's assets.
- Profits from marketing products produced by the joint venture.

In addition, the parent can benefit strategically from the impact on economies of scale in the parent, through sales of components or raw materials to the joint venture, and the resulting reduction in unit costs. Some of the most common relationships are discussed below.

Pooling Technology to Enter a Radically New Market

In Exhibit 9–1, the parent companies have pooled resources to start a new, largely freestanding business. The joint venture purchases raw materials from independent sources and markets its own products. The main financial benefits to the parents are likely to be through dividends and the growth in value of its investment. One or both companies may be able to negotiate royalty payments on the technology provided but, by and large, the parents have an equal interest in the venture's financial success, provided that there is no competition for customers.

Local Manufacturing and Marketing

Often, an overseas company will link up with a local business to sell into the latter's market. In this situation, the joint venture will usually carry out

EXHIBIT 9–1
Relationship between Local Manufacturers and OEM Intermediary

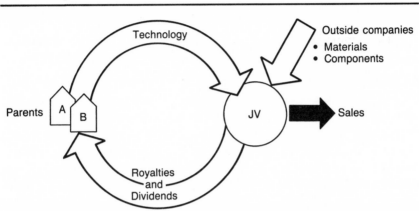

production under license or assemble products from components supplied by the overseas parent.

In contrast to a pooling of technology, the financial interests of the two companies are here quite different. Eastern Europe poses new and unusual questions of income repatriation, but traditionally, the overseas parent can receive income in a number of ways:

- Profits on raw materials or components supplied to the joint venture.
- Royalty payments.
- Dividends.
- Capital growth.

At least in industrialized countries, the overseas parent will probably try to minimize local manufacturing content and set the highest possible transfer price for the raw materials or components it supplies. In many cases the boost to domestic manufacturing profits is the most important source of revenue. However, the local parent can benefit only through dividends and capital growth, and it is in its interest for transfer prices to be as low as possible.

It is clear that there are strong commercial pressures on the local partner to try to bring as much as possible of the added value into its core business—by manufacturing components for the joint venture or gradually appropriating its product-market base. Certainly there is likely to be only limited incentive to continue trading through the joint venture if a wholly owned alternative becomes possible, especially if that also opens up exporting prospects.

Local Manufacturing with an OEM Customer

A third approach is even more complex. In this situation the overseas partner has joined forces with a local company to establish a local assembly operation. Both then sell the product under their own brand names, the overseas partner through a wholly owned marketing subsidiary. This form of joint venture is becoming increasingly common with growing pressures on exporters to adopt an insider position in major markets. Examples include the J2T joint venture, NUMMI, Eurotechnique, and Canon's European office-equipment joint venture with Olivetti. The overseas parent earns a margin on both component manufacture and distribution. The local partner earns only the distribution margin. Both partners can benefit from dividends on the joint venture's profits. The setting of transfer prices is a critical issue here; the interests of the two partners are quite different.

Structuring the Financial Relationship

There are many variants of these examples. It may also be possible to arrange repatriation of profits through the payment of interest on loans made by one or both of the parents or through consulting or management fees. Dividends are often the least important financial consideration. Many of the joint ventures we studied had, in fact, never declared one. Transfer prices, royalty payments, and commissions are set so that profits accrue directly to the parent companies. Clarifying how the commercial relationship will work in different circumstances is, therefore, critical to getting an acceptable financial return.

In many situations, a number of commercial and financial relationships are possible. In choosing among them, each parent needs to evaluate the commercial and tax implications and assess the impact on its P&L and balance sheet. The impact of possible commercial and strategic changes must also be carefully considered. Specific considerations that may need evaluation include:

- The way in which transfer prices will be adjusted in response to exchange-rate changes.

- Expected reductions in manufacturing cost arising from learning-curve improvements in manufacturing—both in the parents and in the joint venture—and the way in which this will be reflected in transfer prices.
- Possible reductions in royalties as the joint venture develops in-house technology or acquires it from other sources.
- Shifts in the procurement of products or assemblies from parents to alternative sources.
- The effects of competition on volume and overall margins.

Different forms of financial relationships are likely to be affected in different ways by these changes.

There are special problems for joint ventures between Western and Japanese companies. Japanese companies usually pay only modest dividends, and venture partners must look for other income streams. Moreover, an initially satisfactory profit can be easily and drastically altered by changes in circumstances. One of the joint ventures we examined was set up to sell products manufactured by a Western partner into the Japanese market. The margin on these products delivered the Western parent a good return on its investment. Over time, however, it became sensible to buy products from the Japanese parent, which had developed a more appropriate product for the local market. While the joint venture was still successful, the revenue flow to the Western parent was reduced to quite unsatisfactory levels.

A further complication is the different attitudes to manufacturing and marketing activities of Western and Japanese companies. Western companies usually regard both as important profit centers. Many Japanese companies look on manufacturing as the principal source of profits; the function of marketing is to achieve maximum market share. Prices may be set in a way that takes into account *anticipated* learning-curve improvements in manufacturing costs. It is then up to manufacturing to deliver those improvements. Such differences in attitude can give partners different financial expectations of joint ventures, although the conflict may become apparent only when circumstances change.

PREVENTURE PLANNING

The next step is to carry out detailed preventure planning, providing the basis on which to decide:

- Whether the venture is financially viable—either in its own right or in terms of its contribution to the parent's business.
- By what means it should be undertaken (e.g., joint venture versus acquisition).
- What resources are required from outside the company.
- The criteria for selecting the partner.
- Key negotiating points.

An appropriate level of flexibility must be built into the strategy. This is particularly important for joint ventures created to exploit novel technologies. The most lucrative applications and the best means of marketing will become clear only over time. Opportunism is a vital ingredient of such businesses.

The need to go through this analytical and planning process applies as much to recipients of joint-venture proposals as to initiators. They must be sure that they have the information with which to match their potential partners in negotiations.

Lack of planning is surprisingly common in strategic alliances. For example, one of the companies we examined had almost concluded a license agreement with a more aggressive commercial partner before a new director initiated an examination of the proposal. Only then did the possibility of using an equity joint venture to get a larger share of the added value become apparent. In another case, a joint venture foundered in its first year because one of the companies failed to carry out a proper market and technical assessment and had not determined how its own contribution should be organized. Operational difficulties rapidly arose, demolishing the trust that had been established between the partners.

Initiatives taken directly by chairmen and chief executives sometimes cause the greatest problems for planners. The automatic support that they tend to generate gives them such momentum that the formal disciplines of planning and feasibility testing used for in-house ventures are abandoned. Top-level backing is vital in order to secure commitment and build a relationship of trust with the other partner, but it must be tempered with normal business caution.

There are two main aspects of preventure planning: preparing an outline business plan for the joint venture and identifying and screening potential partners. In practice, this is an iterative process, the two components often moving in parallel. The precise form of the relationship will depend on what each of the two parties has to contribute, which becomes clear only during negotiations. Also, joint ventures are frequently set up between partners that have already been working together over a long period. This may have been through an OEM relationship or a precompetitive collaborative R&D program. Trial marriages of this kind can provide a good way of establishing whether partners are likely to be able to work together in a joint venture.

In many cases, the number of genuine candidates is limited to two or three companies. Personal contacts and intuition will always be important in business—but, subjective judgments should always be carefully tested against the qualities and characteristics of the other options. The starting point for the selection process is the venture plan.

The Venture Plan

As for any other initiative requiring a major commitment of assets and management time, companies considering a joint venture should first prepare a business plan. This plan should describe the rationale for the initiative and define its objectives. It should also indicate anticipated resource requirements and describe the venture's operations. The plan should relate to the overall operation, not just to the contributions of one parent. Alternative means of achieving the business objectives, through licensing or acquisitions, for example, should be evaluated.

The main topics that usually need to be covered are shown in Exhibit 9–4. In some areas, very little detail will be available at this early stage. It may be necessary to commission studies by external consultants—on technology, market characteristics, competitors, or financial matters. Going through these planning disciplines helps pinpoint areas where information on potential partners must be gathered later.

Preparing the Ground Internally

A collaboration in one area of a major company's business usually has an impact on many different interests and product areas. To be successful, it may need the support of several subsidiaries or divisions. Joint ventures usually need to be championed at a senior level in the company—either by the CEO or by a director who is able to obtain the chief's wholehearted backing. One of the jobs of the sponsor is to make sure that all the key people on whom the success of the venture will depend get a chance to air their views and participate fully in the planning process. Lack of effective consultation was clearly evident in one of the failed joint ventures we examined. In this case, the venture was largely the chief executive's initiative. In pushing the proposal forward, he quickly attracted the support of a variety of executives who could see ways of furthering their careers. The two key divisions, however, remained unconvinced. Politics and planning lapses had doomed it from the outset.

In some cases, the venture may conflict with existing business relationships or undermine other strategies. It may open up other parts of the business to competitive attack. There may even be the opportunity for a broader collaboration with certain partners, bringing benefits to a number of different parts of the organization.

Widespread internal consultation is particularly important in companies that have extensive programs of alliances. It is important to expose these interests at an early point in the planning. This helps to identify potential allies for the proposed venture and address the specific needs of dissenters. Some companies with extensive partnership programs have set up special internal mechanisms to assist this process.

Partner Selection

In drawing up a profile of the ideal joint-venture partner, it is necessary to consider both the resources that will be required to contribute and a variety of less easily measurable characteristics. If the major selection criteria are established at the outset, the partner search and screening exercise will reveal the key sensitivities and stumbling blocks.

Key Resource Analysis
The venture plan should indicate what resources the venture will require overall. Preparing a simple table of needs inputs, as in Exhibit 9–5, helps to identify what the initiating company can contribute to the joint venture and what resources are required from the other partner.

Those resource requirements must be defined in some detail. "Having strong marketing skills" is not the same as "having relevant distribution networks in target markets," for example.

The exact mix of resources provided by each partner varies widely. In the case of BT&D, British Telecom provides its optoelectronics research capability in return for du Pont's skills in commercializing and marketing the results of that research. Siecor involved the contribution of complementary technologies by Siemens and Corning. In the case of J2T, JVC

EXHIBIT 9–2
The Venture Plan

Introduction	• Background • Business need or opportunity • Objectives of business initiative
Product(s)/Service(s)	• General description • Circumstances of use by purchasers • Research and development (current status and work to be undertaken) • Patents, licenses, and other intellectual property rights • Future development plans, including follow-up products
The Market	• Market size and anticipated changes • Market segments • Prospective customers and their needs • Nature of the purchase decision • Distribution chain • Dependence on third parties • Impact of new technologies • Assessment of competition
Business Strategy	• Means of securing and retaining competitive advantage • Technology • Marketing • Cost • Project phasing
Resource Requirements	• Product range (in-house and bought-in products or components) • R&D skills • Production capabilities • Facilities • Marketing skills • Market access/distribution networks • Systems engineering capabilities • Customer support • Management • Finance
Strategic Options	• Structure of commercial and financial relationships with both joint venture and other options (e.g., acquisition, in-house development), and in each case:

EXHIBIT 9–2 (concluded)
The Venture Plan

	• P&L and balance-sheet projections
	• Financial flows to parents
	• Impact on balance sheet of parents
	• Effect on consolidated P&L and balance sheets of parents
	• Financing requirements
	• Return on parent's capital
	• Analysis of alternative strategies
	• Strategic and financial impact
Key Issues	• Principal risks and problems
	• Proposals for coping with these
Funding	• Amount of start-up funding required
	• Return on capital
	• Mileposts
Appendixes	• Technical reports
	• Market surveys
	• Additional detailed information

---

contributed product designs and manufacturing skills in exchange for market access. In the NUMMI venture, Toyota contributed its manufacturing expertise in return for GM's U.S. marketing capability and experience in the U.S. business environment. NUMMI is unusual in that it involves not just a *pooling* of skills in the joint venture, but a genuine *exchange* of skills between the parent companies, with the joint venture the conduit through which that exchange takes place.

Both parties usually contribute financially to a joint venture, although Eurotechnique is the only example we studied where money was the *principal* contribution of one of the partners. In its efforts to diversify into electronics, St. Gobain effectively bought into semiconductors by putting up the cash in exchange for National Semiconductor's design capabilities and semiconductor production technology.

Other Criteria

There are often a number of companies that could provide the skills and resources required for the prospective partnership, but other factors need to be taken into account. These reflect both the criteria for the success of

EXHIBIT 9–3
Key Resource Analysis

	Key Factors for Success	Venture Requirements	Initiating Company Contribution	Ideal Partner Contribution
Product				
Technology				
Manufacturing Capacity/Expertise				
Market Access				
Marketing Capacity/Expertise				
Customer Support				
Management				
Finance				
Other				

the venture itself and characteristics that will limit the risk to the initiating parent's own business.

Size. It is important to consider the size of both the business unit directly involved in the venture and the parent company. The ideal partner must be sufficiently large to provide all the resources that the venture will require, but not so large that it will be able to dominate the initiating partner. At the same time, companies must choose partners for which the joint venture will be of sufficient strategic importance to ensure a continuing high level of commitment.

Management Style and Corporate Culture. How a company is managed should be a major consideration in deciding whether it will make a good partner. Is it capable of making quick decisions? How aggressive is it in pursuing opportunities? Does it take a short-term or long-term view of investments? Can it be relied on to pursue consistent strategies? If the partner is a subsidiary, how much autonomy does it have in decision making?

Where there is a choice, companies usually seek out partners with similar corporate cultures. This makes it easier for executives to work together, though it also reduces the opportunity for learning—an important benefit of carrying out joint ventures. In some cases, companies deliberately seek partners with a very different culture—where, for example, the joint venture is intended to enter a radically new business.

There are distinct differences in national business cultures. The French have a reputation for independence and autocratic decision making. Japanese companies have a reputation for long-term thinking but slow decision making. U.S. companies resort much more to legalistic relationships, while some British companies have a reputation for short-term thinking and lack of dynamism. These simplistic labels may provide a backdrop to the process of partner selection, but there are wide variations around the cultural norm in each country. It is possible by careful searching, to identify potential partners with characteristics not generally recognized as fitting the national pattern.

Profitability. Unprofitable companies can make difficult joint-venture partners. They are more likely to experience changes in management and strategic direction, and they may be unable to afford additional finance if the venture requires it. They may also be vulnerable to a change of ownership.

Partnership Experience. Handling a strategic partnership is not a common management skill. Research shows that collaborations between companies with previous partnership experience tend to last longer than others.[1] Successful partnerships in the past can be a good indicator of how well a company is likely to be able to handle a new relationship.

Competitive Threat. Many joint ventures are undertaken with actual or potential competitors. When a company's technology is not well protected, it is usually desirable to select a partner that lacks the resources and skills to establish a competitive, wholly owned business. For example, when National Semiconductor set up Eurotechnique, the fact that Saint Gobain was not a competitor had an important bearing on the decision to enter into a joint venture. In evaluating the extent of the competitive threat, companies must look at the other alliances in which the prospective partners are engaged and the kind of strategies pursued in the past, as well as at their current in-house capabilities.

Screening and Investigation. The partner selection process usually starts with one or two highly favored candidates. Sometimes the choice is fairly obvious; sometimes it results from a combination of prejudice and ignorance of the alternatives. Even if the front runners ultimately turn out to be the best choices, it is important to carry out a formal search process. The objective is to screen as many candidates as possible, focusing on the most appropriate companies through a process of progressive elimination.

The field tends to be widest when a company wants to join forces with a partner with complementary skills in order to enter a radically new product market. In this situation, screening typically goes through three stages, the amount of information collected on each partner increasing at each stage.

The Partner Search Process

Stage 1   Identification of an initial list of partners from database sources, sector reports, and individual suggestions. The objective is to ensure that no important possibilities are overlooked. Computerized company databases can help to give a very rough ranking at this stage based on size, product range, or other macrocharacteristics.

Stage 2   Investigation of a long list identified in Stage 1. This usually involves collecting company reports, brochures, and press articles. Each partner can be compared with the ideal, using the framework shown in Exhibit 9–5. In some cases, while the most appropriate weightings of different criteria are unclear, it may be possible to establish rules of precedence, indicating which companies provide the best fit, given certain criteria.

Stage 3   Detailed investigation of a short list of perhaps three companies.

A detailed brief should be prepared on each of the final candidates. This should include:

- Background on the company's structure, performance, and financial situation.
- An analysis of the business unit with which the joint venture would be undertaken.
- A history of past partnerships in this and related areas.
- An assessment of overall culture and ability to cooperate.
- An assessment of current strategies and the means by which they are to be realized, including the role of current partnerships.
- Likely partner objectives for the joint venture and its importance in relation to overall strategy.
- Probable relationships between the joint venture and related and future initiatives.
- An analysis of the potential partner's ability to outmaneuver you by competing directly or switching allegiance.
- Notes on key members of the management team.

Besides published data, sources of information include employees previously with one of the final candidates, professional consultants, and distributors and customers. In industries where collaborating with competitors is common, larger companies should continually monitor potential partners.

NEGOTIATION

Joint ventures are very fragile; they are difficult to put together but easy to break.

—Kan Higashi, President, NUMMI

Once the short list of potential candidates has been agreed on and any preferences between them established, the next step is to draw up a negotiating brief and prepare the negotiating team.

As in any other negotiation, companies should go into discussions with objectives for each of the issues to be covered in the final agreement. It is important to identify points that are not negotiable as well as those that, if necessary, are. It is helpful, too, if you can put some kind of valuation on your own contributions to the joint venture—for example, the amount of R&D contributed to the project so far.

It is essential to think about these points in advance. Even though initial discussions are likely to be fairly open-ended, it is easy to get caught off guard. There is a fine dividing line between informal discussion and hard negotiations.

At the same time, negotiating a joint venture is different from negotiating a one-time business deal. Success depends on the partners' continuing to work together in a variety of circumstances over several years. Both parties must know that they are contributing to the planning process in an atmosphere of mutual trust, and both must feel that they will gain from the venture. This means that negotiators must assess the potential value of the venture to the other company and be sensitive to its interests.

Relationships during the negotiations can set the tone for the whole joint venture, and the atmosphere in which they are approached will affect the final agreement. Of the negotiations leading to one highly successful joint venture, a senior negotiator told us: "They were very professional, fully prepared, and very positive in their approach." Of a failed negotiation we were told: "There was no way we were going to agree. We were at each other's throats from the first meeting."

Joint-venture negotiations need to cover every aspect of the business. The negotiating team must include representatives from all the company's main functions—marketing, production, finance, personnel, R&D, and legal. Negotiations should be led by an executive of sufficient seniority to make decisions (subject of course to ratification), and he or she should be accompanied in meetings by representatives of the technical and operations management most directly involved, together with in-house or external legal advisers. Other members of the management team may also need to attend meetings to iron out particular details. If they are not present in person, they must be readily available at the other end of a facsimile machine or telephone to evaluate proposals. When negotiations are conducted overseas the communication arrangements must be set up in advance. If there is a substantial difference in time zones, the visiting team should be able to fax notes on the day's discussions back to home base in the evening and receive comments when they begin work the following morning.

It is particularly important to sort out aspects of competition policy early. Legal advice must cover each of the countries in which the business is registered and in which it operates, as well as cover the parents.

There are wide variations in the role of lawyers in different cultures, and it is important to understand these before negotiations begin. The United States is a highly litigious society, and lawyers tend to be heavily involved in negotiations from the start. In Japan, there are few lawyers; mutual trust is more important than legal agreements. Lawyers should play a less visible role, appropriate to the expectations of the negotiating parties.

Principal Stages

Joint-venture negotiations typically pass through four main stages: initial contact, the start of formal negotiations and the exchange of confidential information, negotiation of the memorandum of understanding (MoU) or letter of intent, and the signing of the formal joint-venture agreement. The broad principles can often be agreed on quickly, and the MoU is sometimes signed within two or three months.

However, completion of negotiations requires agreement across a whole range of different functional areas. It will also usually involve a series of joint planning studies and possibly negotiations with third parties. As a result, from first contact to final signing of the joint-venture agreement commonly takes 12 to 18 months or more.

Initial Contact

The circumstances of initial contact vary widely, in both the degree of formality and the level of seniority of the executives involved. In some industries—consumer electronics and telecommunications, for example—there is an ongoing dialogue on standards among the industry's main companies. In others, such as computers and aerospace, where subcontracting and OEM relationships are common, ideas for collaboration are often discussed informally at the operating management level before top management is involved. When this is the case, the instigator of the informal contact often acts as a champion within his or her own organization to prepare the ground politically.

When collaboration is based on complementary skills from different industries, such information networks do not exist, and initial contact will be more formal in nature, usually through the company chairman or chief executive. What is important is that once you are talking, you are negotiating.

There are often preliminary discussions with several preferred companies to ascertain how interested each would be in a joint venture and to assess their competence as partners. By this stage, there may be little doubt as to these companies' abilities to provide the skills and resources the joint venture needs, and business style may appear to be the most important issue. Yet technical and marketing qualifications must never be taken for granted. Our evidence suggests that partners frequently fail to live up to expectations. Sometimes companies use trial marriages to evaluate partners, using minor collaborations in a related area to make the assessment.

The reasons given for rejecting companies as partners make interesting reading. In one of the cases we examined, one partner was rejected as being "way behind technically," another as "too slow," and a third as "impossible to deal with." In another case, a partner that would have been highly competent from a technical point of view was turned down because it wanted control, was "too bureaucratic," and fielded a poor negotiating team. The company that was chosen gave a response in 24 hours.

Companies approached with joint-venture proposals must realize that they have a beauty pageant. Their technical competences, their corporate culture, and their decision-making capabilities are all on trial.

Information Exchange
Once the partners have agreed to enter into formal discussions, the next stage is to exchange basic information relating to the project. This should normally include an outline business plan for the venture, some preliminary information on technology, and background information on the partners themselves. Recipients should be asked to sign a confidentiality agreement, restricting circulation of sensitive information and preventing its use outside the proposed joint venture. The commercial and technical information provided should be as limited as possible. National laws vary widely in the protection afforded in the event of a breach of confidentiality or misuse of intellectual property, and some potential joint-venture partners may be more interested in looking over your technology than in forming a joint venture.*

Memorandum of Understanding
The next major milestone in the negotiations is usually the signing of a memorandum of understanding (MoU) or letter of intent. The main purpose of the MoU is to make sure that both parties are serious and to set the

---

*The sealed box approach practiced by Japanese companies involved in MITI-financed collaborative R&D projects provides a possible way of resolving disputes over infringement of IPRs that arise from joint-venture negotiations.

framework for detailed negotiations. For this reason, the MoU is usually followed by the first formal announcement of the partners' intentions. There is no legal requirement for an MoU, and it is generally not binding, although it can be used to perpetuate confidentiality agreements and preclude either party from entering parallel negotiations with another company. The document should indicate clearly the conditions surrounding such obligations.

Generally, the MoU outlines the proposed venture, providing the basis for detailed operational planning and the drawing up of the joint-venture agreement itself. It also sets down a framework for the next phase of negotiations and provides the basis for seeking corporate and government approvals. A timetable for the final signing of the full agreement is sometimes established at this point.

MoUs vary in length from a couple of pages to 50. In some cases, the MoU is very detailed (virtually a draft of the final agreement); in others it is very broad indeed. A typical MoU includes the following information:

- Status of negotiations.
- Objectives and key features of proposed joint venture, including activities, location, financing, organization, and legal provisions.
- Organization of working group to expedite negotiations.
- Responsibilities during the startup period.
- Future approvals required.
- Treatment of planning and startup expenses.
- Exclusivity and confidentiality clauses.
- The legal status of MoU.

Once the MoU has been signed, meetings between the parties should be concerned more with planning than with negotiation. It is advisable to channel much of the detail to working groups drawn from the two companies. These should include as many as possible of those likely to be involved in running the venture itself, to build up working relationships and identify possible personality conflicts.

In many joint ventures, partners begin work in parallel during the period prior to signing the joint-venture agreement so that the formal start-up can move ahead as quickly as possible. These commitments are undertaken in good faith, usually with a broad agreement to regularize the sharing of expenditure once the joint-venture agreement is signed.

THE JOINT-VENTURE AGREEMENT

An outline of a typical joint-venture agreement is provided in Exhibit 9-4. It will usually be backed by appendices giving more detailed information, including the agreed-on business plan and the start-up management team. Key aspects of the joint-venture agreement are discussed below.

Definitions
The definitional sections of international joint-venture agreements need to be especially clear to cover differences in national, linguistic and business practices. In most cases, they will be longer and more comprehensive than in agreements between partners of the same nationality.

Scope of Business
The scope of the joint venture's business defines both the types of business it can engage in and the geographic areas in which it can trade. In some cases, these may be defined in exclusive terms, restricting the parents from a similar mode of operation. Other areas may be nonexclusive. For example, the Eurotechnique joint-venture agreement allowed for competition between the joint venture and National Semiconductor in Europe, but prevented Eurotechnique from selling directly into the United States.

All combinations of product or business and geographic markets must be covered, and it is important to try to anticipate changes in technology or market circumstances. These can easily trigger unexpected changes in the operation of one or more parties. Indeed, one or both of the parents may have entered the venture with the intention of leveraging its own operations in related areas. It is important to go through this exercise thoroughly, as it can easily become a bone of contention later, when either of the parents or the management of the joint venture itself wants to change its strategy.

Changes in the parents' objectives can also affect the joint venture's financial performance. For example, one of the ventures we studied had operated for many years as the overseas manufacturing arm of a Japanese parent. Its partner was primarily an OEM distributor for the joint venture's products in Europe. The European partner later decided, however, that to rebuild its own position in the industry, it wanted the venture to manufacture its own designs, even though this was more expensive. In this case, the European partner regarded the effect on the joint venture's profitability as less important than the long-term strategic enhancement of its core business.

CASE 9-2
Siecor—A Model of Joint-Venture Management

One of the world's most experienced joint-venture partners is Corning Glass Works. It has systematically and repeatedly used joint ventures—40 of them since 1924—to develop new businesses and enter new markets. In 1987, joint ventures were responsible for more than half of Corning's operating income; their total impact on corporate performance is probably even more significant.

Corning's joint-venture portfolio includes:

Dow Corning — Set up in 1943 to manufacture silicone.

Ciba-Geigy Corning Diagnostics — Created in 1985 to produce blood and urine analyzers.

Corning Asahi Video Products — Created out of Corning's existing television bulb glass manufacturing operations.

During the early sixties, Corning was one of the pioneers of fiber-optic technology. By 1970 it was spending $1 million a year trying to turn fiber-optics into a viable transmission-cable medium and sought a number of partners to help share costs. Agreements were signed with five companies—Fujikura (Japan), Siemens (West Germany), Pirelli (Italy), Thomson (France), and BICC (U.K.). In return for an annual contribution of $100,000 a year to Corning's R&D program, each company received access to Corning's technology plus certain licensing options.

As work progressed, Corning needed a partner with whom it could work more closely to develop the cable that would clothe the fiber. In the end, Corning chose Siemens, with which it already had a development and marketing relationship. Besides the right complementary technological strengths, there were also important cultural affinities between the two companies. Both were family-owned businesses with a strong sense of tradition; both were technologically driven; and both believed in patient money.

A cooperative R&D agreement was signed in 1973, and work was carried out in parallel in the United States and West Germany. Full commercialization began in 1977 with the creation of a 50/50 joint venture, Siecor.

Milestones in the Development of Siecor

1970 Fujikura, Siemens, Firelli, Thomson, and BICC agree to fund Corning's fiber-optics R&D program.
1973 Corning signs cooperative R&D agreement with Siemens.
1977 Siecor forms an entity joint venture—U.S.-made fiber shipped to Germany for cable manufacture. Initial market is local computer networks.
1980 Corning acquires Standard Cable of North Carolina.
1982 Corning's cable manufacturing business merged into Siecor.

Today, Siecor is the world's largest manufacturer of fiber-optic cable and is active in the market for associated components and equipment. Through the old Standard Cable Business, which was merged into Siecor in 1982, it is also the United States' largest supplier of wire and cable for elevators and lifting equipment.

Up to 1990, Siecor was extremely profitable. For the most part, however, the venture's profits have been reinvested. The principal return to the shareholders is through equity accumulation, royalties, and internal trading (Siecor is Corning's biggest customer for fiber).

Like virtually all Corning's joint ventures, Siecor is a highly autonomous business. The management team owns roughly 10 percent of the equity; the remainder is split equally between the parents.

Corporate Structure and Shareholdings

We always aim to get 51 percent, but in some cases this is not possible. This can lead to problems. Fifty/fifty is fine when things are going well, but in difficult times, somebody has to take control.

—Senior executive, European multinational

Most companies would like to hold a controlling interest, and two of the companies we spoke to insist on this in every joint venture in which they are involved. This may also be required so that the venture can be consolidated in the accounts of one of the parents or for legal or political reasons. For example, the French Government insisted that St. Gobain hold 51 percent of the equity in Eurotechnique, although National Semiconductor had de facto operational control.

In many joint-venture situations, however, an important aspect of the relationship is the equal power and commitment of the parents. Some companies prefer a 50/50 structure for this reason, seeing it as a means of be-

EXHIBIT 9–4
Key Elements of the JV Agreement

1. Definitions (particularly important in *international* joint ventures)
2. Scope of operations of the JV
3. Organization and capitalization
4. Financing arrangements
5. Management:
   Shareholders and supervisory board
   Executive board
   Arrangements in the event of deadlock
   Operating management
6. Contractual links with parents
7. Rights and obligations regarding intellectual property
8. Arrangements for the closing of the agreement
9. Termination agreements
10. *Force majeure*
11. Arbitation
12. Covenants
13. Representation and warranties of each partner
14. Miscellaneous provisions

stowing autonomy on the management team. This is particularly important where the joint venture's task is to attack a new market outside either of the partners' existing domain.

In negotiations, however, companies must be realistic about the degree of power they can command. For example, companies forming joint ventures to assemble or manufacture products under license from overseas partners must often be prepared to accept a minority position. There is no reason why this should not be satisfactory, provided that the commercial arrangements have been set up carefully to ensure that the operation is financially beneficial. Joint ventures are extremely flexible business vehicles. By using different classes of shares and by careful design of the management provisions, it is often possible to reconcile the differing interests of the parties in terms of ownership, management control, and dividend payments.

Whatever the negotiated share structure, it is important that partners believe they are being treated on equal terms by the joint venture's management. An important role of the CEO is to maintain this climate.

Valuation of Parents' Contribution
New joint ventures tend to combine expertise and access to resources, rather than physical assets in their own right. These are extremely difficult to value; therefore companies often tend to value them equally. Exceptions occur when one company contributes physical assets (for example, General Motors' Fremont plant in the case of NUMMI) or one partner has a clear lead in terms of technology and management expertise (for example, National Semiconductor's contribution to Eurotechnique). Problems of asset valuation are more significant in partial mergers. Ultimately, it all depends on negotiating position.

Commercial and Financial Relationships
In many joint ventures, the way in which commercial relationships with the parents are defined and the impact of changes in circumstances will determine whether the venture makes a positive contribution to financial performance. As we saw earlier, the relationships are often complex. This area requires much more careful consideration than it receives in most negotiations. Partners must undertake careful contingency planning to make sure that ventures are structured in a way that will serve their interests over the long term.

Board Structure and Operation
Although different titles are used, most ventures have a dual-board structure—a supervisory board drawn from senior directors of the parents and an executive board to oversee the day-to-day business. As in other businesses, as much as possible of the decision making and managing should be delegated to operational management. The role of the supervisory board is both to ensure that the venture is successful in its own right and to protect the parents' positions. It should normally meet between two and four times a year, and its tasks should include:

- Approval of the annual operating plan.
- Review of budgets.
- Approval of major investments.
- Approval of increases in capital.
- Appointment of the CEO.
- Approval of major commercial agreements entered into by the venture.

- Changes in the scope of business.
- Changes in the joint-venture agreement.

In a 50/50 venture, the supervisory board would have equal representation from each of the parents (perhaps two or three from each). Members would normally be chosen to reflect the main contributions of each parent. Regular negotiations on transfer pricing and other aspects of the financial and commercial relationship may be necessary. The detailed work for these negotiations would normally be carried out by line managers from the partners, reporting to their respective board members. The CEO of the joint venture will normally sit on the supervisory board, although not always with full voting rights. For example, at the time of our study, the Siecor board consisted of nine members:

From Corning	— Chairman
	— General Counsel
	— Senior Vice President, Finance
	— Senior Vice President, R&D
From Siemens	— Vice President, Public Telecommunications
	— Vice President, Cables Division
	— Chief Finance Officer, Cables Division
	— Head, U.S. telecommunications subsidiary
From Siecor	— Chairman and CEO

In the case of deadlock, the Chairman of Siecor has the deciding vote, although at the time of writing, all decisions have been unanimous.

In contrast, at BT&D each partner provides two directors. The joint venture's CEO has no vote. There are various possibilities, but whatever the structure, unanimity is the key test of the joint venture's continued viability.

The J2T venture had a supervisory board that consisted of two members representing each of its three partners. Because of the complexities of trading relationships among them, the board's three monthly meetings also considered transfer pricing.

Sometimes the partners require different levels of information. In one venture we examined, a briefing session is usually held for the representatives of one partner before the full board meeting.

The supervisory board provides the principal means of ensuring that the venture is being well run and that the partners' interests are served. The selection of its members is critical. They must reflect the partners' technical and marketing interests in the venture and have the broader business background needed to monitor the changing strategic and commercial relationships with the parents' activities. They must be of sufficient seniority to take a corporate view, and they must have time to discharge their responsibilities effectively. Making this time available will often require a high degree of support at the parent staff level.

It is important that the board include members who have been involved in planning the venture and negotiating the agreement. This is necessary in order to provide continuity, parent commitment, an understanding of what it is the parties wish to achieve, and a knowledge of likely problem areas. Frequent changes in the composition of the board over time can give rise to problems.

Breaking Deadlocks

When you are making money, there ain't no problem.

—Joint-venture CEO

The resolution of disputes is frequently given inadequate consideration during joint-venture negotiations. Deadlock in the supervisory board is a rare but serious occurrence. It is important to build a formal procedure for resolving disagreements into the agreement.

There are three principal arrangements: passing the problem up to top management; dissolution of the venture if the dispute remains unresolved for a period of, say, 12 months; and a cutthroat provision. The last of these, sometimes called a "Texas auction" or "sudden-death clause," allows one partner to take over complete ownership. One party sets the share price at which the transaction will take place; the other decides whether to buy or sell.

Termination

A dispute between the partners is one reason for terminating a joint venture. The need to end any agreement can, however, arise in a number of ways, many of which are difficult to predict. The changing nature of parents' operations can result in the venture's becoming irrelevant to one of the partners. The competitive relationship between the parents can become more intense, making a venture no longer tenable, or one of the parents may be acquired by another company for which the joint venture represents a duplication of activities. Or something totally unpredictable may occur (such as the nationalization of St. Gobain and the resulting transfer of National Semiconductor's share in Eurotechnique to Thomson). Some ventures are set up to achieve specific temporary objectives, and in certain cases a third-party regulatory body may require the termination of a venture. For example, antitrust considerations persuaded the U.S. Federal Trade Commission to limit the life of the NUMMI joint venture to 12 years and that of GMF Robotics to 10 years.

Every joint-venture agreement should deal adequately with the possibility of termination. This may appear overly pessimistic and irrelevant during the heady period of optimism when plans are being laid for the future, but failure to agree on appropriate ground rules can lead to problems later. The joint-venture agreement must specify precisely what will happen if termination becomes desirable or necessary. (The most common outcome of dissolving an agreement is for the joint venture to survive as a distinct operating unit, one partner purchasing the other's interest at a negotiated price.)

THE START-UP PERIOD

Starting a joint venture is in many ways just like starting any other business operation, once strategy and operational arrangements have been agreed on. Some features, however, require special attention.

Early Implementation

The start-up process really takes place in parallel with the final negotiations. Once the MoU is signed, the management teams from the two parents must work closely together to agree on details. There is, of course, some danger that this openness may prejudice a company's negotiating position but, provided that there is proper control and that risks are identified and monitored, it can provide a valuable opportunity for people from the two companies to work together to identify and resolve potential areas of conflict before it is too late. The risks are much greater in partial mergers, where valuation issues are more important.

Companies usually begin putting key components of the venture in place before the agreement is signed, particularly when negotiations with third parties are required. In one case we examined, the two partners undertook substantial coordinated R&D programs and started work on a new factory. When AT&T Philips (strictly a partial merger) was formed, AT&T trained more than a hundred of Philips' staff before the agreement was signed. In the NUMMI joint venture, millions of dollars were spent between the signing of the MoU in February 1983 and the receipt of government approvals for the project. The major investment was the virtual rebuilding of the old Fremont plant in California, which was almost complete before the Federal Trade Commission granted its approval. Similarly, Toyota negotiated labor agreements with the UAW, first nationally and then at local levels. In addition, Environmental Protection Agency approval was required for the new model. This involved establishing the sources of parts. By the time the joint-venture agreement was actually signed, NUMMI was virtually ready to produce its first cars.

Start-up operations for international joint ventures in particular tend to be big and complex. They can pose major problems of project management. Negotiations take time—time in which the window of commercial opportunity may be closing. Getting into the practical details early provides an opportunity to incorporate allocations of responsibility into the agreement if necessary.

Managerial Power and Balance of Interests

Another major aspect of joint-venture start-ups is the transfer of decision-making powers from the parents to the joint venture's management team. The degree of autonomy that the venture's management will be able to exercise should have been largely agreed on during the negotiating period. However, the reality will always depend heavily on personalities. On y when the venture's top management is in place will the decision-making power it is able to exert become clear. Involving members of the eventual management team in the planning process is essential if they are to have a complete ownership of the plans they are charged with implementing.

The management team must be sensitive to potential cultural and commercial conflicts, balancing the interests of the operation with the interests of the parent companies. Its members must be selected partly for their ability to handle these conflicts. Lengthy discussions may be necessary to resolve them at the start.

Recruitment

Running an international joint venture requires a demanding combination of skills. Besides being able to set up and manage a substantial business operation, it is also likely to involve motivating a team drawn from different business cultures and trying to satisfy the interests of both parents. Joint-venture CEOs must not only have the normal general management experience—industry experience, a strong track record with profit-and-loss responsibility, and leadership skills. They must meet a number of special requirements as well.

First, they must have superb project management skills. Joint ventures usually involve expensive and very rapid start-ups aimed at entering or creating a new market or exploiting a new technology. Expenditures of several hundred millions of dollars over just one or two years are not unusual. A joint venture would probably have been unnecessary after all, if the task were not a demanding one.

Second, they should have operating experience in different cultures. Previous exposure to a joint venture, perhaps in another part of the world, can help in anticipating and dealing with problems of culture clash.

Third, they must have the diplomatic and interpersonal skills necessary to manage the conflicts between parents that may emerge, without bias or prejudice to the venture itself.

And *fourth,* they must have the personality and vision to inspire confidence in their teams and create a culture that is independent of either parent.

In most cases the CEO is supplied by the partner in whose territory the venture is to be based. The person selected must have a strong belief in the potential of the venture itself and will ideally have been involved in the planning and negotiating stage.

There are also cases where the CEO appointed was not affiliated with either partner. The main criterion is "the right person for the job;" there should be no compromises if a suitable internal candidate is not available. All partners must be happy with the choice. If they cannot fully endorse any candidate from among their own organizations, an outsider should be sought.

Recruitment of other senior operational directors should be largely the responsibility of the CEO, subject to ratification by both parents. Sometimes the MoU will indicate that certain positions are to be filled by people from one or other of the partners. The CEO, in turn, must be sure that the people chosen are adaptable enough to work with managers from differing business cultures. When the purpose of the venture is to import technology from an overseas parent, it is common for that parent to provide a team of advisers to work alongside local management during the start-up period.

As a general rule, it is advisable to link the CEO's compensation firmly to the performance of the joint venture as an independent entity—through share participation and performance-related bonuses. It must be made clear that his or her career depends on the success of the joint venture. This is especially important to the partner that does not provide the CEO. It must be certain that his or her allegiance is undivided. Whenever possible, the remuneration of other members of the management team should also be performance linked.

The arguments for and against temporary transfers of parent personnel are conflicting. The promotion of a successful independent business is best served by keeping such assignments to minimum. Whenever possible, managers should be employed by the joint venture itself, rather than by one of the parents. This position is, however, often difficult to square with the career aspirations of the staff. It may also conflict with parents' objectives of using the joint venture as a learning vehicle to benefit their own operations. The composition of the venture management team must be the subject of negotiation and will depend on the precise circumstances.

Cultural Independence

Joint ventures vary widely in their degree of managerial and cultural independence from the parents. For the majority of strategic joint ventures between companies of roughly similar size, there are usually strong arguments for a largely autonomous style of operation. Such ventures are created, after all, to undertake an activity in which neither of the parents could succeed alone. If their objective is to exploit new markets, they will probably demand much more entrepreneurial styles of management than those of their larger parent organizations.

The start-up period provides an opportunity to break with the tradition of the parents, though inherited cultures will exert a strong influence. One of the main roles of the CEO and his or her senior managers is to create a culture that is appropriate for the joint venture and that overcomes potential conflicts arising from the different management styles of the parents.

SUCCESS FACTORS AND LIMITATIONS

Successful joint ventures are the result of a combination of circumstances. Good technology, good people, a fast start-up, and opportunistic timing are all important—just as in any other kind of new business. A precise cultural match between the partners is not so important. The combination of opposites can sometimes be more powerful than permanent consensus,

CASE 9-3
Fanuc's Joint Ventures with General Motors
and General Electric

Fanuc is best known as the world's largest supplier of computer numerical control (CNC) systems for machine tools. It was established by Dr. Sieveman Inaba as a division of the Japanese computer maker Fujitsu, using technology licensed from the Massachusetts Institute of Technology. By 1972, it had reached sales of $49 million and employed more than 600 people, and it was decided to spin the business off as a separate company. It was listed on the Tokyo Stock Exchange four years later. Fujitsu still holds 39 percent of the equity.

The new company grew rapidly, using a highly focused product-development and manufacturing strategy to achieve technological and cost leadership in its chosen market. Between 1972 and 1985, sales growth averaged 29 percent a year, and by 1985 it was supplying roughly half of the world market, with revenues of some $1.2 billion.

This huge growth has been achieved with only a modest increase in employment—about 1,700 by 1987—a feat achieved by the use of wholesale automation. Roughly 30 percent of Fanuc's staff is involved in product development.

Fanuc's strengths in CNC systems and servo motors have opened up a number of diversification opportunities. The most important is in industrial robots, although this still represents only about 10 percent of total sales.

Since 1982, Fanuc has entered into two important joint ventures with U.S. companies to promote its diversification strategy and improve overseas market penetration. The first of these is GMFanuc Robotics, a 50/50 joint venture created in 1982 with General Motors. Automobile manufacturers are leading users and in many respects innovators in the use of robotics in the West. General Motors had already developed a numerically controlled paint robot and was launching a $40-billion modernization program involving the purchase of 20,000 robots by 1990.

A joint venture gave GM the opportunity to save money on its own modernization program, increase its control over a key technology by backward integration, and diversify into new markets. After a careful search of the potential candidates and preliminary discussions with five companies, GM approached Fanuc with an offer. For Fanuc, GM offered an ideal partner to exploit the U.S. and Canadian markets and increase its existing $2-million U.S. robot sales. It accepted the proposal almost immediately.

By 1985 GMFanuc was the leading supplier of robots in the United States with sales of $180 million, roughly three quarters going to General Motors itself. About half the hardware is supplied by Fanuc in Japan and accounts for about 40 percent of sales. Software is developed jointly by GMFanuc and Fanuc.

Early in 1986, Fanuc was again approached, this time for a joint venture with General Electric's factory-automation business. Despite an investment of $500 million, this had been a disappointing business for GE; losses had totaled $120 million in the previous three years. A joint venture offered the opportunity to combine GE's integration skills with Fanuc's individual machines.

GE Fanuc Automation is really a partial merger. It combines GE's existing business units, employing some 1,500 people, with a much smaller team—about 50 people—from Fanuc. Fanuc contributed a balancing cash sum to achieve a 50/50 equity split. The company is based in Charlottesville, Virginia, with operating divisions in North America, Europe, and Japan.

provided that sufficient effort is put into planning for the accommodation of the cultural differences.

In many ways, joint ventures provide a rather better mechanism for creating new businesses than the wholly owned start-up. Their unusual nature ensures (or should ensure) careful planning and top-level commitment from the start. They are then free to execute the business plan and exploit emerging opportunities swiftly.

Many joint ventures are created with built-in obsolescence. They usually have a tightly defined mission, making them particularly vulnerable to market and technological changes. Unlike their parents, which are free to diversify and change direction as circumstances change, they have no mandate to adapt to their environment. In fact, if they try to do so, there is a strong chance that they will impinge on their parents' other interests and cause conflict.

On the other hand, partners can take steps to realize other sustained benefits. In particular, joint ventures provide an invaluable opportunity for each parent to learn management skills from its partner. Medium-to-long-term assignment of parent personnel probably provide the best means of achieving this. The loaned employee should always be necessary to the venture rather than a supernumerary, thus ensuring that he or she gains the maximum practical benefit and minimizing disruption. At NUMMI, where this learning process is formally planned into the operation, two- or three-year assignments are augmented by observers who spend up to six months with the company.

This learning opportunity can be exploited only if it is planned for. Managers returning from joint ventures should be encouraged to share their experiences, and career paths must be structured to ensure that their knowledge is used elsewhere in the company. Programs should be established to push through changes in practice or develop new technological competences.

CHAPTER 10

THE PARTIAL-MERGER PHENOMENON

What counts is not necessarily the size of the dog in the fight—it's the size of the fight in the dog.

—Dwight D. Eisenhower

In 1970, the Dutch aircraft maker Fokker and the German manufacturer VFW agreed to merge. Economically, the union made eminent sense. VFW, strong in military aircraft, needed help in marketing its revolutionary new civil jet. Fokker was strong in civil aircraft. At this time, size was becoming increasingly important in the industry, and the venture offered a European solution with muscle in the European market. Encouraged by their respective governments, the companies joined forces in a 50/50 joint venture and a new headquarters was established in Dusseldorf, staffed by some 70 people from the two companies.

The venture was a disaster from the start. The merger took place on paper only. The operation of the two companies' business units was unaffected. What went wrong? Government pressure effectively precluded factory rationalization, and nationalist pressure meant there was little or no internal subcontracting. Moreover, both management groups were reluctant to give up control. Each retained its own supervisory and executive boards, even though all assets were in theory pooled within the new company. The board structure for the merged holding company consisted of the combined boards of the two parents. Fokker-VFW ended up with two of everything.

The difficulties were complicated by product problems. VFW's new aircraft, the 614, was plagued by disaster. The prototype crashed—as it turned out, a result of pilot error rather than technical fault. And further uncertainty was caused by the collapse in 1971 of Rolls Royce, which was developing the engine. In any case, the 614 was in direct competition with well-established Fokker aircraft, provoking intense rivalry between the previously separate companies. Fewer than 30 614s were built, and roughly half were scrapped.

By 1975, the German subsidiary of the venture was heavily in debt to the government and in severe financial difficulties. A German government report recommended a full merger of the two companies. But by this time, that solution was wholly unacceptable to Fokker, and it withdrew its key people from the central holding company. However, it was not until 1979 that the two companies were finally disentangled. Throughout the period, each senior management team retained its allegiance to its parent company, and while middle management worked well together in the joint holding company, there was little attempt to establish personnel systems that would create a unified management.

The Fokker-VFW merger illustrates some of the difficulties with international mergers. It was typical of a whole series of unsuccessful pan-European mergers and joint ventures that took place in the 1970s.

Academic studies indicate that between half and two thirds of all mergers fail to achieve their objectives,[1] and one third of all merger failures result from an inability to bring about an integration of the parent companies' operations.[2] When divisions or discrete operations of different corporations merge—partial mergers—the opportunity for ambiguity is rampant and can be deadly. Partial mergers are the most complex, challenging form of strategic partnership. As long as joint ownership remains, there are always two or more separate major interest groups at board level. They are often in head-to-head competition in other parts of their business. When they are international, the difficulties are magnified.

Setting up and managing partial mergers is much the same as it is for new joint ventures (see Chapter 9). They require an understanding of the partners' objectives and adequate planning activity. But there are also two important, distinguishing factors: there is usually much more scope for negotiation on price, and there are immense integration problems that have to be dealt with.

PARTNER OBJECTIVES

Partial mergers are used when each party wishes to improve its competitive position but both prepared to give up only a limited amount of control over their operations. There may be a number of reasons. For example, both partners may wish to capitalize on the synergy available from a partial merger. Achieving economies of scale and therefore the critical mass necessary to fund R&D is one of the most important motivators in partial mergers. Access to each other's national markets and product synergies are also important. The 1988 merger of Komatsu and Dresser's North American construction-equipment operations gives Dresser access to Komatsu's products and as much as $300 million to upgrade factories. It gives Komatsu much-needed manufacturing capacity by enabling it to assemble in the United States, and it helps to sidestep problems caused by the currency differential and protectionist threats to sales in the United States.

Whirlpool's 53 percent stake in Philips' domestic-appliance business achieves a similar objective—giving it a much-needed entry to the European market and paving the way for increased economies of scale in R&D and manufacturing in what is fast becoming a quasi-global market.* In another situation, one of the parties may wish to withdraw from the industry but may find this difficult to accomplish in one move, for reasons that may be political or commercial. A national government may find the complete disposal of a domestic champion to an overseas buyer unpalatable, especially if it has been given strong financial support. Potential conflicts with labor unions can sometimes be more easily handled by approaching divestiture through partial merger.

One of the main commercial constraints is company identity or branding. Sometimes companies wish to dispose of one part of their business but retain use of the brand elsewhere. A partial merger provides an attractive means of phasing the disposal and changing branding and corporate identity at a judicious pace.

Sometimes it is not possible to make a clean break from the rest of the company. Potential acquirers may be unwilling to make a 100-percent acquisition because of dependence on components made elsewhere within the parent. A partial merger provides the means of ensuring continuity of component supplies, something of interest to both parties.

Or it may provide the only practical way of achieving restructuring in

---

*For example, the main difference between refrigerators designed for different countries is the need to accommodate milk containers of different shapes and sizes. Flexible manufacturing is fast making it possible to produce different national versions under one skin. Production economies are already enormous in this industry. Whirlpool, with a 15-percent share of the U.S. market, has only one washing machine factory for its entire output. ("Preparing for a Debut on the International Stage," *Financial Times*, August 22; 1988.)

an overcrowded sector, eventually allowing the new business to be fully acquired by one of the parents or a third party at a higher price.

There may be tax reasons why a disposal is difficult. For example, it is common for German companies to value overseas subsidiaries on their books at cost. This means that an acquiror could be faced with a large capital gain. Phasing in an acquisition through partial merger provides a means of mitigating the tax charge.

Partial mergers can also be a way to make major changes in the strategic direction of the business gradually, releasing funds for major acquisitions in new areas before the final disposal is completed.

Finally, a partial merger can provide a powerful protection against takeover—except, of course, against one by the partial merger partner.

Those are the logical reasons for partial mergers, but many of them actually reflect top management's inability to come to terms with changes that are forcing a new strategic direction on the company and with the resulting need to give up a traditional area of a business. A straight disposal might actually be the more rational approach; a partial merger provides time for the emotional adjustment.

In practice, few partial mergers continue in operation with shared ownership for any significant time. Their usual role is to provide a vehicle for divestment by one of the partners, although neither party may envisage this when the merger is negotiated.

PREMERGER PLANNING

The special sensitivities of the partial-merger arrangement demand thorough planning. After clarifying their own objectives, partners should carefully examine the options open to them, formally select potential partners, thoroughly prepare a negotiating position, and include any special provisions in the formal agreement that will smooth the road to a successful partnership.

> Mergers are about corporate strategy, but they are also about the top men.
> —Planning director, European company

Examining the Options

Partial mergers are particularly important in mature industries, those in which global competition is forcing more and more attention on scale and unit costs. Companies unable to match the R&D programs of the industry leaders must find ways to share economies of scale. It is no longer possible simply to hide behind national market barriers and hope that competitors will take the battle elsewhere.

Acquisition, disposal, and partial merger are the obvious solutions to this problem, but other forms of strategic partnership can buttress cost competitiveness. OEM contracts can enable a company to buy certain products, helping it to provide a full product range and concentrate in-house resources on the things it can do well. Parts of the supply chain can be shared with competitors. For example, in the automobile industry, economies of scale are most significant in engines and transmissions.[3] There are also economies of scale in final assembly, but the effect of volume on cost is less severe. By sharing the development or manufacture of components with competitors, a company can sometimes reduce unit costs while retaining independence and the ability to differentiate the final product in the market.

Alternatively, when products have a high price per unit, it may be possible to agree on some form of work sharing. Airbus Industrie is responsible for running virtually all aspects of the business except manufacturing. However, its members retain their independence by working as subcontractors.*

Technology, globalization, and the pace of innovation have rewritten some of the commercial logic of the 1950s and 1960s. It is time to reappraise some of the make-or-buy decisions of the past and consider the new options that involve sharing projects or facilities to acquire scale. Before considering a partial merger, the reasons for a company's cost or volume

---

*The Groupment d'Intérêt Économique is a peculiarly French business vehicle. The GIE does not itself give rise to the making or division of profit, but is intended to enable its members to avail themselves of all the means to develop and improve their own economic activity. It has substantial flexibility with respect to its organization and administration, while at the same time having a full corporate personality and legal capacity. In the GIE, the accounts are subject to external audit but not to general disclosure to third parties. All expenses and revenues are allocated to its members. One of the major aspects of the GIE that is particularly relevant to producers of high-unit-cost products, such as aircraft, relates to liabilities. The members are liable for the debts of the GIE, jointly and severally. Thus, the creditors of the GIE could take action to recover from a number of the partners separately, after unsuccessfully serving a formal summons for payment by the GIE. In the Airbus GIE structure, partners are of equal ranking. No partners are more equal than others; there is not single dominant entity. The company is made up of a special group of individuals who no longer report to a particular partner, but solely to the GIE. The operating costs of the joint organization are borne in relation to membership work-sharing rights.

disadvantage must be analyzed carefully, and those aspects of its business that differentiate its products in the marketplace must be identified. The dissection must go horizontally and vertically. Each part of the supply chain must be considered separately, and the different options for offsetting the size disadvantage should be considered along with the other, more conventional options—acquisition and disposal. This exercise has an important role, even if a partial merger is determined to be the best strategy for acquiring scale economies. It helps to establish the criteria for partner selection and provides a basis for preparing a business plan for the merged operation.

Partner Selection

In the vast majority of partial mergers, partners find one another. There is no systematic search process. They are often the result of a long association, as with Honeywell-Bull; sometimes they arise during discussions of other forms of collaboration. The idea of merging their European truck interests emerged when Fiat and Ford were discussing collaboration in automobiles. It was discussion of possible OEM deals between CGE and ITT that led to the decision to merge their telecommunications businesses by forming Alcatel.

Usually these discussions are initiated at the top. It is essential that these ideas be subjected to the same rigorous analysis as any other major strategic decision. And there may be alternative partners. Partner selection criteria should be established as a part of the formal planning process and potential suitors measured against them.

Preparing the Negotiating Position

Each company should prepare for its own use an outline plan of its goals for the venture—as a business entity in its own right and in terms of its contribution to the parent company. Many of the key issues to be negotiated are the same as in a new joint venture, and they are not reexamined here. In a partial merger, however, there are five important complicating factors.

First, there is likely to be a complex set of interconnections between those parts of the company to be merged and those to be retained. *Second*, the assets contributed by each partner are likely to be very much larger than they typically are in new ventures, offering considerable scope for negotiations on valuation. *Third*, one of the keys to the commercial success of the new business is likely to be the efficiency with which it restructures to cut costs. The cost of restructuring can be borne in several ways, with differing financial impacts on the parents. *Fourth*, the investment may have a continuing and significant effect on the parent's profit-and-loss and balance-sheet positions. *Fifth*, the size and nature of the transfers gives considerable scope for tax planning.

Who Contributes What?

The operations of a business considered for a partial merger are often not clearly separated from the parent company's other businesses. For example, two different businesses may be run from the same factory, or they may share some of the same administrative staff. Even if operations are completely separate physically, they may be incorporated into the same legal entity. For example, the IVECO-Ford joint European truck venture acquired Ford's U.K. truck manufacturing operations. Ford kept the engine manufacturing capability in-house because the same engines are also supplied to its commercial van business, which was not part of the deal. Honeywell Information Systems, in which Bull and NEC acquired substantial equity positions in 1987, was structured as a division of Honeywell Inc., not as a separate subsidiary company.

It may take a significant amount of time to define the boundaries of the business, and important tax implications must be considered. As with new joint ventures, it is important to assess the continuing impact of commercial trading relationships between the parents and the joint venture.

Asset Valuation

International company valuations are notoriously difficult. One company may have adopted a more cautious approach to accounting than the other. There may be different treatment of stock, work in progress, debt, R&D expenses, depreciation, and income. Undervaluations in company books are common, particularly where real estate is concerned.

Each component of the business contributed to the merger must be valued as a going concern, but with major physical assets valued separately. Intangibles such as brands and distribution networks leave plenty of room for negotiation. A common method of calculation must be agreed on by the partners, and outside accountants should make or validate the calculations. Before starting this exercise, each partner will wish to establish clearly what approach is in its best interest.

Restructuring Costs

The merged company may be expected to be financially more successful as a result of restructuring and scale effects. There is considerable room for negotiation on how restructuring costs and financial synergies are to be treated. For example, it is possible for restructuring costs to be borne either by the parent companies or by the new company itself.

In negotiating the best financial deal, it is in each partner's interest to maximize the amount of investment and restructuring costs that the other will assume and thus minimize its own outlay. Building a sound negotiating position therefore involves making an honest assessment of one's own business and building up as full a picture of one's partner's business as possible. If either party is in a weaker position (and is looking for a phased disposal), it is often possible to include at least part of the restructuring costs in the agreed price.

Financial Structure of the Deal

A substantial partial merger can have a correspondingly substantial impact on both the balance sheets and the profit-and-loss statements of the parents. Differences in valuation can be offset by cash payments to achieve the equity split required—usually 50/50 (Exhibit 10–1). Earnings may be either improved or diluted, depending on the relative profitability of the components before the merger. It may be necessary to offset this by adjusting the price or through special dividend payments. The profit or loss from the businesses before merger can be either rolled up into the purchase price or brought onto the parents' profit-and-loss statements.

The treatment of exchange-rate movements also needs consideration. The planned merger of the medical-equipment businesses of GEC and Philips fell through in 1988 because GEC would not agree to the valuation differential (between $150 and $200 million) asked by Philips, following a decline in the dollar during negotiations.

There are many variations in how financial arrangements can be structured. Payments may be phased to cover uncertainties. The mixture of loans and equity must be decided. Complex share structures can be used to provide the balance of ownership, control, and dividends that the parents seek.

Taxes

Early tax planning is vital. Each partner will be affected differently; each must negotiate from a position of strength, knowing its own best interests.

EXHIBIT 10–1
Partial Mergers—A Temporary Staging Post

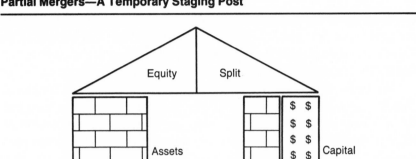

Tax and corporation laws in different parts of the world may require that subsidiaries be merged over a given period. Depending on generally accepted accounting principles in different countries, it may be possible to handle the restructuring of costs as an extraordinary item or a direct charge to reserves.

Tax and financial benefits may be offered by host governments. This is likely to be the subject of negotiation and may depend on where the head office is located. The options must be weighed carefully. Once the decision is made, the business must be operated in a way that does not attract double taxation. Companies whose operations are predominantly limited to their domestic markets tend to lack the in-house international tax skills needed to tackle these issues.

Partial-merger negotiations tend to be tough, and brinksmanship is not uncommon. There are clear winners and losers. Planning is the key to success, and companies entering partial-merger negotiations must be sure they have the best possible legal, financial, and strategic advice.

The Formal Agreement

The formal merger agreement should cover broadly the same ground as does that for a new joint venture (see Chapter 9). Special sections are often required to cover matters discussed above. In some cases, side agreements with third parties may also be required to ensure continuity in the supply of key components or raw materials.

Political or other constraints can sometimes lead to clauses in the merger agreement that restrict the extent of integration. For example, the French and Italian governments made the SGS-Thomson merger conditional on splitting R&D efforts equally between the two countries.

As we have seen, partial mergers are frequently a vehicle for phased withdrawal by one of the partners. The arrangements for eventual purchase of one party's shares by the other are, therefore, of special importance. Valuations and expectations can change dramatically once the postmerger restructuring process gains momentum.

As with joint ventures, a Texas-auction or sudden-death clause provides a possible solution. Arrangements in which only one partner has an option to buy out the other should be avoided. Lack of possible counterbid makes negotiations one-sided, especially if the prospective seller needs the cash urgently to invest elsewhere.

International mergers also need to establish a formal working language. English is the most common choice; where the dominant parent's working language is not English, executives soon learn what they must speak to get things accomplished.

POSTMERGER INTEGRATION

> For those who have developed a taste for life in the fast lane, there really is nothing quite like a merger.
> —Director of a Unisys subsidiary

The extent of the postmerger integration task depends on the extent of overlap between the two companies' operations. Where they have similar product ranges and geographic marketing strengths, difficulties are fewer. Since the objective of partial mergers is to create scale economies, however, they can be successful only if management succeeds in creating competitive advantage by combining the capabilities of the companies. Thus, management of the immediate postmerger period is key to the success of the merger. Integration typically requires the consolidation of each element in the parents' value chains—from R&D and purchasing to distribution and after-sale service. The changes required are massive and probably one of the hardest project-management tasks that a company can take on.

One of the most difficult judgments relates to timing. Rapid change may confuse and demotivate people, and managers who have been with a company for many years may find it hard to adapt to new ways of doing things. It may be tempting to try to retain management support by making changes slowly. But if changes are undertaken too slowly, the synergies and potential improvements in competitive advantage will not be realized. The evidence of our study is that rapid action is essential. Delay only creates more uncertainty and a sense of lack of direction among staff.

Much must be done in a very short space of time—to realize potential economies of scale, reassure customers, remotivate staff, and reestablish strategic direction. Strong leadership is essential. This is most easily achieved in partial mergers that are covert acquisitions or where one of the partners is acknowledged as having responsibility for management.

To ensure that the integration process proceeds smoothly, clear timetables must be established, taking into account the interdependencies between different aspects of the business—sales force, brands, product range, distribution outlets, manufacturing facilities, components, R&D programs, and management information systems. To the extent possible, preplanning should be done between the signing of the memorandum of understanding and the final agreement. Getting staff involved early in the planning process contributes greatly to the creation of commitment to the new business. Complete openness is not possible until the final agreement is signed. There may be some tough areas of negotiation, and the companies remain competitors still. Discussions between the parties must usually be restricted to the corporate level over this period; the merger deal may ultimately not go through. Many issues, however, can be handled in some detail, using special task forces drawn from the companies involved to work on specific issues, such as the integration of manufacturing operations.

Management and Personnel

The most urgent aspect of integration is management, especially where there is a considerable degree of structural similarity between the companies. Once the merger is announced, there are two people for virtually every important job in the organization, and each of them will know it. This period therefore, is one of real personal uncertainty for senior managers. The strategic direction of the business probably seems unclear. Morale is low. Productivity may be affected. It is a time for making major career moves.

The headhunters know this too, and will hover like vultures, waiting to pick up the new company's most talented managers.

Putting the new management in place must be done quickly if the rest of the integration program is to be carried through. The normal approach is to cascade the selection process down the organization's hierarchy. The two partners jointly appoint the new company's CEO, and he or she, with appropriate consultation, selects the top management tier. These executives, in turn, select the people reporting to them, and so on. The problems are complicated where there are extensive overlapping geographic operations. Appointments for the key positions in each country need to be agreed on before the merger takes effect locally. The phasing in of subsidiary mergers over time, to comply with different tax and legal requirements, can help by delaying some of the more difficult decisions.

When Unisys was formed through the merger of Burroughs and Sperry, joint teams for management selection were set up in each national subsidiary. Burroughs' CEO, Michael Blumenthal, was the merger's architect and new CEO. He was determined that the selection of the new management team should be based on ability rather than on company origin. In some countries, it took three months to make all the appointments down to supervisory level.

In another case, one of the parents of the partial merger gave each employee the right to choose whether to stay with the parent or join the newly merged company. The other partner, which was to take the lead in management, had to put a great deal of effort into identifying and moving the people it wanted, starting with the well-respected personnel director.

A vast range of more-detailed personnel issues must be tackled. Combining the two organizations' structures requires changes of position, job description, remuneration, reward systems, and terms and conditions for hundreds, possibly thousands, of people. Outside advisers are usually required to help bring grades and remuneration structures into line. Union agreements must be examined, and any needed renegotiations should be planned in advance. Inevitably, these changes will lead to some redundancies and to the departure of some people. Redundancy legislation varies widely from country to country, and large costs can be involved. Again, it is important to get professional advice on these complex, specialized areas at an early stage.

The same applies to fringe benefits. Combining pension plans without reducing the benefits of any individual takes careful planning. Not all pension plans are adequately funded, and the integration costs need to be worked out before the merger agreement is signed.

One purpose of partial mergers is to provide the dominant companies with operations in countries with which they are unfamiliar. There is much to be learned, including how to work with different unions and under different labor laws. Maximum synergy is inevitably associated with minimum ingoing knowledge.

It is essential that the personnel function be involved from the outset of the merger planning. As many potential problems as possible must be discovered before the merger takes effect so that postmerger actions can move ahead rapidly. In the most effectively managed partial merger we reviewed, a special joint subcommittee was set up to work on personnel issues in parallel with the main negotiations.

Communications and Corporate Identity

After reorganization of the management structure, the most urgent task is to inform people about the changes taking place. Partial mergers usually follow periods of uncertainty. The parents may well have become disillusioned with the businesses involved and starved them of investment and management talent. They may even have been more or less openly up for sale. Morale and image must now be rebuilt. Optimism tinged with realism is the order of the day.

Customers and shareholders alike are looking for a revitalized management team, determined to solve the company's problems and provide improved products and services. Staff members are looking for direction and reassurance of management competence. Coordinated internal and external information campaigns are needed.

Corporate identity programs are often one of the first public actions of the newly merged company. They provide a valuable means of repositioning it in the marketplace, and they also help to communicate a new strategy to the workforce. A new name can provide the opportunity for a major relaunching of the business. This may be a combination of the two parents' names—Honeywell-Bull and IVECO-Ford, for example—or an entirely new name. The choice depends on the strength of the existing brands, the nature of the continuing activities of each parent, and whether products are sold under the company or a brand name.

When Burroughs and Sperry merged in 1986, they initiated a major corporate-identity program. Employees were invited to invent a new name for the combined company. Suggestions far exceeded management's ex-

---

CASE 10–1
Partial Mergers—A Temporary Staging Post

AGFA-Gevaert—From Equality to Buyout

Bayer merged its Agfa subsidiary with the Belgian company Gevaert to form a European photographic group in 1964. Each party had a 50-percent holding. The pan-EEC legislation on which the companies counted to allow the transfer of losses across national borders did not materialize, however. Consequently, little integration took place. The Belgian operations reported profits, and the West German company continued to incur losses.

Nevertheless, in 1980, when the combination needed capital, it was the stronger Bayer that was able to provide it and thereby raise its stake to 60 percent. Then it was only a matter of time before the stronger company took full control. In 1981, Bayer paid Gevaert Photo-production DM325 million for its 40-percent stake when the Belgian company was unable to pay its share of a further capital injection of DM200 million.

FBC Holdings—From Equality to Selloff

In 1980, Fisons and Boots of the United Kingdom merged their agrochemical interests into a joint company called FBC Holdings. Each company had a 50-percent share and three board representatives. The merger was intended to provide greater scale to support the research costs involved in agrochemicals.

In 1983, Boots and Fisons reached an agreement to sell the company to Schering AG. Fisons and Schering AG had closely collaborated since 1970 through a cooperation agreement. Proceeds of the sale were equally split between the parents.

---

pectations and included Burrovac, Sparrow, and Burros. Unisys was chosen only after a massive worldwide trademark and name search.

When CGE (Compagnie Générale de l'Électricité) and ITT merged their telecommunications operations to form the world's second-largest telecommunications company on January 1, 1987, it was decided to use Alcatel, the name under which CGE's telecommunications activities were already trading. The choice of name and the new corporate image were seen as critical in motivating employees, communicating the new core values of the group, and providing a focus in the marketplace for the compa-

CASE 10–2
ST—Building a World-Scale Semiconductor Company

Thomson SA of France and SGS Microelectronics SpA of Italy began talks in 1986 on a merger of their semiconductor interests. The merger was announced on April 30, 1987.

The operations were of comparable size before the merger. The resulting company, equally owned by the parents, had sales of $806 million and was the second-largest European chip manufacturer after Philips. Both parent companies were state-owned, and the deal needed approval by both governments. At one point, a minority third party was considered, but the idea was rejected.

The aim of the deal was to create a semiconductor company with sales approaching $1 billion, a level considered necessary to finance the tremendous development costs associated with the industry. The new company was initially called Unisem, but the name was changed to SGS Thomson Microelectronics (ST).

The two companies had largely complementary product lines; only 25 percent of products overlapped. The annual research budget for the merged company is about $200 million. Half of this is provided by the partners, the other half by Italian and French government research projects.

The first post-merger priority was to rationalize production facilities. In a little more than a year, the new company had closed or sold three factories in France and two in the Far East, eliminated 2,000 redundant positions, and reorganized its production.

The breakneck speed of this effort paid off. Results for 1988 exceeded budget, with ST achieving a modest net profit of $2.2 million, before the cost of the restructuring, after a $132-million loss the year before. Sales of more than $1 billion also exceed targets.

Since then, sales and net profits have continued to grow. In 1989, ST earned $10 million on revenues of $1.3 billion, and the company's 1994 sales target is $3 billion. ST expanded by acquiring the British semiconductor company Inmos from Thorn EMI. And it installed an international R&D approach by participating, along with Siemens of West Germany and Philips of the Netherlands, in the $3.3-billion Joint European Semiconductor Silicon (JESSI) project. At the time of this writing, ST is looking hard for an alliance with a Japanese company.

> The Thomson-SGS venture is a good example of a partial merger in an industry undergoing a shakeout. It was formed between two parties that were both committed to the industry but were incurring losses before the merger; each realized that by itself, it could not afford the investment necessary to stay in the business over the long term.

ny's long-term marketing efforts. Three major guidelines were established:

- The Alcatel name would be used with the various subsidiary names, either directly or as an endorsement, and it would be introduced progressively when the national identity of companies needed protection.
- Alcatel would be the dominant brand name for all product lines; secondary brand names would be used only in special circumstances.
- The new corporate identity was to be implemented immediately, except where specific circumstances required a phased introduction.

Marketing and Distribution

The next phase in the integration process is usually the creation of a unified marketing and distribution strategy for existing products. The extent of integration depends on the degree of product and geographic synergy between the parents, on the type of products involved, and on the nature of the distribution channels. The higher the synergy, the easier the integration is to manage. The longer the product life, the slower integration will be. Existing distribution agreements may have a long period to run, slowing integration of the supply chain.

Integration of Distributors and Sales Force
After IVECO was formed in 1975, the distribution networks of its two main constituents, Fiat and KHD, were continued in parallel for several years. There was still a KHD distributor in Italy in 1980. As a result of this earlier experience, IVECO's senior management team was determined to proceed with the integration process much more quickly after the creation of IVECO-Ford. As a result of careful premerger planning, the members

CASE 10–3
Honeywell-Bull—Passing the Baton

The formation of Honeywell-Bull in 1987 marked the creation of one of the world's first truly "Triadic" strategic partnerships. The relationship between the participants has a long history. Both NEC and Groupe Bull owe their existence as major computer manufacturers to Honeywell technology.

Since the early 1960s, the French government has been Groupe Bull as one of the primary instruments for building a strong electronics industry. Machines Bull (as it was then called) first sought technical assistance from General Electric, which invested in it in 1964. This investment passed to Honeywell in 1970, when it took over General Electric's computer division. The 1970s saw several attempts to reorganize the French computer industry, together with the creation and failure of Unidate, the pan-European computer venture in which Bull was involved. Honeywell's stake in Bull progressively declined, first to 47 percent, and then in 1982, to 20 percent, with an option under which the French government could acquire the remaining shareholding over the next five years.

Meanwhile, there had been a whole series of technology-exchange agreements between Honeywell and Bull and between Bull and NEC. NEC's computer business was, in fact, created on the back of a 1962 agreement giving access to Honeywell products and technology. For many years, NEC sold Honeywell-designed mainframes under license in Japan. Throughout the 1960s and 1970s, it continued to invest in its own R&D and participated in a number of MITI-sponsored collaborative R&D projects.

Over the years, Honeywell found it more and more difficult to fund the R&D required to compete with IBM, and the roles became reversed. In 1984, NEC signed agreements allowing both Honeywell and Bull to distribute NEC mainframes under license. Honeywell's withdrawal from the commercial computer business followed rapidly. In 1985, it sold NEC its Japanese computer subsidiary, and in March 1987 it completed the sale of a majority shareholding in the rest of the business to Groupe Bull and NEC. The deal gave Honeywell and Groupe Bull each 42.5 percent of the equity and NEC the remaining 15 percent, though Honeywell had an option to sell a further 22.5 percent to Groupe Bull during the following two years.

In exchange for the shareholdings, Bull and NEC paid Honeywell $527 million, $350 million of which was financed by a consortium of French, U.S., and Japanese banks. The cash provided a timely boost to Honeywell, which had just spent $1.4 billion on purchasing Sperry Corporation's Aerospace Group. The deal made Bull potentially the most powerful computer company in Europe, almost doubling the sales and R&D over which it had effective control, and giving it access to marketing networks in the United States, the United Kingdom, Italy, and Australia.

The combined computer operations of the three parent companies amount to well over $12 billion.

Honeywell will continue to take Honeywell-Bull machines for resale by its building and industrial systems business. It has also retained responsibility for U.S. government sales. It is likely, therefore, to remain Honeywell-Bull's largest OEM customer for some time. Furthermore, Honeywell remains committed to a joint venture established with NEC in 1986 to sell supercomputers in the United States. Honeywell retains its 50-percent investment in this business.

Honeywell-Bull is headed by an eight-man board led by Jacques Stern, Chairman of Groupe Bull. Bull has five seats, Honeywell two, and NEC one.

of the two existing distribution networks knew whether the new company had renewed their contracts on the first day of the joint venture. Those selected were able to offer a complete range of trucks almost immediately.

A great deal of detailed planning is required to integrate two distribution chains. A unified approach to pricing discounts, promotions, and the financing of customer stock must be adopted. New promotional material must be developed. Distributors must be selected and retrained. Contracts must be renegotiated.

Similar issues are involved in marrying the two companies' sales forces. One of the most difficult personnel issues is often sales-force remuneration. There may be wide differences between the incentives and "perks" available to employees of the two companies.

Promotion and Repositioning

Once the new company's marketing organization has been restructured, it is in a position to launch new promotional programs. Special efforts are required to rebuild the merged company's image in the marketplace and inform customers of its policies. In one case, the merged company doubled the combined advertising budgets in support of this objective.

A major promotional campaign may also provide the opportunity to reposition certain products or services, although this depends on the industry and on how much strategic thinking has already been done. Unisys chose the opportunity to focus much more on vertical markets, the combined strengths of Sperry and Burroughs providing an ideal platform from which to do so. This is one instance in which new market strategies could be developed quickly. In most cases, the time required is longer. The main strategic thrust comes from the need to rationalize existing products and production facilities, and to integrate product development programs. When IVECO-Ford was first formed, it carried separate but not completely overlapping product lines from the five member companies. Developing a completely unified product range, with a single product offered for each market segment, took some 10 years.

Alcatel's product rationalization program has been greatly facilitated by the long-term purchasing policies of the National Telecommunication Network it serves, which enabled it to announce that it will retain production of its two ranges of public switches for many years. For products with shorter lives, Alcatel's various national subsidiaries (predominantly ITT outside France) were allowed to select the products they will sell from the combined ranges of the two parents.

R&D Programs

As with other forms of joint venture, one of the main motivations for partial mergers is the need to achieve sufficient critical mass to support a competitive R&D effort. Getting the most bang for your buck is as much about how the R&D program is integrated with the rest of the business as it is about the management of the R&D operation per se. The postmerger period provides a unique opportunity to reconsider the entire role of R&D within the new organization and to make sure that effective linkages with the rest of the business are put into place.

In constructing a larger and, presumably, more effective R&D program, there are five issues to be considered:

- The extent to which duplicated projects can be eliminated or combined.

- The extent to which duplicated facilities can be rationalized.
- The way in which the R&D pipeline as a whole should be managed (including, for example, linkages with universities and corporate venturing).
- The integration of R&D production engineering.
- The integration of R&D with marketing and business development.

Saving money in the short term by merging R&D programs is more difficult than it looks. R&D projects burn up the most money when they are about to bear commercial fruit; combining different designs is next to impossible at this stage. In many cases, projects will be at different stages of development—each performing a useful role in the continuing R&D program. Where two genuinely competing projects exist, the only way of saving money may be to cancel one of them, though even this may be difficult if orders have already been taken or customers are dependent on a particular system or standard. It may be necessary to use OEM alliances to fill product gaps while long-term product strategy is being reformulated. Otherwise, common upgrade strategies should be developed where possible.

Any physical rationalization of the R&D organization must be carried out with great care, to avoid losing good scientists or disrupting important projects.

Production

Many partial mergers begin with overcapacity. Swift action is required to bring this into line with expected sales, though the interactions between production and marketing in the modern multinational are so complex that careful analysis is required to ensure that the best result is achieved. Honeywell-Bull commenced operations with twice the U.S. capacity it needed. Rationalizing production offered a 10 percent saving in the labor costs of manufacturing, worth $40 million a year.[4]

Production rationalization is closely linked with product-range rationalization, and this often dictates the pace at which sustained progress can be made. The process may start with the adoption of common components, though even this is possible only when for instance a consistent parts-numbering system has been introduced and the information systems are in place to provide effective stock control.

Combining two product lines offers useful production economies of scale, though substantial investment in new facilities and equipment may be required to develop the new generation of plant required to realize these economies. The physical rationalization program is likely to be long and continuing. It requires a combination of planned product obsolescence (taking into account any contractual obligations for supply of existing products or spares) and phased new-product introductions.

Single-source production of components, subassemblies, or final product is often one of the ultimate objectives. The potential for economies of scale in production must obviously be balanced against increased distribution costs and the higher risk of dependency on a single source of supply. In the 12 years after IVECO-Ford was set up, the original companies' plants were totally restructured and specialized, so that every product had a single source for worldwide distribution.

Information Systems

The management of the new business will need information to make decisions and monitor performance. At the same time, both parents will require sufficient information to monitor their investments in the merged business. The two components of the merged business will have their own management information systems, quite possibly fully integrated with the remainder of each parent's business and relying on its hardware. A plan for developing a new information system for the merged business is needed. This may involve either adopting one of the existing company's systems or constructing a totally new one. In the case of Alcatel, it was decided to implement ITT's highly sophisticated reporting systems right across the new company.

Achieving full systems integration takes time—often as long as two years. In the short term, a temporary system must be created, combining information from the two businesses' existing systems through simple aggregation programs. Outside assistance will normally be required to speed up the development process. Even temporary systems can take several months to install, forcing management to rely on special exercises for key decisions.

This issue must be addressed early in the new company's life. Preliminary work can be carried out before the formal merger agreement takes effect—selecting potential consultants to carry out the integration process and drawing up terms of reference, for example.

Business Culture and Style

Anyone who has worked in a merged corporation knows that its component parts continue for many years to operate in their own idiosyncratic styles. Achieving a common culture is the greatest challenge of all.

Managers in the component businesses will have grown up with different value systems, especially if they have worked for the same employer for many years. One company may have practiced a strongly intuitive style of decision making, with most important decisions coming, in effect, from the CEO. The other company may have been accustomed to carrying out sophisticated planning studies before any new business initiative is taken. There will have been differing degrees of consultation within the two parent organizations, and managers will have different and perhaps conflicting understandings of their levels of authority. There will be different and perhaps conflicting attitudes toward risk and investment. One company may have stifled innovation by a regimen of excessive cost cutting; the other may have been too profligate.

All these attributes are part of the culture that flows through an organization. It affects every individual's perception of what he or she must do to be successful, how he or she must relate to other parts of the organization. And it has enormous impact on motivation. Beyond this, many detailed aspects of operations will be different—from budgeting systems to ways of designing products.

These differences create important barriers, impeding the realization of potential synergies. They prevent people from communicating effectively, they create disharmony, and they make cooperation very difficult. The business problems may be compounded in the early years by language barriers and differences in national culture.

The establishment of a common culture requires considerable investment in communications, training, and personnel development. The objective is to create trust between managers and develop a single approach to decision making. Standard information and communication systems must be established to speed the integration process.

Getting managers from different parts of the business to exchange ideas and get to know one another socially can play an important role. This can help break down barriers and rebuild the informal communications channels that are the essence of effective cooperation in any company. Ultimately, the objective must be to achieve a complete mix of managers from the two component businesses, although this will often take 10 or 20 years.

After IVECO-Ford was formed, six monthly meetings were held to foster teamwork among some three or four hundred managers from all over Europe. In another, more recent partial merger we examined, there was no real attempt to bring the two line-management teams together. In fact, the more internationally oriented partner found that managers in the other company were unaccustomed even to meeting colleagues from other parts of their own company face to face. The lack of a genuine, internal postmerger communications strategy, in this particular case, seriously damaged the motivation of managers.

Partial mergers are the most complex of any of the forms of strategic partnership that we have studied. Planning and negotiating skills are at a premium during the set-up stage. The achievement of potential synergies requires precise and detailed project management across every function of the business. All of this must be carried out in a way that removes uncertainty quickly, remotivates staff, and encourages customers. Above all, the partners must find a way of managing their involvement that gives maximum autonomy to the new management, while safeguarding their own interests. In a complete merger, there is ultimately only one management team; in a partial merger, there are potentially at least three. For corporate parents, as for biological parents, giving up control is perhaps the most difficult decision of all.

CHAPTER 11

VERTICAL SUPPLY ALLIANCES AND STRATEGIC INVESTMENTS

Unlike joint ventures and partial mergers, which focus on new business initiatives or restructuring, many partnerships are concerned with cementing a purely trading relationship. No new entity is formed in this process.

Clearly, only a few such commercial relationships deserve to be called strategic partnerships. However, the trends we have examined in this book point to an increase in the degree of strategic interdependency between businesses as the process of international specialization and concentration continues. Companies are seeking to put important trading relationships on a much firmer (and more public) basis. In this respect, these partnerships are strategic.

We use the term vertical supply alliances to cover a variety of situations in which a closer degree of collaboration is involved than in the conventional buyer-vendor relationship. These are alliances between manufacturers and:

- Companies supplying key components or subassemblies.
- Companies carrying out R&D under contract to them.
- Their distributors.

Four features distinguish vertical supply alliances from more traditional buyer-vendor or subcontracting relationships. *First*, in contrast to a conventional subcontracting relationship, the buyer is often highly dependent on the specialized R&D skills of the seller for initial product development. *Second*, close collaboration is usually necessary to ensure that each partner maximizes end-user sales. *Third*, these alliances involve trading relationships of long duration; it is difficult for the partners to switch their allegiances quickly. *Finally*, the partnership has a significant impact on the competitive position of one or both of the partners.

Companies increasingly tend to use equity investments to cement relationships of this kind. In Chapter 8, we looked at the reasons for corporate venturing, the taking of minority investments in young companies through participation in the venture-capital process. The term strategic investment describes the taking of minority investments in medium-sized and large strategic partners. This approach is becoming more and more common in many kinds of manufacturing. Because of the close relationship between vertical supply alliances and strategic investments, it makes sense to examine them together.

OEM RELATIONSHIP

The most common form of vertical supply alliance is the OEM (original equipment manufacturer customer) relationship. OEM relationships take many forms. They range from the supply of standard products for rebranding by customer companies to the design and manufacture of highly customized products designed to meet the OEM customers' specific requirements. The balance of power between the partners and the degree of collaboration required vary widely from case to case.

There is a fine dividing line between an OEM relationship and conventional subcontracting. In the latter, the product is manufactured entirely to the customer's design. In the consumer electronics industry, for example, large Japanese and Far Eastern corporations supply many Western companies with products for marketing under their own brand names. These can be either standard models or versions specially designed for the OEM customers' markets. Once the design had been agreed on and the contract worked out, this kind of relationship is relatively straightforward. There is no reason why the manufacturer should be involved in more than an arm's-length relationship with its OEM customers' marketing activities.

Where more specialized equipment is concerned, the situation is rather different. The young, entrepreneurial company often leads the way. Sun, formed in 1982, was rapidly able to establish a leading position in advanced work stations, and Stratus did the same in fault-tolerant computers. These are both relatively new segments of the computer market that were either overlooked by the industry majors or in which they had been unsuccessful in developing satisfactory products.

Both Sun and Stratus make extensive use of OEM alliances in their marketing, in addition to selling directly to end users. OEM customers include much larger and more powerful companies, which are able to combine their products with in-house equipment to produce complete systems for specific customers or market segments. Close collaboration is required to make such relationships work.

We therefore will examine two forms of OEM relationship—first, those involving specialized products that will help the customer to sell its own product in certain situations and, second, those in which the product will simply be rebranded or incorporated as a standard item into every product the OEM customer sells. In both cases, the supplier may well be selling directly to end users as well as through OEM customers. In each, the perspectives of the buyer and seller are very different.

Supply of Specialized Equipment: The Supplier's Perspective

> An OEM relationship between a small company and a multinational is rather like an elephant mating with a mouse. For the elephant it is pretty comfortable. But for the mouse it is downright dangerous.
> —Senior executive, small high-tech company

Specialized OEM relationships often involve small companies, operating at the leading edge of technologies that will eventually be of critical importance to their customers. OEM contracts may provide the only way in which they can reach a wide market and achieve rapid growth. They are often associated with a venture-capital investment by the OEM customer, although an investment is by no means essential (see Exhibit 11–1). For example, Olivetti made a 10-percent investment in Stratus during the latter's second round of venture-capital raising, before a product had ever been demonstrated. It maintained its investment after the company went public. Yet IBM, Stratus' other main OEM partner, had not invested in the company.

An OEM alliance with a much larger company poses important challenges for the smaller supplying company. It must:

- Structure the relationship in a way that avoids overdependence on one or two channels of distribution, and retain freedom of action in the future.
- Manage the conflicts that arise from competing for end-user customers with its OEM partners.
- Discourage competitive R&D within the parent.

- Ensure that its OEM customers are themselves generating maximum end-user sales.
- Cope with the inevitable company differences in culture, business style, and priorities.

The contract defines the framework within which the relationship will operate, but how it is managed is just as critical.

The Contract

The objective of any OEM contract is to secure the maximum financial and strategic benefit with the minimum loss of flexibility. The supplying company should resist giving exclusive marketing rights to the OEM customer unless there is strong evidence that the OEM offers an enormous advantage over alternative channels of distribution. Where exclusivity is granted, it should be confined to specific vertical or geographic markets in which the OEM is strong, be of limited life, and be linked to sales-performance criteria. The rights to future products should be excluded from OEM agreements, although upgrades of existing products will need to be covered.

The supplying company will have to provide a substantial discount to offset the OEM's marketing efforts. It may be possible, however, to structure discounts in a way that contributes to performance—by linking them to volume or using them to pay incentives to the OEM salesmen.

The contract should, if possible, prevent the OEM customer from developing directly competitive products. In practice, a company can count on an OEM customer's support only as long as it has real benefits to offer. New technological developments can rapidly render products from specialized suppliers irrelevant; the responsibility for continuing the relationship over the long term remains with the supplying company's R&D team.

It is essential to understand the role that the product will play in the OEM customer's strategy before drawing up the agreement. In which particular end-user market segments will the product be important? What leverage does it give the OEM customer in achieving sales of its core products or of total systems? How can the supplier contribute to this marketing effort?

The OEM agreement may need to include specific provisions, to cover such issues as technical support and sales training, to ensure that maximum benefit is achieved from the relationship.

CASE 11-1
Stratus and Its OEM Customers

Stratus Computer Inc., founded in 1980, is a Boston-based manufacturer of fault-tolerant computers for on-line transactions processing (OLTP). It sells products both directly to end users and through two important OEM contracts with IBM and Olivetti. Stratus also has a number of VAR (value-added reseller) agreements with smaller companies. Fault-tolerant computers are designed to sit at the center of a network of work stations and other equipment, so the potential benefit to the OEM customer is many times the margin on the Stratus machine itself.

The history of Stratus' development is typical of successful U.S. companies backed by venture capital. The initial venture capital, some $1.5 million, was raised in May 1980. Soon after, Burgess Jamieson, one of the original investors, introduced William Foster, the company's founder, to Elserino Piol, Olivetti's new strategy director. Olivetti was actively looking for computer companies with which to establish strategic partnerships, and Stratus offered an entrée to an important segment of the date-processing market. Although Stratus was still some way from having a commercial product, Piol decided in January 1981 to support the venture with a $1.5 million investment, giving Olivetti roughly 10 percent of the equity. This decision was crucial to the success of the second round of financing. In all, some $5.5 million was raised. Investors committed a further $8 million soon after. Olivetti sold its stake in 1988 for $50 million but retained the OEM relationship. It never had a seat on the board.

Stratus launched its first products in November 1981. Initial market interest was not encouraging. The only order was from a Boston creamery, a market segment very different from the one intended. The relationship with Olivetti proved to be something of a lifesaver.

Negotiations on the details of the OEM relationship with Olivetti started in 1981, although the final agreement was not signed until the spring of 1982. It gave Olivetti exclusive marketing rights to Stratus products in Italy and France and exclusive rights in other European countries for a limited time. the announcement of the deal gave Stratus a valuable PR boost, and Olivetti accounted for 30 percent of Stratus' $5-million first-year sales. Most of the products were bought for Olivetti's own use, and these orders helped Stratus over a difficult quarter.

Two years later, in 1984, Stratus began to look around for other OEM outlets and approached, among others, IBM. After an initially disappointing response, a second approach to a different part of the IBM organization was more successful. IBM's own R&D team had failed to develop a satisfactory product for the OLTP market, and by this time it was looking at other means of market entry. An agreement was signed in January 1985, just a few months after the start of serious discussions. Unlike Olivetti, IBM does not have an equity investment. IBM sells the Stratus machines as System 88. An important feature of the agreement is that IBM has the right to announce its Stratus-based products almost immediately after Stratus. On one occasion, the lag was just one day.

Stratus went public in 1983, and by 1987 it was the world's second-largest fault-tolerant superminicomputer company, with sales of $184 million and net income of $19 million. Today IBM and Olivetti account for some 25 percent and 5 percent of sales, respectively.

In both cases OEM sales were much slower to take off than Stratus expected. In the case of Olivetti, Stratus had to fight an internal propaganda battle against a computer from DEC, Olivetti's traditional OEM supplier. As a result, Stratus committed a significant support team to the two OEM relationships, and the effort expanded as the importance of selling to its customers' own sales teams was recognized.

EXHIBIT 11–1
Relationship between Small Supplier and Large OEM Customers

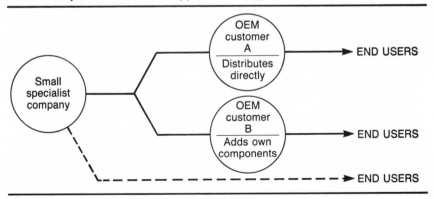

Managing the Relationship

Most small companies totally underestimate the difficulty of selling through OEMs. When the contract is first signed, the product is likely to be seen by the customer's marketing team as of only peripheral interest. Salesmen are primarily interested in selling core products. Brought-in items, about which they are likely to have received much less sales training, are relevant only when they help achieve this end. Top-management time is required to ensure that major OEM contracts are fully exploited. Each major OEM requires a full-time account manager, possibly supported by a sizable team. The result of failure to manage the relationship actively is often that OEM customers provide access to only a fraction of their customer base.

When the OEM customer is a foreign company, it helps considerably if the account manager has some familiarity with the language and business culture of its people. There must be a clear picture of the strategic role the relationship is expected to play, as well as sales targets.

The first year of an OEM relationship is likely to be a getting-to-know-you period. It is vital to establish the right relationships at the marketing and technical support levels quickly. The OEM contract is likely to have been negotiated at a senior level, contacts being mainly with the OEM's technical or product management team. Selling is likely to involve entirely different parts of the organization.

The account manager must establish strong communication channels with the OEM customer during this critical launch period, and spend time studying how the customer's sales team operates. It must invest in sales training to make sure that the OEM's sales force is properly equipped to sell its products. In some cases, it will be necessary to make joint sales calls and provide direct customer support.

It may also be necessary to negotiate separate incentives with the OEM's sales force to encourage the passing back of leads where potential orders are too small or too specialized to interest the OEM customer's own sales team. Direct access to the customer's sales force is also important in the longer term to provide market feedback and guide new product development.

The problem is especially complicated if the contract extends to a number of international markets and management is decentralized. One solution is to concentrate on the most promising markets, where key individuals within the OEM sales organization are prepared to make a special effort for the supplier. Helping them achieve their own goals can provide a demonstration of the value of the product to other parts of the OEM customer's marketing network.

A common problem for OEM account managers is how to handle competition with the customer. It is quite common in the computer industry for several OEM customers to be active in a market in competition with the company's direct sales team. A company cannot prevent its OEM customers from competing with one another, but it can try to minimize the damage caused by competition with its own sales force. The key here is to recognize that benefits accrue whether sales are direct or indirect. Sales teams must, therefore, be constantly on the lookout for conflicts and make an early informed judgment as to whether a direct or an indirect sale is most likely to secure the order. Where the OEM customer is best placed, it should be given all the support possible. This is sometimes difficult for salesmen to swallow. Incentives must be carefully designed to encourage them to adopt cooperative behavior.

The account manager also has a more strategic role to play in spotting threats and opportunities. Working with the OEM customer's sales team provides the opportunity to monitor its development program and identify openings for the supply of other products. He or she must also be alert for changes in the OEM's organization and power structure and for other alliance negotiations that could threaten the relationship.

Coping with an Overseer

An OEM relationship with a major multinational can give an enormous boost to a small company—providing access to an international marketing and distribution network and the credibility that goes with supplying an important customer. The announcement of an OEM deal can even have a significant effect on share price.

The relationship sometimes also creates an interdependency that limits freedom of action in the future. Certain alternative distribution channels may be cut off, and increasing priority may have to be given to meeting the OEM customer's technical and marketing requirements. The customer may want to have a major influence on future product development. If the supplier has no direct contact with end users, it will lose touch with changing customer requirements and fall behind in product development. If it also sells direct to end users, its OEM customers will object to the direct release of new products.

Dependence on a single OEM customer also opens a company to pressure on margins. As sales grow as a proportion of the OEM customer's total business, it will come to regard what was, perhaps, once a specialized product as increasingly central to its core business. It may want to participate more directly in the manufacturing profits and increase control of product development. This can lead it to develop second- or third-generation products internally or to try to acquire its supplier.

This is the downside of the OEM relationship for the small company. The pressures are stronger when the OEM customer has a substantial equity holding. To avoid being swallowed up, the supplier should cultivate a number of OEM customers and balance a high degree of cooperation with a fiercely independent and pragmatic view of long-term strategy.

At the same time, a small company must also be realistic about what it can do on its own. Only a few companies can grow to be major multinationals. Even the development of a world-class product typically gives a company only three or four years in which to achieve the economies of scale required for long-term viability. For most small companies, eventual acquisition by a larger group is the most logical way of achieving the goals of their growth strategy.

The Customer's Perspective

While the partners' short-term interests run in the same direction in an OEM alliance, over the longer term their objectives are likely to be precisely opposite. The ideal supplier is often one so dependent on the business you give it that it must react rapidly to your every need. This is an important component of the Japanese manufacturing system: a network of highly responsive and subservient subcontractors provides the foundation on which the success of many of the large manufacturing companies is built. When output falls or competition forces a cut in prices, subcontractors bear the brunt. They know that in return they can expect favorable treatment from their customers when times are good. If, however, a brought-in product becomes more and more successful or critical to a company's business, it is natural to try to internalize it—to buy the company or take over product development and manufacturing. Both considerations must be tempered, however, by one important constraint—the need to remain at the forefront of innovation. Either trampling on the most innovative suppliers or acquiring them can destroy their will or capacity to innovate.

A strategic investment can provide a sufficient degree of influence without destroying the independence or entrepreneurial power of the supplier. It can also reduce the impact of many potential conflicts of objectives: the more successful the supplier, the greater the financial return to the OEM customer.

A strategic investment also opens a valuable and cost-effective door to acquisition, if this is the ultimate goal. It makes the supplier the natural source of extra capital during an OEM customer's temporary financial difficulties. It ensures that the investor will be in the best position to know what an acquisition would contribute to its business, and it helps to determine timing.

Where poor financial performance is in danger of undermining the overall strategy, a strategic investment can provide the means to intervene in a partner's management. Such intervention must be undertaken with great care. Turning a company around is a rare and specialized skill. It demands a great deal of management time and patient application of investment capital. An independent company doctor will probably have to be brought in to achieve success.

As the interdependencies between companies become stronger, more and more OEM relationships are likely to be backed by equity investments. In effect, corporations all over the world are beginning to see the advantages of the kind of structure that exists in Japan, where circumstances have led major companies to make strategic investments in a whole network of suppliers. Toyota is one case in point. It owns a substantial share (ranging from 43 to 62 percent) of 3 key suppliers and varying lesser percentages of 20 others.

Supply of Standard Products

Many OEM relationships involve the supply of large volumes of products for sale under the brand name of the OEM customer—for example, computer peripherals such as disk drives and printers, consumer products such as television sets, telecommunications equipment like private office exchanges (PABXs), and even automobiles.

As we have seen, these products are at a stage in the product-market life cycle when competitive advantage depends on market share and manufacturing efficiency. OEM alliances can play a powerful role in this situation, enabling companies whose strength lies predominantly in manufacturing to build overseas market share rapidly, while converting potential manufacturing competitors into dependent distributors. Launching new categories of products with mass market potential provides a means by which companies can establish a de facto international industry standard.

The Supplier

For the supplier, getting the best out of these OEM relationships depends on the efficiency with which marketing programs are managed—signing up the best OEM customers in each major market and helping them to plan and execute their own marketing campaigns when necessary. The basic disciplines are well established. Good products and good management are the ingredients of success.

In the longer term, commercial profitability depends on maintaining a close and friendly relationship that gives OEM customers a fair return, without encouraging them to move back up the supply chain and acquire some of the manufacturing capability. While it may ultimately be tempting for a company to try to squeeze out its OEM customers if it is already selling in the same market, this could result in the creation of alternative sources of manufacturing that would undermine its own position in the sector.

As with specialized suppliers, there may be an argument for making an equity investment in certain important OEM customers, especially if they are relatively weak or open to takeover by competitors. However, making strategic investments in other multinationals is expensive, and the anticipated strategic benefits often fail to materialize.

The OEM Customer's Perspective

Clearly, the OEM customer depends heavily on its supplier, but as the product-market life cycle matures and products become more standardized, distribution becomes more straightforward and offers less and less profit. Ultimately, the brand of the overseas source company may be even better established than that of the OEM customer, giving it a local marketing advantage. Procuring stand-alone products from more-powerful suppliers is therefore a dangerous strategy. It gives away the very part of the battlefield—manufacturing—on which the competitive battles of the future will be fought.

There are certain ways in which this threat can be diminished. One is for the OEM customer to retain a strong design and engineering capability in-house and to make sure that brought-in products are manufactured to its own specifications. This restricts the supplier more closely to the role of subcontractor and gives the customer greater control. It also retains the possibility of alternative sources of supply, the second means of retaining control.

In the longer term, the OEM customer may be able to negotiate participation in local manufacturing, perhaps through a joint venture or a license agreement. This can preserve the option to learn some of the supplier's technical skills and ultimately provide the opportunity to rebuild internal R&D and manufacturing capabilities. Thomson's reentry into the VCR business after several years of involvement in the J2T collaboration was a move of this kind.

STRATEGIC INVESTMENTS

Minority investments in specialist OEM suppliers are becoming increasingly common. They provide some measure of influence over the supplier's strategy and performance, while giving the OEM customer a share of the profits generated. However, multinationals are also making an increasing number of investments in much larger companies, often in anticipation of a wide range of benefits. The size and scope of the investee company's operations make managing these strategic investments very different from the corporate venturing in start-up and high-growth companies discussed in Chapter 8.

Bolstering Strategy

There are many variations on this theme. For instance, in the competitive battle currently being waged in the world telecommunications market, Canada's Northern Telecom has made a 25-percent investment in Britain's STC, seeing it as a means of gaining a much-needed distribution channel into Europe. NEC has a 15-percent investment in Honeywell-Bull. It was already supplying both companies with mainframe computers, and when the venture was formed, an equity investment provided the means of exerting some influence over the continued supply of products to the new company.

The extensive cross-shareholdings between Japanese companies could in some ways be described as strategic investments. Certainly, they have a considerable influence on business relationships. In general, they are the result of progressive spin-offs of new ventures rather than of proactive investment programs. Much smaller share purchases are made as a gesture of goodwill between partners, but the acquisition of companies, wholly or in part, is not common in Japan. Opportunities arise only as a result of financial difficulties or other special circumstances.

Financial problems provided the opportunity for General Motors and Ford to acquire major holdings in Isuzu and Mazda, respectively, and for Philips to buy 50 percent of Marantz, the Japanese consumer electronics company. Honeywell's investment in Yamatake arose because the company offered to pay with equity for overdue license royalties accrued during World War II. Yamatake now has a 50-percent share in Yamatake-Honeywell, probably its most successful nondefense operation.

One of the most interesting examples of a strategic investment is ES2, a pan-European semiconductor company formed in 1987 with about $133 million in grants and equity from seven major manufacturing companies, including Philips, British Aerospace, Groupe Bull, and Olivetti. Two years after its formation, ES2 had risen to fourth in the global league of specialized chip manufacturers. The company succeeded in attracting two more partners in 1989, though it is not expected to become profitable before the end of 1990. Each ES2 partner hopes to benefit from access to a quasi-internal source of Applications-Specific Integrated Circuits (ASICs). In-house ASIC facilities are likely to be of increasing importance to manufacturers of "intelligent" products. Many of ES2's investors could not justify setting up this kind of facility for their own use alone.

Not all vertical supply relationships are backed up by equity investments. They are relatively unknown in the aircraft industry, for example, where there is a complex network of subcontractors for each major project.

In sum, the circumstances in which a strategic investment is appropriate are clearly rather special and go beyond the goal of participating in the financial benefits that an alliance bestows on a smaller company. There are, in fact, three main reasons for making a strategic investment in another company:

- To exert some degree of control over a supplier or distributor of strategic importance to the business and on whose allegiance or performance the company cannot otherwise depend.
- To prevent an important supplier or distributor from being acquired by a competitor.
- To provide a framework for future collaboration across a range of projects.

Excluded from this list are unfriendly share purchases, often the prelude to a full acquisition. Raiding parties are rarely described as allies, and the problems of strategic management are not complicated by conflicting objectives.

Market Access

Acquiring a major piece of a multinational company is expensive. When AT&T invested in Olivetti in 1983, its 26 percent cost $280 million. Its investment in Sun cost $400 million—a high price for potential access to semiconductor technology. NEC's 15-percent stake in Honeywell-Bull cost $50 million, and in 1971, General Motors paid more than $50 million for its 34-percent stake in Isuzu.

Investments of this magnitude are unlikely to be justified as a simple cementing of a relationship with an OEM supplier. The most important objective of strategic investments in other multinationals is nearly always to provide access to overseas markets, although a variety of potential synergies are often cited as justification.

In AT&T's case, the investment was a key component in a major change of strategy. Before 1984, the company had been essentially a U.S. telecommunications operator. When its monopoly was broken up, it was permitted to enter the computer market, and AT&T's chairman declared that the company would "redefine the industry." With such an ambitious objective, AT&T clearly needed a European partner to provide market access and help tailor products to European standards. Olivetti had a similar need to gain access to U.S. technology and sell into the U.S. market. AT&T's investment provided a useful cash infusion.

General Motor's investment in Isuzu also offered a variety of benefits to both parties, though the opportunity arose through an unusual combination of circumstances. During the 1960s, Japan's market was virtually closed to Western manufacturers wishing to set up facilities there. A series of reforms in the late 1960s and early 1970s made inward investment progressively easier, and beginning in 1967, executives of the three major U.S. car manufacturers—Ford, General Motors, and Chrysler—began to look for possible partners. Meanwhile, MITI was trying to rationalize Japan's highly fragmented automobile industry (it still has nine manufacturers) by creating two new groupings around Toyota and Nissan.

Mergers were, and still are, virtually unheard of in Japan, and these moves have aroused intense feeling. Over the next few years, however, they helped to force a number of the Japanese car manufacturers into the arms of Western partners. Mitsubishi linked up with Chrysler. Ford took a 24-percent stake in Mazda, and General Motors bought into Isuzu, best known for its light and heavy-duty trucks. Besides offering potential access to the Japanese market, General Motors' investment also gave it access to a source of trucks for sale into markets outside Europe and the United States.

NEC's investment in Honeywell-Bull was also opportunistic. It paves the way for NEC to take a much more active role in the computer-systems business outside Japan. As an exporter of hardware boxes for the computer and telecommunications markets, NEC has been extremely successful, pioneering in marketing thinking in its C&C strategies for the integration of the two technologies.

Future developments in semiconductors and the trend toward industry standardization will make it harder for companies in countries with high labor costs to compete. The real opportunity is likely to be in systems integration—meeting each customer's requirements case by case. Achieving volume requires strong engineering resources. NEC's investment in Honeywell-Bull provides a foothold in the systems-integration market outside Japan, as well as the opportunity to supply products on an OEM basis.

Benefits and Demands

While the primary objectives of strategic investments may be quite clear, the size and diversity of the organizations involved makes realizing them quite difficult. The partners remain independent organizations that may well compete in certain geographic or product markets. Their ultimate strategic goals will almost certainly conflict to some extent.

There are likely to be a variety of further opportunities for collaboration and mutual benefit. Identifying and exploiting these requires interaction across many different parts of the organization. Careful thought must be given to how the relationship is going to be managed. Before making a strategic investment, a company must address the following questions:

- What are the strategic and financial benefits of the investment, and what are the competitive risks?
- What degree of influence and control does it wish to exert over its partner's strategy, and how should this be exercised?
- How will collaboration be organized on a day-to-day basis across the two organizations?

Strategic and Financial Benefits

Investor. The strategic benefits for the investor might include:

- Supplying products into the investee company's domestic market (on an OEM or part-assembled basis or by licensing local manufacture).
- Procuring products from the investee company or using them to supply an overseas distribution network.
- Learning the investee company's technological or management skills.
- Joint R&D projects.
- Downstream joint ventures in specific product or geographic markets.
- Preferred access through the investee to new suppliers.

In addition, financial benefits will accrue if the investee company is successful. As with joint ventures, the financial calculations must allow for the impact of commercial trading, dividends, and capital accumulation. Dividends and capital appreciation are likely to be more important than they are in a joint venture, but the investor must carefully consider relevant tax and corporation law (regarding dividends, for example) in the investee's country.

To be weighed against these potential benefits is the risk that it will simply be too difficult to agree on and implement subsidiary trading agreements and collaborations. Of course, the potential for capital appreciation greatly reduces the long-term risk of strategic investments in joint ventures. If the investee company performs as well as the investing company and there are no significant changes in exchange rates, the investment will be broadly neutral, compared with retaining the capital for in-house projects. If the partnership improves the performance or valuation of the investee company, the impact can be considerable, although it may be difficult to get out of the relationship in later years.

Investee. The potential strategic benefits to the investee company mirror those to the investor. There is, however, one important asymmetry in the financial benefits. Whereas the investing company benefits financially from an improvement in the performance of its investment, for example, by helping it sell products into its own domestic market, the investee derives no such benefit from taking the investor's products. There is thus always a much stronger incentive for the investee company to defend its own market position and retain as much of its business internally as possible. It will also be less inhibited from working outside the relationship by signing new joint ventures or making its own strategic investments.

This is the great paradox of strategic investments in major manufacturing companies:—While the commercial objective is usually for the investing company to access the investee company's markets, the financial objectives tend to operate in completely the opposite direction. (This is not the case, of course, if the objective is to source products, the usual situation for investment in smaller companies.) The most obvious way around this problem is for companies to exchange shares so that the financial incentives are equally balanced and the asymmetry in interdependence is removed. However, this form of partnership has not been widely used.

Gaining the full benefits of strategic investment in large companies is often much more difficult than it first seems. The investing company must consider carefully what degree of influence and control it can exert over the investee company, and it must ensure that the benefits do not flow only in one direction.

Influence and Control

A minority investment in a company creates a power relationship completely different from that of a majority shareholding. A 51-percent investment gives the shareholder the power to ensure that the investee operates only in the interest of the investor. A 49-percent shareholding provides only influence. The investee remains, in principle at least, a free agent, able to pursue an entirely independent strategy.

Once an investor has determined the degree of influence it requires and over what aspects of the business, it then has to structure the organizational apparatus of collaboration to provide the required weight.

The degree of influence sought will often affect the amount of equity purchased, and investors must study company law and practice in the country in which the investee is registered. In Japan, for example, ownership in excess of one third gives the investor the right to veto changes in corporate bylaws and major assets.

Strategic investments generally give the investor a right to board participation. NEC's 15-percent investment in Honeywell-Bull gives it a seat on the main board—one of the most truly international in the world, with members from the United States, Europe, and Japan. Fujitsu negotiated three seats on Amdahl's board. General Motors has 6 directors on Isuzu's 38-member board, with an executive vice-president and a senior financial executive based permanently in Japan. It is also represented on important policy and operating committees. AT&T had six directors on the Olivetti board.

Board participation does not, however, guarantee privileged involvement in decision making. It may not provide access to sensitive cost information, for example, and there is no assurance that it will provide prior warning of really major strategic decisions. By the same token, there is no necessity for the investing company to provide advance information of its own decisions, though the more open it can be, the better the relationship that is likely to develop. When decisions that could affect the relationship are made, the investor should make sure that its partner is given advance notice and does not have to rely on press announcements and speculation.

Organization
Board participation is not enough. Involvement at lower levels is required if all the benefits of collaboration are to be realized. Frequent one-to-one consultation between chairmen or CEO's is essential, and a great deal of top management time is required to make the relationship work.

Olivetti and AT&T have structured their relationship at three levels. Beyond board discussions, there is a steering group of three or four decision makers from each party. This meets every two or three months to review the status of existing subsidiary alliances and look at possible new areas for collaboration. Cooperation at the operational level is structured through a series of vendor-buyer relationships.

General Motor's investment in Isuzu is managed through a team of eight senior executives, based in Tokyo, whose role is to ensure the smooth running of different aspects of the relationship, provide technical help to Isuzu, and identify new areas of collaboration.

One of the most demanding areas of management is to achieve consistency of approach between different parts of the companies involved. It takes a long time to understand how a major organization works and to appreciate its strengths and weaknesses.

Transfer pricing is a contentious area at the best of times, and it is particularly sensitive in long-term strategic relationships. Prices are subject to a variety of influences—exchange-rate fluctuation, efficiency improvements (rapid and continuous in well-managed manufacturing companies), and competitive pressures. A company making a strategic investment should try to obtain access to detailed costing and pricing information if it plans to procure product from the investee. Of course, reciprocity may be demanded.

Building Flexibility

As more companies adopt truly global strategies, strategic investments are likely to be increasingly common. But no alliance between competitors will be ideal. There will always be changes in strategy and in relative competitive strength. Both partners will start the alliance with specific expectations of how they expect it to help them achieve their strategic goals. In many cases they will eventually be disappointed by what has been achieved in certain areas and may seek to make alternative alliances to plug gaps. It is almost inevitable that these alliances will be with the investment partner's competitors. It may be easier for the investing company to accept being cuckolded in this way if it still expects to gain financially, but tensions are bound to creep into the relationship.

Companies must not be afraid to make difficult decisions and adapt their overall strategies to changing circumstances. If necessary, alternative partners that can be of more help in meeting objectives should be sought.

Besides acquiring a valuable source of products, General Motors was also able to learn some important lessons in Japanese methods of manufacturing management from its investment in Isuzu.

In 1981, General Motors bought a 5.3-percent share in a second Japanese manufacturer—Suzuki—which was followed by a small exchange of shareholdings between Suzuki and Isuzu and a move toward three-way collaboration in certain areas. More recently, both GM and Isuzu have taken new partners to establish manufacturing joint ventures in the United States. GM has formed NUMMI joint venture, described elsewhere, with Toyota. In 1987, Isuzu formed a 49–51 joint venture with Fuji Heavy Industries, which manufactures Subaru automobiles. This will produce at least 120,000 automobiles and pickup trucks in Lafayette, Indiana.

CASE 11-2
General Motors' Strategic Investment in Isuzu

In 1971, General Motors paid $58 million for a 34.2-percent equity stake in Isuzu Motors, today Japan's sixth-largest automobile and truck manufacturer. GM's objectives were threefold:

- To gain increased access to the Japanese market.
- To gain access to high-quality Japanese components (particularly in light trucks).
- To earn a reasonable profit on the investment.

For Isuzu, the marriage provided a response to competitive and political pressures for a merger at home, access to General Motors' technology (particularly in passenger cars, in which it was weak), and an injection of capital. At the time, Isuzu had virtually no overseas sales, and it also hoped to export through the General Motors network.

Various commercial relationships and secondary alliances have flowed from the initial investment.

- The two companies have supplied each other with components. For example, Isuzu won the contract to build the manual transaxle for General Motors' J car (Opel Vectra in continental Europe) outside North America. In return, GM supplied automatic transaxles for Isuzu's J car.
- Isuzu adapted the Opel J car for sale in the Japanese market. It also agreed to distribute Opels built in Europe beginning in 1989.
- Isuzu has supplied General Motors with light and medium trucks and with small front-wheel-drive cars for Chevrolet for distribution in the United States on an OEM basis.
- In 1987, Isuzu took a 40-share in General Motors' United Kingdom Bedford light-van subsidiary. The new company, IBC Vehicles, manufactures four-wheel-drive vehicles as well as vans, and it has been profitable since its first full year in operation.
- The two companies have formed a number of joint marketing ventures, including Convesco, a European distribution company owned 60 percent by GM and 40 percent by Isuzu.

Isuzu's exports have increased substantially since 1971 (see Exhibit 11-2) directly, through OEM agreements, and through joint ventures. It has also received substantial technical help from General Motors. GM now holds 38 percent of Isuzu equity.

EXHIBIT 11–2
Isuzu Vehicle Sales (Number of Units)

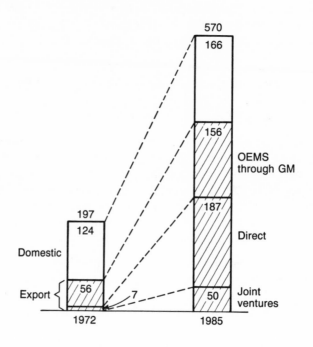

CHAPTER 12

THE GLOBAL DIMENSIONS
OF STRATEGIC PARTNERSHIPS

> The economic system is more and more like one single interacting organism.
> —Akio Morita, Chairman, Sony[1]

Differences in economic, political, and social environments have caused multinationals in the Triad regions to pursue widely divergent patterns of development. There are also significant variations in business culture and management practice.

Today, companies in each region face different kinds of challenges. For Japanese companies, it is the challenge of building genuinely international organizations that operate at the leading edge of technology and are welcome everywhere in the global marketplace. For European corporations, the issues are largely about scale and how to create companies of sufficient size to compete in world markets with larger U.S. and Japanese operations. For the United States, the problem is rather one of a loss of the advantages it has enjoyed in the past, particularly in technology leadership and market size.

These different challenges require different strategic responses, but companies in all three regions are turning to strategic partnerships as an important component of the solution to their problems. This chapter examines some of the special factors influencing multinational strategies in the three regions of the Triad and looks at the role of strategic partnerships in achieving companies' objectives.

LESSONS FOR WESTERNERS

In 1964, when the Olympic Games were held in Tokyo, Japan was a relatively small, highly protected market. The per-capita Gross Domestic Product was $840, roughly a quarter of the United States' level, and half that of the United Kingdom. Today, Japan contributes some 19 percent of OECD GDP, and its GDP per head is on a par with that of the United States.

Since then, too, Japan has changed from being a heavy importer of technology through licenses and joint ventures to one of the most powerful industrial nations in the world. By the early 1970s, Japanese companies were already selling more technology abroad, in terms of new contracts, than they were buying. Today the overall inflows and outflows are more or less in balance (see Exhibit 12-1). In 1964, Japan spent only 1.5 percent of its GDP on research and development, half as much as the United States. Today that proportion has doubled. During the first half of the 1980s, Japan's R&D investment grew more rapidly than that of either Europe or the United States, growth largely financed by industry. Japan now spends a higher proportion of GDP on civil R&D than any other major industrial nation. It trains more than 70,000 engineers a year, twice as many per capita as the United States.

Evolution of Japanese Partnerships

Strategic partnerships between Japan and the West evolved in three phases. The first phase, lasting well into the 1970s, was predominantly one in which Japanese industry was catching up with the West. The vast majority of partnerships during this period took the form of licensing agreements or joint ventures based on Japanese soil. They provided Japanese companies with much-needed access to products and technology, and a stepping stone to improving their own internal R&D capabilities and manufacturing skills. Until the early 1970s, joint ventures represented the only way in which a Western company could establish a presence in Japan.

By the end of the decade, this catching-up process was largely complete, and Japan had obtained leadership in some important areas, notably in the management of large-scale manufacturing. The second phase had already begun, characterized by a much greater flow of technology in the other direction. Many Western companies have since come to rely heavily on joint development and OEM relationships with Japanese companies to fill parts of their product ranges in which they have lost the battle for competitiveness.

We are now entering the third phase, and the competitive environment is rather more complex. There are four important features of this new situation.

EXHIBIT 12–1

Japanese Balance of Payments for Technology Transfer (Receipts and Payments)

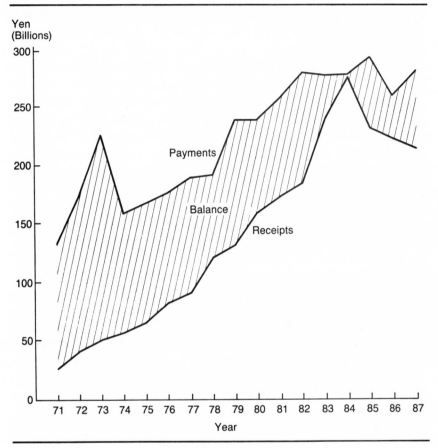

Source: OECD Science and Technology indicators.

First, the Japanese market is becoming much more open than it used to be, and the government and industry are actively seeking imports from overseas companies. As the second-largest market in the non-Communist world (more than half as many consumers are packed into 4 percent as much space as in the United States), Japan is of strategic importance to all multinational companies. It is also slowly becoming easier for Western companies to establish management control over their Japanese operations.

Second, Japanese companies are being forced by circumstances to develop more comprehensive international operations—both to support marketing of the more sophisticated products into which they are moving, and to overcome political and economic constraints. Acquisitions, joint ventures, and strategic investments have an important role to play in this transition.

Third, there is greater parity in the level of technology on which Japanese, United States, and European businesses now base their strategies. All must operate at the leading edge of technology if they are to maintain economic growth. All are now in competition to develop and acquire the most advanced technologies. For Japanese companies especially, the old licensing routes are less productive. Western companies are more reluctant to make technology available, and it is less likely to be sufficiently advanced. Again, strategic partnering has an important role to play in gaining access to technologies from overseas partners.

Fourth, is a feature of Japanese industry that is of special significance to strategic partnerships: the competitive strengths of many of its companies. Productivity, value engineering, quality, flexibility, and product development have all been used with great success as competitive weapons by Japanese companies, frequently enabling them to outmaneuver their Western competitors. These strengths derive largely from the way the companies are organized and managed. The long-term future of Western companies depends on implementation of these new standards of management in the United States and Europe.

Such lessons can really be learned only by experience, and partnerships with Japanese companies provide one of the best means of gaining that experience. Some Western companies have already established alliances with these objectives in mind. Learning the Japanese approach to automobile manufacturing is an important reason for General Motors' participation in the NUMMI project, and some of Philips' partnerships, for instance those with Marantz and Kyocera, also have this as one of their objectives.

Alliances with Japanese companies often offer attractive benefits to Western companies. However, these relationships can be one-sided; Japanese companies often have longer-term objectives than their Western partners. In all but two alliances between Western and Japanese companies studied by a team of European and American researchers, the Japanese had started out as the weaker partner but ended as the stronger.[2]

The Japanese dimension represents one of the most fascinating aspects of the strategic-partnership phenomenon. Alliances between Western and Japanese companies create challenges for both partners. The differences in culture and business practice are at their widest. Before examining the issues involved, it is important to appreciate what these differences are. We look first at the situation from the perspective of Western companies, focusing particularly on the use of strategic partnerships to gain access to the Japanese market.

Economic Structure

Before World War II, the Japanese economy was virtually controlled by 10 major industrial conglomerates, or Zaibatsu, of which four—Mitsubishi, Mitsui, Sumitomo, and Yasuda—accounted for roughly a quarter of Japanese industrial assets.[3] After the war, the United States government forced the dismemberment of the Zaibatsu. However, the repeal in 1949 and 1953 of antimonopoly laws resulted in a gradual reestablishment of these associations. A number of new business groups have also been formed since, so that Japanese industry is today characterized by loose business groupings, each consisting of companies in widely divergent activities.

There are now 6 major industrial groups, or Keiretsu, and 11 lesser groups. Taken together, the sales of companies in these groups are responsible for roughly 25 percent of the activity of all Japanese companies. Seven of the largest industrial groups include both major banks and general trading firms. The general trading firms have played an important role in the businesses of client companies, using their global information and marketing networks to help set up overseas subsidiaries and joint ventures. However, as the sophistication of Japanese exports has increased, direct control of the distribution chain has become more important for its manufacturers.

The range and complexity of the relationships are illustrated in Exhibit 12-2, which shows the main members of the Mitsubishi Group.[4] It is led by Mitsubishi Bank and Mitsubishi Heavy Industries, the country's largest machinery manufacturer, with interests ranging from aircraft to air-conditioning equipment. Altogether, the Mitsubishi Group involves some 160 companies, of which 124 are listed on the Tokyo Stock Exchange. Each is entirely independent, with its own board of directors.

It is a common practice for Japanese companies to acquire a small shareholding in businesses with which they have commercial dealings. However, the original role of the extensive cross-shareholdings between

EXHIBIT 12–2
Complexity of Keiretsu: The Mitsubishi Group

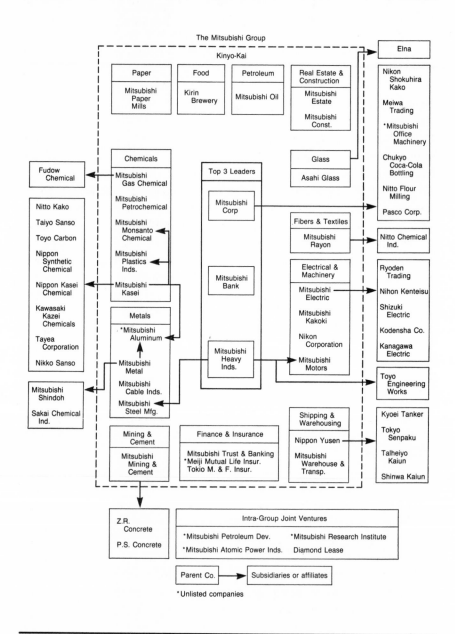

The Mitsubishi Group

Kinyo-Kai

Paper	**Food**	**Petroleum**	**Real Estate & Construction**
Mitsubishi Paper Mills	Kirin Brewery	Mitsubishi Oil	Mitsubishi Estate / Mitsubishi Const.

Elna

Nikon Shokuhira Kako

Meiwa Trading

*Mitsubishi Office Machinery

Chukyo Coca-Cola Bottling

Nitto Flour Milling

Pasco Corp.

Chemicals
- Mitsubishi Gas Chemical
- Mitsubishi Petrochemical
- Mitsubishi Monsanto Chemical
- Mitsubishi Plastics Inds.
- Mitsubishi Kasei

Glass
- Asahi Glass

Top 3 Leaders
- Mitsubishi Corp
- Mitsubishi Bank
- Mitsubishi Heavy Inds.

Fibers & Textiles
- Mitsubishi Rayon

Electrical & Machinery
- Mitsubishi Electric
- Mitsubishi Kakoki
- Nikon Corporation
- Mitsubishi Motors

Fudow Chemical

Nitto Kako

Taiyo Sanso

Toyo Carbon

Nippon Synthetic Chemical

Nippon Kasei Chemical

Kawasaki Kazei Chemicals

Tayea Corporation

Nikko Sanso

Mitsubishi Shindoh

Sakai Chemical Ind.

Nitto Chemical Ind.

Ryoden Trading

Nihon Kenteisu

Shizuki Electric

Kodensha Co.

Kanagawa Electric

Toyo Engineering Works

Metals
- *Mitsubishi Aluminum
- Mitsubishi Metal
- Mitsubishi Cable Inds.
- Mitsubishi Steel Mfg.

Mining & Cement
- Mitsubishi Mining & Cement

Finance & Insurance
- Mitsubishi Trust & Banking
- *Meiji Mutual Life Insur.
- Tokio M. & F. Insur.

Shipping & Warehousing
- Nippon Yusen
- Mitsubishi Warehouse & Transp.

Kyoei Tanker

Tokyo Senpaku

Talheiyo Kaiun

Shinwa Kaiun

Z.R. Concrete / P.S. Concrete	Intra-Group Joint Ventures
	*Mitsubishi Petroleum Dev. *Mitsubishi Research Institute
	*Mitsubishi Atomic Power Inds. Diamond Lease

Parent Co. ——▶ Subsidiaries or affiliates

*Unlisted companies

Keiretsu members was to maintain their financial independence. Cross-shareholdings were greatly strengthened after the laws on overseas capital investment were liberalized in the late 1960s and early 1970s. Today, some 25 percent of Keiretsu members' shares are held by other companies in the group.

The cross-shareholdings of Keiretsu companies support a subtle blend of financial independence and commercial cooperation. Additional mechanisms to promote cooperation include senior personnel exchanges and regular discussions of trade and investment policies.

Shacho-Kai

A number of Japanese industrial groupings have formed Shacho-Kai, or Presidential Councils, to discuss issues of mutual interest. For example, the 28-member Mitsubishi-Kinyo-Kai (Friday conference) meets twice a month. While the Shacho-Kai do not have the policymaking power of the board of a Western conglomerate, they exert enormous influence. Discussions are confidential, but cover such topics as new joint-venture opportunities, R&D, personnel appointments, and support for members in financial difficulties. They also provide a powerful forum within which group members can meet one another regularly, simply to get to know one another and exchange ideas.

Joint Investments

The Keiretsu concept provides a strong and varied resource base from which to enter new industries. The formation of new joint ventures and spin-off companies has been a common feature of Japanese companies' diversification strategies since World War II. This has often involved collaboration between the eight more traditional groups and the newer, industrially led independent groups such as Toyota and Toshiba.

Barriers to Acquisition

The structure of Japanese industry makes acquisition extremely difficult. Because of the extensive cross-shareholdings and long-term positions taken by institutional investors, only a small proportion, often less than half, of shares in Japanese public companies are actually traded on the stock exchanges. For example, a company wishing to acquire Japan's third-largest tire maker, Sumitomo Rubber Industries, would find that 69 percent of shares were held by the 10 largest shareholders—56 percent by other members of the Sumitomo Group, with the largest single share-holder, Sumitomo Electric Industries, holding 40 percent.

Perhaps more important are the fundamental cultural barriers to acquisition. Japanese companies are bound together by strong bonds of loyalty, which pass through all levels of the organization. Directors are not appointed from outside, but grow up within the organization. Their primary objective is the health and welfare of the people for whom they are responsible, not shareholder interests. Japanese companies guard their financial independence fiercely. Loss of control is synonymous with loss of face. And the emphasis on independence is reinforced by a hierarchical perspective that goes right through Japanese society; a subsidiary company has less status than its parent organization.

In the business culture of Japan, the sale of a company to an outsider is virtually unthinkable. Hostile takeovers are particularly distasteful—so much so that none ever succeeded until 1989. The very words that describe them—*notori*, meaning hijack, and *baishu*, meaning bribery, sum up Japanese attitudes. This distaste is not restricted to Western buyers, although foreigners are still regarded with some suspicion, and those seeking to acquire 10 percent or more of a Japanese company are subject to government scrutiny. Only companies in financial difficulties tend to be for sale, and bankruptcy is more likely to be avoided by the intervention of a company's bank. Another deterrent is that, while MITI exerts much less direct control and influence over industry than in the past, it would be unlikely to let foreign companies take a controlling interest in the country's most important companies.

All this means that acquisitions and strategic investment must in most instances be negotiated on a friendly basis. The building of long-term relationships is a crucial part of the business environment in Japan. This must be the first focus of the Western company wishing to penetrate the Japanese market. Direct acquisition will continue to be rarely available as a strategy, but a strategic partnership can provide the prelude to full ownership through gradual acquisition of equity.

The Japanese business environment is clearly changing. The proportion of new investment and joint-venture situations in which overseas companies had a controlling interest increased significantly (see Exhibit 12–3). Similarly, in recent years there has been an increase in equity investments in and foreign acquisitions of Japanese companies.[5] There is little doubt that this trend will continue, if only because Japanese companies now take part in it. But despite persistent American pressure, foreigners remain at a

EXHIBIT 12-3
Changing Patterns of Direct Foreign Investment in Japan

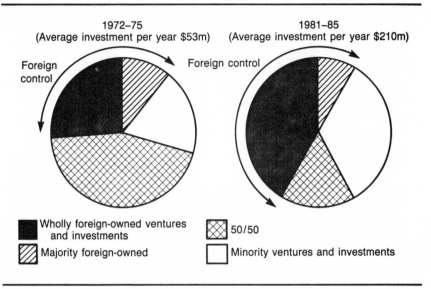

1972–75
(Average investment per year $53m)

1981–85
(Average investment per year $210m)

Foreign control

Foreign control

■ Wholly foreign-owned ventures and investments

▨ 50/50

▨ Majority foreign-owned

☐ Minority ventures and investments

disadvantage, and the number of companies involved is still small. A study carried out in 1985 identified only 32 foreign acquisitions of Japanese companies that had taken place since 1955, together with a further 33 in which there was a substantial foreign ownership.[6] Between 1985 and 1989, foreigners took control of 97 Japanese companies, mostly smaller ones. Today, only the weaker companies in a given market sector are available. Indeed, weaker companies often see a Western company as a more amenable partner than another Japanese company. It offers them a stronger degree of independence and an important place in the new parent's global network. Japanese acquisitions therefore tend to require a good deal of aftercare, with further injections of finance, products, and management time.

There is still a large and increasing imbalance between the level of foreign investment in Japan and investment by Japanese companies overseas (see Exhibit 12-4). As Japan's economy becomes more international and its financial markets become more closely integrated with the West, the scope for Western involvement in Japanese companies will also expand. Some Japanese investment bankers already have a substantial number of clients for whom they are actively seeking outside investment. How-

EXHIBIT 12-4
Foreign Investment in Japan and by Japan

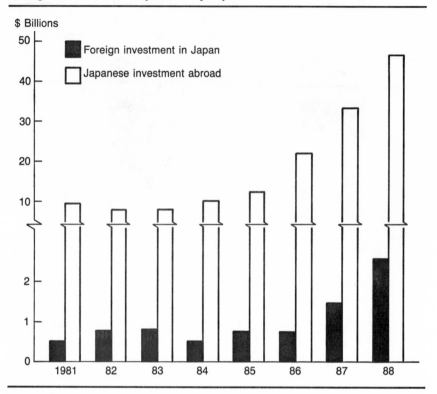

Source: Japanese Ministry of Finance

ever, it will be a long time before Japanese companies fall to the raiding-party tactics prevalent (at least until recently) in many Western economies. CEOs wishing to buy Japanese companies must learn to do it the Japanese way and brush up their strategic-partnership skills.

The Practicalities

Any Western company considering entering an equity relationship with a Japanese company, either as an investor or as a joint-venture partner, must be aware of the impact of Japanese commercial practices and of cultural differences. It must also be wary of the dangers of teaming up with powerful competitors.

Higher Prices—Lower Profits
Every aspect of the investment equation is affected by Japan's commercial practices—equity prices, expected returns, dividend policy, budgeting, and intracompany pricing. Failure to understand the differences in practice can lead to unpleasant surprises later on, either during negotiations or, worse still, after the investment has been made.

Cheap at Half the Price. The first important difference is the price of shares in Japanese companies. Price/earnings ratios are typically several times higher than in U.S. and European companies. There are several reasons for this difference, and they affect the treatment of both revenue and valuation.

There are strong incentives to keep profits low by investing surplus cash in assets and R&D. This practice reflects both the traditional bias toward growth and the high rate of corporate tax (56 percent in 1988). Moreover, taxable corporate income is generally greater than profits as reported to shareholders. At the same time, reported Japanese earnings often include only those of the parent company. Consolidated earnings would typically be 50 percent to 100 percent higher.

Coupled with this is a tendency to undervalue company assets. Many Japanese companies have huge hidden assets, especially in real estate and shares in associated companies. Both are reflected in the balance sheet at cost, often dramatically undervaluing the real worth of many companies. Informed (Japanese) investors recognize these hidden assets, even if it is difficult to put a value on them. Together, these factors serve both to increase share prices and depress reporting earnings,[7] making it difficult for Western companies to justify investments by reference to conventional capital-budgeting criteria.

Yet another difference is the yield offered by Japanese equity investments. The position of the ordinary Japanese shareholder is much closer to that of the preferred shareholder in U.S. companies. Barring company bankruptcy, there will be a dividend every year. However, it is likely to be relatively small and, to make things more confusing for Westerners, it is usually expressed as a percentage of par value. Many companies pay a dividend equal to about 10 percent of the par value of their shares, although this may work out at less than 1 percent of the share price, a fraction of average U.S. yields.

Japanese shareholders are happy to accept this position, not just because of the economic success and share-value appreciation that have been achieved through growth-based policies, but also because capital gains on share sales are generally tax free to individuals in Japan, whereas the tax on dividends is some 20 percent.

The result is that an investment in a Japanese company is likely to generate far less in the way of repatriated income than would a comparable investment in the United States or Europe. Investors must find other ways of deriving income—through interest on loans or consulting fees, for example, or through royalties and commercial trading.

Transfer Prices and Budgeting.   The setting of transfer prices is an important point of negotiation in any buyer-vendor relationship. Chapter 9 explained how the complexity of the commercial relationships in joint ventures affects partners' interests in different ways. The setting of transfer prices has a major impact on the overall cake and how it will be divided.

Partnerships with Japanese companies are further complicated by different philosophies about where a company makes its profits. In Western companies, marketing is regarded as having a major and usually quite explicit role in profit generation, and it is common for both production and marketing departments to be treated as profit centers. Manufacturing may be treated as a cost center, products being transferred to the marketing function at cost.

The Japanese approach is very different. For Japanese managers, manufacturing is the source of company profits; the role of marketing is to achieve the highest possible volume of sales. This thinking is responsible for the focus on manufacturing economies of scale and the continuing cost-improvement programs that are characteristic of many Japanese companies. This difference in philosophy can easily lead to misunderstanding or even conflict in joint-venture situations in which partners enter transfer-price negotiations with genuinely different profit expectations.

> There would be the most bloody damn battle you have ever seen every time we got down to negotiating prices.
> —U.S. executive on transfer-price arrangements with Japanese partner

Budgeting is also approached in a different way. Budgets in Japan tend to be viewed as demanding targets rather than as operating standards to which management will be held. Again, this can lead to misunderstanding, though here too the gap is narrowing. A number of Japanese companies have adopted Western budgeting and planning methods. Some we interviewed had imported those of their strategic partners.

Cultural Differences

One of the greatest sources of concern for Western companies doing business in Japan is the great difference in styles of management and business culture, differences that stem from the fundamentally different philosophies of life in the two societies. Even Westerners who have lived and studied in Japan for many years find it difficult to articulate the differences and admit to being frequently surprised by what they see and hear. Communication is made more difficult by the poor English of many Japanese businessmen (and, of course, the even poorer Japanese of most Westerners). Many words do not translate well from one language to the other, so it is important for anyone negotiating a strategic partnership to try to understand these differences and work out methods of dealing with them in advance.

Perhaps the most significant characteristic of Japanese culture is the emphasis on personal obligation—obligation to the company, to employees, to the peer group, to suppliers and customers, and to the nation. Obligation implies mutual trust, and for the Japanese the building of mutual trust is the first item on the agenda in any business relationship.

Closely linked is a strongly hierarchical view of the world. Individuals and companies see themselves in relation to those lower and higher in the hierarchy. There are strong cultural pressures to work hard to move up the ladder. For companies, the hierarchical perspective extends to their positions in their industries internationally.

The emphasis on personal obligation means that, once created, personal and business relationships tend to be long-lasting. For example, one recent study indicated that Japanese firms obtain 55 percent of supplies from trusted vendors with whom they have long cooperated. Supplies obtained from such sources by U.S. companies amount to just 6 percent of the total.[8] Thus it is extremely difficult for Western companies to break into Japanese markets. It can take years to build up the required network of human and commercial relationships with customers and business partners. A strategic partnership may be the only way to find a place in one of these networks.

The Negotiating Table.   For many Westerners, their first real encounter with Japanese business culture is at the negotiating table. The process of decision making in Japanese companies is traditionally different from that in the West. It is perhaps best described as a middle-up approach. Major decisions are subject to painstaking analysis, and discussions may be protracted, which is often highly frustrating for potential partners. Specialists will be involved from all parts of the organization that are likely to be affected. Western negotiators may find themselves sitting down opposite a Japanese team of a dozen or more people, with no idea of where the real decision-making power lies. Once a decision is made, however, this consensus-building process ensures that implementation—the most difficult part of any strategic plan—is likely to be swift and efficient.

Another important reason why negotiations with Japanese companies tend to take much longer than with Western companies is the effort put into creating good relationships at a human level. Everyone on the negotiating team must be fully briefed on the importance of this process, and only those with the capacity to build good relationships should be included.

Relationships between company presidents and their senior executives responsible for negotiating the partnership are particularly important. They are also enduring. In the event of later difficulties, it is the managers who presided at the birth of the partnership who are likely to be consulted by the Japanese partner, even if they have moved on to quite different lines of responsibilities in their own companies. Their responsibilities as architects of the partnership remain. A move by a key executive to another company—common in the West, but virtually unheard of in Japan—creates considerable uncertainty, and an immediate effort must be made to rebuild human relationships between the partners.

The fundamental importance of obligation in Japan also underlies the different attitude to legal contracts. A resort to litigation constitutes a loss of face for a Japanese businessman. The sense of honor dictates that great effort be put into fulfilling obligations. There are only 15,000 lawyers in Japan, compared with 500,000—about 15 times as many per capita in the U.S. Lawyers do not play the major role in negotiations that they do in the U.S. A philosophical belief in the indeterminacy of the future may lead the Japanese side to prefer that contractual obligations be left as vague as possible so as to provide future flexibility. In the event of a dispute, it is far more likely to be settled by conferral rather than confrontation.

For the Western negotiator, this emphasis on trust must be balanced against the realities of any commercial negotiation. No aspect of a deal can be left unexplored before it is signed. Key technologies must be validated, distribution networks analyzed, and management competences considered. Japanese companies tend to go through a far more detailed process of checking than is typical in Western companies, with wide internal discussion to examine the impact on their businesses. Western businesses must do the same.

An increasing number of companies have adopted a more Western style of business and are able to make decisions rapidly. A number of the Western companies with Japanese partners that our team interviewed had quite deliberately searched out partners of the new breed, finding companies with a more entrepreneurial style of management much easier to deal with and quicker to respond to proposals.

Recruiting Staff.   One of the problems for Western companies wishing to set up in Japan is the difficulty of obtaining personnel. Major Japanese companies recruit predominantly at the graduate-school level. Companies offer graduates the prospect of lifetime employment, with steady career advancement and virtually no prospect of redundancy. Midcareer recruitment is virtually unheard of.

The practice of lifetime employment also means that there is no ready pool of more experienced staff on which a company can draw in order to expand—much less set up an operation from scratch. And Western employers may appear more risky; Japanese managers know that once they have entered the Western business community, they must stay there.

Again, the pattern is slowly changing. Headhunters are beginning to be active in more specialized fields such as computing, and discrimination against women in Japanese business makes the female population a useful source of recruits for Western companies. But the basic problem remains.

Strategic partnerships provide a means of overcoming these difficulties. Acquiring or investing in a Japanese company supplies a ready-made vehicle for recruitment, provided that the company image can be built up sufficiently. Joint ventures provide access to the partner's management talent.

Strategic partnerships do not provide an automatic solution to recruitment problems. Subsidiaries tend to be regarded as inferior in status to the parent, and it can be difficult to attract committed management. Worse, subsidiaries can provide a dumping ground for second-raters.

A Tiger by the Tail

Perhaps more important than these operational difficulties are the longer-term strategic implications of partnerships with Japanese companies. The Japanese manufacturing base is now the strongest in the world. The economy has immense reservoirs of engineering talent. Companies spend more per head on R&D than any major Western competitor, and the commitment to research is growing. Staff development programs turn out some of the best general managers in the world, with experience in many different parts of the business. Lifetime employment and cultural attitudes create an intense loyalty to the company. The Japanese approach to innovation and group problem solving means that both products and processes are continually being upgraded and improved. The way in which engineers are trained ensures that products are designed for manufacture. Low interest rates and passive shareholders underpin a bias toward growth that few Western companies have been able to match. Aggressive competition in the large, protected Japanese market gives its companies a powerful springboard from which to sell overseas.

Finally, Japanese companies are extremely effective at strategic management. They tend to be far more active than their Western counterparts at searching for new technological and business opportunities. Not-invented-here prejudices—prevalent in some countries of the West—are much less evident. Diversification is the norm in Japan, not the exception.

These are the realities of the Japanese manufacturing industry. Companies are not equally efficient, of course, and as the process of internationalization proceeds, many aspects of the Western business culture are becoming more common.

Any Western company considering a strategic partnership with a Japanese manufacturer must decide how it is going to handle the potential competitive threat that goes with it. It must expect that its partner will try to learn from the venture, that it may try to develop better technologies or products, and that it may try ultimately to bring a larger share of the manufacturing in-house, enabling it to build a long-term competitive advantage in the technology introduced.

This is good business sense anywhere. It is just that more Japanese seem to realize it, and their businesses are better equipped to exploit opportunities. As an academic study concluded, after commenting on this asymmetry in partnerships between Western and Japanese companies, "there is no anti-Japanese bias; it is just that along the three dimensions of strategic interest, transferability of contribution, and receptivity of the organization, Japanese competitors may enjoy an advantage over their partners."[9]

Western companies must find out how to reverse this pattern and use partnerships with the Japanese to learn new management skills—just as the Japanese learned from the West in the 1950s and 1960s. The West will continue to lose ground in the battle for world markets unless it can match Japanese companies in terms of quality, value engineering, product development, efficiency, and manufacturing cost improvement. Even the Japanese approach to strategic management has important lessons for Western companies. Using strategic partnerships to improve competitive advantage in these areas should now be on the agenda of the CEO of every Western multinational.

LESSONS FOR JAPANESE COMPANIES

As commercial success has pushed up Japan's labor costs, it has become less and less competitive in many of the products on which that very economic success was founded. Its key export industries have been progressively subjected to low-cost competition, particularly from the NICs. Over the last 30 years, textiles, shipbuilding, steel, and consumer electronics have all been affected. The competitive pressure has been aggravated by *endaka*, the rapid increase in the value of the yen, itself a result of Japan's trade imbalance, and by the difficulty experienced by Western companies in selling into Japanese markets.

A gradual erosion of price competitiveness is not a new experience for Japanese businessmen. They have had to live with it for years. However, the space for maneuvering is now small. Japan is no longer going through a catching-up process; simply improving efficiency and moving to products with greater perceived value is not enough. More fundamental changes in strategy are required, and international strategic partnerships have a major role to play.

Going Offshore

Japanese companies must first be prepared to move production to lower-cost manufacturing locations offshore. This in fact is already happening. An increasing proportion of the production of more-basic manufactured products—those that do not require a highly skilled workforce or close linkages to R&D—is being transferred. Many Japanese companies plan to increase overseas production significantly. Matsushita, whose overseas operations were supplying only about 30 percent of the goods sold in their own markets in 1989, plans to raise this proportion to a minimum of 50 percent. This is part of a plan to raise overseas production to about a quarter of the company's total. NEC, which has long assembled products in the markets where they are sold, has forged a new overseas manufacturing strategy; a mesh of regional manufacturing operations now work for one another with or without the support of NEC plants in Japan. Some economists predict that 20 percent of the country's manufacturing will take place overseas by the turn of the century, compared with well under 10 percent in 1989.

The newly industrialized countries are likely to be important beneficiaries of this move. They are eager to follow Japan's path and use overseas technology to accelerate economic development. Japanese companies must learn how to work with these economies for mutual advantage.

Korea is particularly active in seeking Japanese investment, keen to acquire Japanese technology and finance in exchange for lower labor costs. Japan is Korea's most important source of technology, responsible for 50 percent or more of technology transfer deals signed by South Korean companies. And Japan provides more than half of Korea's inward development.

Most investments take the form of joint ventures. The initial target is usually the Korean market itself, with 42 million people and an average annual GDP growth rate over the last five years of 8 percent. Many important joint ventures, however, have a significant exporting role, as they must if Korea is to pursue its objective of export-led growth in products ranging from cameras to light trucks.

Operating at the Leading Edge

Another strategic response of Japanese companies to increased wage costs must be a move into higher-technology products. In many ways this represents a continuation of existing trends. Industries currently targeted for development by the Japanese government include aerospace, nonpetroleum energy sources, information processing, biotechnology, and new industrial materials.

There is an important difference between these new industries and the earlier pattern of economic development. From now on, Japanese industry will be competing at the very edge of technology; competitive success will depend to a great extent on a company's innovative skills. Because of this, and because of the West's growing awareness of Japan's technological strengths, it will be far more difficult than it used to be for Japanese business to acquire appropriate technology through licensing and joint ventures.

Japanese executives are only too aware of the restrictions their own corporate culture places on innovation. It provides an ideal environment for incremental engineering improvements, but deters the kind of independent individual action that lies at the root of most major breakthroughs. For example, the concept of a product champion, an icon of current management thinking in the West, is unknown to the majority of senior Japanese executives. The severe problems in starting a new company, the seedbed of many commercial innovations in the United States, mean that there are very few entrepreneurially driven small companies in which a more fertile environment might exist.

Early access to leading technology developed in the West will therefore be crucial to the next stage in Japanese economic development. Research collaborations, university sponsorship, and corporate venturing must form important elements in Japanese business strategies. Some aspects of these new strategies are already well advanced. Japanese companies already have good contacts with many university centers of excellence. Many send their best scientists overseas to carry out research and build up networks of contacts. Some 15,000 Japanese students and researchers enter U.S. institutions every year, and Japanese companies actively support a variety of overseas university research programs.

While contact at the academic level is strong, most Japanese companies have been fairly slow to develop corporate-venturing strategies. The role of the small company in innovation is not widely understood, and many Japanese executives find it difficult to see the point of carrying out this kind of activity systematically. However, there are already signs of a growing interest in small companies, particularly those in the United States. Kyocera, Canon, Fujitsu, and Kobe Steel are among the companies that have made such investments, but these instances are still atypical. The use of corporate venturing to gain access to new technologies is one of the key business skills that Japanese companies must learn if their thrust into high-tech is to be successful.

Building New Channels of Distribution

Besides the need for access to external R&D, there is another important implication of the move into high-tech products. It has to do with the other end of the supply chain. Most of Japan's export success has been in mass-market products—that can be produced in quantity in Japan and shipped to the West for marketing, through such conventional Western distributors as retail stores and car dealers.

As the unit price of electronics collapses and Japan moves into more sophisticated types of product, an increasing proportion of the perceived value will lie not in mass production but in customizing systems to meet particular purchasers' requirements, and in aftersale service. The arm's-length, mass-market approach to distribution will no longer be appropriate. Closer ties will be needed to provide the complex design, installation, training, and customer service associated with these products. To take advantage of these downstream opportunities, Japanese companies must invest in their distributors on the ground. But, it is difficult to build this kind of operation from scratch. Acquisitions, strategic investments, and joint ventures are likely to be more and more important.

Fanuc is a company that has shown the way. Its policy is always to export through joint ventures with local companies. NEC's investment in Honeywell-Bull is another important example. In the short term, its investment cements the OEM relationships that already exist. In the long term, it gives NEC a foothold in the U.S. and European computer-systems market.

Acquiring these value-driven marketing channels in the West is likely to be key to the internationalization of Japanese companies. In the next five years they must learn how to make and manage strategic investments and acquisitions to achieve this goal.

Addressing Political Pressures

The pressures described so far are essentially economic. Just as important for Japan are the political and commercial pressures to locate production in overseas markets. The concentration of Japan's export success in fairly narrow industries such as automobiles and consumer electronics has led to strong political pressures for quota restrictions in the United States and Europe. Antidumping measures can have the same effect or worse. Japanese businesses are acutely aware of the problems of trade friction and are anxiously trying to locate production and assembly in local markets. Some companies have already adopted an international philosophy. A leading example is Canon, which encourages subsidiaries around the world to reinvest the income where it is generated.

The trend toward offshore production is most pronounced in the U.S. automobile market, in which Japanese joint ventures and investments will provide the capacity to produce 2.4 million cars a year by 1991, nearly a million in plants jointly owned with U.S. companies.

In Europe, pressure is growing on the European Commission to use

1992 as an opportunity to introduce or tighten restrictions on imports from Japan. Further, they want to make it more difficult for Japanese companies to establish screwdriver plants that merely assemble imported components. For example, European car manufacturers have demanded that as much as 80 percent of the components be locally manufactured if cars are to qualify as being of European origin.

Moving production offshore helps Japanese companies bring down the price of labor and get around import quotas, but simply building a local production plant may not be sufficient to satisfy local interests. The prime source of political pressure is often local companies, perhaps companies that have surrendered much of their manufacturing capability by remarketing Japanese-manufactured goods on an OEM basis. Forming a local joint venture with an indigenous company, perhaps to assemble products from a mixture of Japanese and local components, can help alleviate the political pressure while providing the local management skills on which success depends.

There are many intrinsic conflicts in ventures such as these. Nonetheless, local manufacturing joint ventures in the West are likely to play a much bigger role in Japanese strategic thinking.

The New Japanese Multinationals

Internationalizing their operations will be the most significant challenge facing Japanese companies over the next decade. Commercial, financial, and political pressures are all combining to force the transition to multinational, which is now entering its fourth phase. Initially, overseas sales were made through the large trading companies like Mitsui and C. Itoh. Later, manufacturers tended to set up their own overseas distribution subsidiaries to manage dealerships and conduct marketing campaigns. The third stage was the creation of local manufacturing or assembly plants, the most successful being greenfield operations into which a strong element of the Japanese management style could be transplanted. (The Japanese make much greater use of Japanese expatriates in overseas subsidiaries than do U.S. companies of U.S. citizens.) To reach full multinational status, Japanese companies must now establish a full-function presence in major markets, including R&D engineering, customer service, planning, investment, and personnel.

This presents some major difficulties. Few Japanese companies have enough people with the language skills and management experience to operate outside Japan. The idiosyncratic management style to which most Japanese executives are accustomed ill equips them to manage a team of senior American or European executives. Recruitment, though easier for a Japanese company than for a foreign company setting up from scratch in Japan, has its own pitfalls—pitfalls that can partially be avoided only by using professional recruitment consultants. The low status traditionally accorded overseas employees by Japanese companies will continue to make it difficult to recruit and retain the best people. Personnel practices will need to be sharply revised before Japanese companies can operate as effectively in Silicon Valley, where job-hopping is as easy as changing your car, as it is in Tokyo, where it is as difficult as changing your personality.

Acquisition overcomes many of these problems, enabling companies to buy a ready-made management team and operations base. However, acquisition puts responsibility for top management squarely on the shoulders of the acquiring company. Motivating and retaining key executives, and ensuring that the political and commercial wheels are being properly lubricated, require familiarity with the local business culture. Keeping foreign subsidiaries on track will be as tricky for the Japanese as it is for Westerners if they don't understand the culture of the people that run them. Acquisition means that the new owner must deal with these problems directly—from day one.

Japanese companies are largely unaccustomed to the concept of using acquisitions to expand business, and their experience in the West has been disconcerting. The results of two of the largest attempts to date have hardly been auspicious. After much delay, Fujitsu's 1986 bid for Fairchild was rejected by the U.S. government. In the very week in 1988 when Bridgestone acquired Firestone, it lost its most significant customer, General Motors. Strategic investments and joint ventures offer valuable alternatives to acquisition. They give Japanese companies the opportunity to come to grips with the Western business environment at greater leisure, to avoid the political problems that may be associated with outright acquisition, and to share the tiller with a more experienced Western hand.

THE EUROPEAN DIMENSION

It was obvious that Europe was not going to be able to make it competitively in the computer industry, so I thought the participants would be able to see

the merits of a cooperative effort. But again they were not really interested.
They could see their problems, but thought they could solve them alone.
—William Norris, Chairman and CEO, Control Data Corporation,
speaking about a visit to Europe in 1979

The United States of Europe?

With nearly 500 million people, Europe's population is twice that of the
United States. While 324 million of these live within the European Community and another 140 million live in Eastern Europe, the United States
of Europe does not yet exist. Europe has long been a highly fragmented
market with individual national champions in its leading industries, often
buttressed by preferential treatment by national governments. The leading
companies are, on the whole, much smaller than their U.S. and Japanese
competitors. Few are really strong enough to compete globally. In many
sectors, U.S. and Japanese manufacturers have a stronger presence in Europe than the largest indigenous companies do.

The primary objective of the European Economic Community is to
redress this balance—to create a single market within which European
companies can build a scale of operations to take on their stronger U.S. and
Japanese competitors. It will have taken 35 years for the political aspirations expressed in the formation of the Community to be translated into
economic reality, but the speed with which the integration process is now
proceeding, and the emergence almost overnight of a powerful cluster of
Newly Industrializing Countries in Eastern Europe, raise new challenges
for European and non-European businesses alike.

Political Imperatives and Commercial Strategy

By the last day of 1992, the European Community intends to have dismantled all internal barriers to trade between member states. The extent to
which this leads to new industrial structures—and who will be the winners
and losers—will depend on how companies react to the challenge.

The potential of European collaboration has already been demonstrated
by projects like Airbus, Tornado, the military-aircraft project, and the European Space Agency.[10] All of these projects have depended on political action,
however, and on financial support from member governments. The overhead
of international cooperation has probably added significantly to their cost.

The next stage in the process involves restructuring through ordinary commercial mergers and acquisitions. The process has already begun, with the formation of partial mergers such as SGS Thomson Microelectronics and increased cross-border acquisitions activity.*

Pan-European mergers can help companies achieve two objectives: uninhibited access to European markets and the opportunity to build economies of scale. However, the history of European cooperation is littered with failures.

Hoechst and Hoogovens, the German and Dutch steel companies, merged in 1972 and parted acrimoniously a decade later, in part because of an apparent reluctance by the West German government to support a company that was not 100 percent German-owned. VFW and Fokker merged in 1969, but separated in 1980 because of conflicting national interests. The 1964 merger between Agfa, a subsidiary of Bayer, and the Belgian photographic company Gevaert, ended with Bayer taking full control in 1981. Unidata, a mainframe-computer collaboration involving Bull, Siemens, and Philips, collapsed in 1975 before producing a single product and amid bitter recriminations over French government attempts to acquire control and a failure to consult either Siemens or the German government before taking independent action.

Economies of scale can be achieved in other ways than intra-continental merger. Merger with a U.S. company of comparable size has exactly the same effect on scale, but with the added benefit of providing access to the U.S. market, still at least five times bigger than that of any European country, and to U.S. technology. It may also raise fewer political difficulties and be easier to manage than a pan-European alliance. For example, Groupe Bull's merger with Honeywell Information Systems Inc. probably provides it with a potential for building scale economies that are greater than those which any other European information-technology company might have of-

---

*Cross-border M&A activity within the European Community soared in the late 1980s. In 1983, the number of mergers and acquisitions involving EEC companies was 117. By 1989, it was well in excess of 800. The most active cross-border acquirer both in and outside the EEC in 1989 was Britain, with 743 transactions valued at $27.3 billion. Of these, 295 involved non-British EEC companies, valued at $4.6 billion, and 355 involved North American companies, valued at $32.4 billion.

French companies, too, have been energetic in European acquisitions. In 1989, they acquired 183 non-French EEC companies—only half the number acquired by British firms—but their value, $7.8 billion, far outstripped that of British EEC M&A activity.

EEC companies that were merged with or acquired by companies from non-EEC countries in 1989 numbered about 500.

fered. And because the two companies already shared common technology, integration problems were far less troublesome than would have been the case with other partners. Of course, choosing a U.S. partner first does not preclude the later use of acquisitions, joint ventures, and marketing agreements to spread geographic market access within Europe.

The idealistic view of pan-European cooperation promoted by European governments needs careful examination. What might be the best move for the economy of the European Community as a whole is not necessarily the best for a company's shareholders.

Moreover, the importance of cultural and language barriers should never be underestimated. The speed with which West German companies have reacted to the commercial opening-up of East Germany is orders of magnitude faster than their reaction to 1992—underscoring the importance of a common heritage and language.

Before undertaking a partnership within Europe, a company must, therefore, go through exactly the same decision-making processes as in any other investment situation. It must identify the primary strategic requirements for building or rebuilding competitive advantage (the seven strategic goals described in Chapter 3) and evaluate alternative means of achieving these goals. It should then develop criteria for a strategic partnership, if that is the option chosen. Selecting the partner should be the final step in the process—not, as is often the case, the first. Existing relationships and personal contacts will always be important factors, but the systematic screening and investigation of potential partners is an essential part of the restructuring process that every European country must now be considering.

Europe's companies must react to the twin pressures for Europeanization and globalization. European partners will often be the best candidates, if only because they are likely to be more willing brides, but strategic planning must be global in reach. The political imperatives of the Common Market and the current focus on European restructuring must not be allowed to impair sound strategic thinking.

Unit-by-Unit Strategies

Many large manufacturing companies consist of a variety of businesses, and it is important to develop strategies for each of these separately. In the European context, this may mean that companies will need to undertake partial mergers with a variety of partners in order to build the scale necessary to compete internationally. Some of Europe's more diverse multinational companies may need to be virtually dismantled. Philips has already embarked on this route, with a partial merger-joint venture in telecommunications under its belt, the sale of a 53 percent interest in its domestic appliance business to Whirlpool announced in 1988, and an attempted merger with GEC in medical electronics.

Besides partial mergers, there are also other ways in which European companies can create the scale economies and, perhaps more important, eliminate duplication of effort.

Collaborating at the R&D level is one way of providing shared scale. Another is to make joint investments in strategic-component suppliers. For example, an in-house semiconductor design and manufacturing capability is vital to success in many areas of electronics. Companies with internal sources of supply are likely to bring new products to market earlier than competitors who do not have this advantage. They are able to use proprietary designs as a barrier to imitation by competitors. European Silicon Structures (ES2), described in Chapter 11, is a fascinating illustration of how co-investment by semiconductor-using companies can provide much better access to key components while spreading the cost. The joint development by Philips and Siemens of memory chips—the Mega and JESSI Projects—has achieved much the same end without, so far, the creation of a new entity. Shared production through a consortium arrangement like Airbus provides a further option.

Exploiting Collaborative R&D Programs

Over the next 10 years, many opportunities for the joint development and marketing of commercial projects will flow from the collaborative R&D taking place under European programs like ESPRIT and EUREKA. The challenge for participants will be to create products and businesses that remain competitive in global terms. The Japanese collaborative R&D projects, on which European programs are largely modeled, rely on the individual participating companies to carry through commercial exploitation. Once this stage is reached, competition between partners is usually fierce.

In Japan, the primary purpose of this most important Japanese program is to make the best use of a limited pool of technical specialists and provide strategic guidance to the carefully selected group of participating companies. The goal of the European programs is quite different: to avoid duplication of research spending and encourage commercial collaboration at a later stage. Many projects entail horizontal collaboration between direct competitors, and a large number of companies are involved—the weak as well as the strong. If precompetitive collaboration is followed by rampant competitive exploitation, the whole point of the exercise is missed. This leaves four main options for commercialization.

The companies involved can concentrate on different application areas, largely removing the competitive element. For example, it is the relatively small overlap between Siemens' and Philips' businesses that enables them to develop semiconductor technology together. Each will be able to customize the resulting products and apply them in different markets.

Another option is for one of the companies involved to take primary responsibility for exploiting particular products, perhaps in exchange for license royalties, supplying the other partner on an OEM basis. Similarly, a quite new entity can be formed to manufacture, and possibly to market, products derived from the R&D collaboration. This could be through a 50/50 joint venture or some more complex arrangement.

Corporate venturing also has an important role to play in the exploitation of collaborative European projects. Many will generate spin-off opportunities, too small initially to merit direct commercial exploitation by the sponsoring companies, but of possible long-term importance.

Finally, some collaborative R&D projects may be so significant to the participating companies that they merit a partial or even total merger of their operations.

Participants in collaborative programs need to evaluate each of these options. European manufacturing companies must be prepared to adopt imaginative new approaches to developing their businesses if the investment in joint R&D is to bear fruit.

Barriers to Acquisition in Europe

The aggressive takeover practices of the British and American conglomateurs in the 1980s have not been characteristic of other European economies. Large bank shareholdings in major companies, interlocking share structures, poison pills, and other devices make buying public companies almost as difficult in some European countries as in Japan. In Germany, hostile bids have been virtually unheard of, a result of the long-term equity positions held by banks, high corporate tax rates, and wide legal freedom for companies to engage in tactics designed to frustrate and prevent would-be bidders. A common device is the use of different classes of shares, with a minority position carrying pre-emptive voting rights. The use of similar tactics is prevalent in France, the Netherlands, and Spain; indeed, across Europe, acquisition activity has been largely limited to friendly takeovers.

A practical factor that limits acquisition activity in continental Europe is the availability of reliable company information. Auditing standards tend to be far less stringent than they are in the United Kingdom and the United States. In Spain, for instance, there is no legal requirement that accounts be audited at all, and many private companies carry hidden tax liabilities. In Germany, only large companies are audited, and the publication of detailed, reliable information is not required. Central registration systems are few; detailed financial data are not, as a rule, available.

Proposals for an EEC merger policy in advance of the 1992 single market will bring about some harmonization of merger-and-acquisition activity in European countries.*

But so-called Euro-regulation will not bring down all, or even most of the existing obstacles to acquisition, at least not for some time. Reporting requirements, accounting standards, and shareholding structures, for example, will continue to vary and to frustrate would-be bidders. What appears to be changing very rapidly—and largely in response to the impending single market—are attitudes toward mergers and acquisitions. While continental Europeans have not yet been converted to the American and British enthusiasm for M&A activity, they have become more interested in acquisition as a strategic tool. This has been reflected in an upsurge of M&A activity across Europe. French companies have become particularly aggressive. Not long ago, they acquired 30 to 40 foreign companies a year; in 1989 they acquired nearly 300.

This is not to say that all European companies will soon be up for grabs. Many highly desirable ones will remain out of reach of even the most determined pursuers. CEOs who really want to play the 1992 game will have to adopt a subtle approach.

---

*The European Commission's proposal in the regulation of mergers and acquisitions should make life easier for acquisitive companies. The proposal is essentially that if each of the following three thresholds is reached, Brussels, rather than national authorities, would do the scrutinizing:
- Worldwide revenues of the combined companies would be more than 5 billion ECUs ($4 billion).
- Revenues in the EEC would exceed 250 million ECUs ($200 million).
- Not more than 60 percent of either partner's business would be in any single member state.

The Commission estimates that under these rules, it would probably take charge of 35 to 46 mergers a year.

EXHIBIT 12–5
Barriers to Acquisition in Europe

Policy	Belgium	Germany	France	Italy	Spain	Netherlands	U.K.
Regulatory Review Period	15 days	None	5 days	20 days	5 days	None	None
National Anti-Trust Laws	No regulations as such exist, but public bids are subject to the discretionary approval of the Minister of France and review by the Belgian Banking Commission.	Premerger notification must be submitted to the Kartelmat (Federal Cartel Office) only in the case of large companies: a. Consolidated worldwide turnover in excess of DM 1bn. b. Two or more of the companies involved have an aggregate turnover of more than DM 2bn.	La Conseil de la Concurrence may investigate if: a. resulting market share of more than 25%. b. The combined turnover is above FFr 7bn (net of taxes) and each company has a turnover of FFr 2bn. c. Limited sanctions up to 5% of turnover; no veto.	No	No authorization requirements except in areas where state sovereignty is affected, i.e., defense, radio, air transport, gambling.	In addition to EC rules, M&As may come under rules laid down in Economic Competition Act of 1958 which applies to cartels and dominant market positions.	In transactions where assets in excess of 530m are to be acquired or where more than 25% of any market in any particular goods or services is involved, government has power to delay transaction until investigated by Monopolies and Mergers Commission.
Public Share Registers	No[1]	No	No	No	No	No	Yes
Nonvoting Share Structures	Yes	Yes	Yes	Yes	Yes	Yes	Yes
Bearer Shares	Yes	Yes	No	No	Yes	Yes	No
Practice of Aggressive Bids	No	No	Yes	Yes	No	No	Yes

[1]Shareholders only

Sources: *Sunday Times*, May 22, 1988; *Euro News*, June 6, 1988; James Capel in turn from Lombard Associates.

Opportunities in Eastern Europe

The creation, beginning in 1989, of a cluster of near-capitalist trading economies on the European Community's eastern border has transformed the political and economic maps of Europe. Yet most Triad companies have been slow to respond.

The dramatic exception, of course, has been West Germany. That nation's attention has shifted firmly away from community issues and specifically toward East Germany. There has been an enormous surge of partnership activity between the Germanys, and when reunification is complete, Germany's economic dominance of Europe will be even stronger than it had been.

It is still too early to assess the full economic impact of the democratization of Eastern Europe. What is clear, however, is the magnitude of the commercial opportunities Eastern Europe offers western countries—both as attractive, fast-growing markets in their own right and as potential sources of low-cost manufacturing.

There are, however, immense barriers in place that make exploiting the opportunity of Eastern Europe difficult. There is a dire lack of hard currency; engineering and manufacturing skills are either out of date or out of practice.

The obstacles and opportunities presented by Eastern Europe, together with approaches to addressing them, are discussed in this book's Epilogue, "Perestroika."

Making It Work This Time

> Many European projects failed because people thought the important thing was to create a large company. They forget that what was important was to have a large market.
> —Jacques Masonrouge, former Chairman, IBM Europe

Language problems, cultural differences, and national pride have historically been barriers no less forbidding to collaboration between European companies than to transoceanic alliances. The failed mergers of the past resulted largely from a reluctance by companies to give up control, and from the political support for this position from governments.*

---

*Government has often been more the problem than company management. For example, the industrialists involved in the creation of Unidata wanted to set up a separate company. It was the French government that prevented this.

The merger between Dunlop and Pirelli in 1973 provides a classic example. The fit between the two looked perfect. As we have already noted. Dunlop's market strengths were in Europe and the British Commonwealth; Pirelli's were in southern Europe, the Middle East, and Africa. After the merger, the new business went deeply into the red, and the partners were unable to agree on what to do. The Pirelli family wanted to continue investing; the U.K. board members were more cautious. The easiest decision was to split up.

There is as yet no European Companies Act, and businesses must still be incorporated in one of the European national jurisdictions, aggravating the political difficulties that still exist with some mergers.*

If genuinely pan-European companies that can stand alongside the U.S. and Japanese giants are to be created, companies and politicians alike will need to put aside the nationalism of the 1970s. But building a strong Europe is just the first stage in tackling global markets. The strong European companies that will emerge in the 1990s must forge partnerships with companies in the other parts of the Triad.

For European companies, the process of restructuring has only just begun. The next five years are likely to see radical realignment. Multinationals will need to make sure that they have the strategic management resources to make and implement the tough complex strategic decisions that lie ahead. The winners are likely to be the companies run by CEOs with the greatest international vision.

THE U.S. DIMENSION

Fifteen years from now the world's third greatest industrial power, just after the United States and Russia, may not be Europe, but American industry in Europe.

—J. S. Servan Schreiber: *Le Défi American*, 1967

---

*On July 1, 1989, it became possible for companies to form European Economic Interest Groupings (EEIGs) to undertake cooperative cross-border projects. These can be anything from joint buying, selling, or manufacturing to political lobbying. EEIGs allow for the creation of a business entity whose regulation is common in most respects throughout the EEC. Though profits may arise from an EEIG, its primary purpose must be to facilitate or develop the economic activities of its members.

European Commission proposals for a European company statute allowing any company, whether of European origin or not, to incorporate under EEC rather than national law, are still being discussed. Such a law would cut through much of the present EEC cross-border red tape, thereby making mergers and joint ventures easier, but the hoped-for passage in 1990 now looks unlikely.

During the 1960s, there was a real concern in Europe that U.S. industry was buying its manufacturing base, and direct U.S. investment overseas exceeded $200 billion a year during the 1980s—reaching $327 billion in 1988. U.S. companies are among the most international of any in the world. America invented the global multinational. Companies such as IBM, 3M, and Coca Cola have fully fledged business operations in many different parts of the world. Now this pattern has been emulated by European and Japanese companies.

It was a long time coming. Only in the last 10 years or so have many European companies started to build up their U.S. and Japanese operations. As recently as 1970, Philips, Europe's largest maker of consumer electronics and semiconductors, had only 3 percent of sales in the United States. One impact of this trend is the growth of overseas direct investment in the United States, which in 1988 exceeded direct U.S. investment abroad for the first time since 1914. Between 1980 and 1987, the proportion of U.S. manufacturing industry directly owned by foreign companies increased one and a half times (see Exhibit 12–6). Japan's direct-investment position in the United States has shown one of the largest increases, up from $4.7 billion in 1980 to $53.4 billion in 1988.[11] Foreigners now own more than 12 percent of U.S. industry and, with dollar rates creating bargain-basement prices for inward investors, this proportion is likely to continue growing over the next few years with acquisition and strategic investments playing a greater role.

Decline in Economic Leadership

> Technology is America's only competitive advantage.
> —John Young, CEO, Hewlett Packard

The buying of America is just one symptom of a steady reduction over the last decade or more in the competitive advantages that U.S. industry has traditionally enjoyed over other economies—advantages that so worried Servan Shreiber in the 1960s. The change in relative economic positions is most starkly illustrated by the high-tech trade balance. Exhibit 12–7 shows how the ratio of exports to imports has declined over a range of different R&D-based products since 1970.

In the 1960s and 1970s, U.S. industry was in a clear position of technological leadership over other economies, a situation deliberately fostered by Pentagon policy in the 1950s and the space program of the 1960s

EXHIBIT 12–6
Foreign Investment in the United States and by the United States

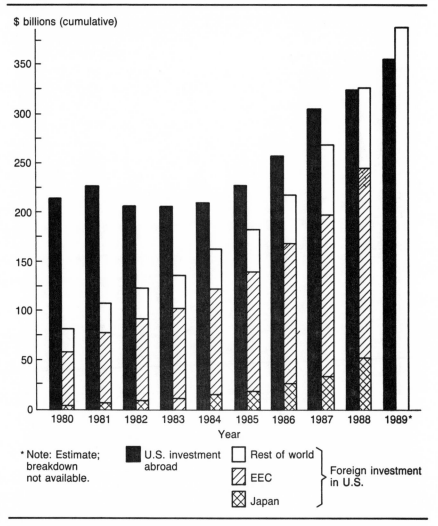

* Note: Estimate; breakdown not available.

■ U.S. investment abroad

□ Rest of world

▨ EEC

▧ Japan

} Foreign investment in U.S.

and 1970s that resulted in huge commercial spin-offs. U.S. industry became used to occupying the high ground of technology—a position essential for a manufacturing economy that supported wage levels up to two and three times those of its European and Japanese rivals. As the Presidential Commission on Competitiveness concluded in 1985, "Technology propels our economy forward. Without doubt it has been our strongest com-

EXHIBIT 12-7
U.S. Trade Ratios in Technology Products

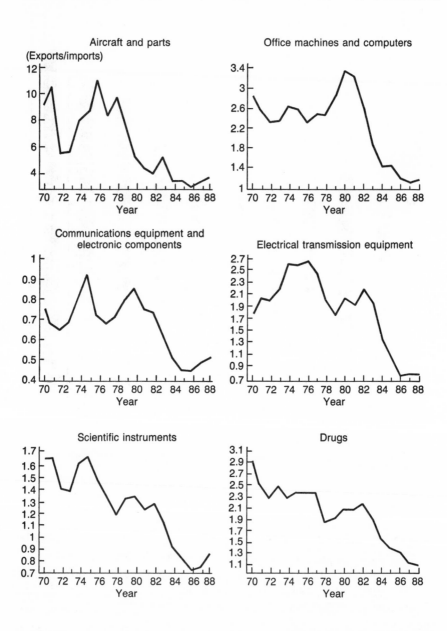

petitive advantage. . . . America owes much of its standard of living to its pre-eminence in technology.''

There were three principal reasons for past U.S. successes in technology markets. The first is the pure scale of the national R&D effort. The U.S. outlay for R&D is greater than that of any other country—about $145 billion in 1988—more than 40 percent of the total R&D expenditure of all the OECD countries combined. Half of this is funded by the Department of Defense and other government agencies.

But the supremacy of the U.S. R&D effort is being eroded, particularly by Japan. Throughout the last 15 or 20 years, industrially sponsored R&D has grown more than twice as rapidly in Japan as in the United States and Western Europe. Its share of world technology markets has tripled since 1965. Furthermore, the quality of research has changed drastically in recent years. Both government and industry are pushing for an approach that produces major innovations as well as engineered improvements in product and process ideas developed in the West. Europe is also becoming a stronger force in technology, its fragmented research effort at long last being pulled together.

The second reason for U.S. historical success is the nation's highly entrepreneurial business culture. Many of the new technologies to emerge from its research base have been exploited first by new companies—spin-offs from research institutions or larger businesses. Job mobility and the nation's sophisticated venture-capital community have supported this process. Companies including DEC, National Semiconductor, Genentech, and many other forces in high technology owe their origins to this financing mechanism.

The environment that fosters new-company formation in the United States is only just beginning to appear in Europe, and it is still largely lacking in Japan. The situation is changing, though, and government policies now stimulate the kind of thriving small-company environment that exists in the United States.

The increasingly global reach of European and Japanese multinationals will also erode the advantage that the U.S. economy gets from its small-business community. Small companies are seldom in a position to manage the full commercial exploitation of their technology by themselves. The most desirable partners are those that bring complementary strengths in international marketing and in manufacturing. Strategic partnerships can be formed as easily with overseas companies as with domestic ones, and the increasing strength and cohesion of the Japanese and European economies will make their companies more desirable partners.

The third reason for U.S. success in high technology is the sheer size of the U.S. market. Few people seem to understand how significant this factor is. The effect is often relatively unimportant during the early stages of any new market opportunity when competition tends to be restricted largely to national players. It is only later, as the costs of successive product developments increase, that the benefits of a U.S. base become apparent. Successful U.S. start-ups soon reach 10 times the size of their French or British equivalents, though they may have started at the same time and with roughly equivalent technology. The size of the U.S. market has a twin benefit: Companies have *less need* than their French equivalents to seek international sales to pay for increasing R&D costs, *and* they have a better base from which to finance the investment in overseas operations. The growth of the Japanese economy, now more than half the size of the U.S. economy, and the emergence of a genuinely unified European market will do much to alter this imbalance.

The Narrowing Window of Competitive Advantage

There are also some areas in which the United States has suffered a more fundamental loss—more fundamental because these areas relate to the way in which companies are managed. The greatest threat, as always comes from the Japanese.

First, product development times are shortening. Japanese consumer-products manufacturers reckon that new products will face equivalent competitor products within less than six months in Tokyo's fiercely competitive market. Reverse engineering has been tuned to a fine art. In Asia there are 80 manufacturers that can turn out exact copies of U.S. personal computers in three weeks.[12]

Strong strategic partnerships with subcontractors play an important role in the new Japanese approaches to product development, and parallel as opposed to sequential scheduling of development and marketing tasks reduces the delays that occur as new products move from the development to the production phase. Honda developed its Today minicar in 42 months, compared with the Detroit norm of about five years.[13]

Coupled with the attack on product-development efficiency is the Japanese approach to manufacturing management. What the West does not appreciate sufficiently is that the Japanese approach is one of continuous improvement. It involves constantly seeking out areas in which change can improve competitive advantage, then setting targets to bring it about. The same philosophy applies to quality, inventories, numbers of parts, throughout model changeover times—in fact, to every aspect of the production process.

When combined with the general upgrading of Japan's technological capabilities, these developments spell three kinds of danger for U.S. companies. *First*, the window of technological advantage, during which premium prices can be charged for leading-edge products, is shrinking. *Second*, the effective international exploitation of new products becomes that much more important. And *third*, cost more quickly becomes the dominant factor in competition.

Coming to Terms with Being Equal

Over the next five years, Japanese strategic thinking will be dominated by the process of internationalization. European companies will be concerned with the unification of Europe. Both economies are facing challenges that derive from success—economic success in the case of Japan and political success in the case of Europe.

The fundamental challenge to U.S. industry stems not from internal change, but from change taking place in these other parts of the world economy. The problem is not so much a loss of U.S. economic power as it is a catching-up elsewhere. The major strategic issues for U.S. companies are about how to come to terms with the stronger overseas competitors they now face.

The response to these changes demand is in large measure the wider application of strategies that many U.S. companies have been using for years—international corporate venturing to capture the best technology wherever it emerges, more active global marketing, and the deployment of the whole range of strategic alliances to build global economies of scale.

U.S. companies will also need to procure more products and components from countries with low labor costs. There are dangers here, however, that are now becoming apparent. Moving production abroad can lead to a hollowing out of corporations, leaving only R&D and marketing in the United States. Eventually, those very suppliers may be powerful enough to take over that part of the business as well. To protect their own long-term interests, U.S. manufacturers must make sure that they have some control over suppliers and can benefit from the boost they are giving to their own businesses. This means linking the supply contract to investment and ensuring that procurement managers are brought fully into the global strategic-planning process.

ENDNOTES

Chapter 1

1. *Technical Co-operation Agreements Between Firms—Some Initial Data and Analysis* (Paris: OECD Directorate for Science, Technology, and Industry, May 1986).

2. Karen Hladik, *International Joint Ventures: An Economic Analysis of U.S. Foreign Business Partnerships* (Lexington, Mass.: Lexington Books).

3. "Direct Foreign Investment in Japan: American Chamber of Commerce in Japan," September 1987.

4. Graham Turner, "Inside Europe's Giant Companies—Olivetti Goes Bear Hunting," *Long Range Planning*, 19, No. 2, 1986.

5. Kenichi Ohmae, *Triad Power, The Coming Shape of Global Competition*, (New York: *The Free Press*, 1985).

6. General Electric, *1986 Annual Report*.

7. Kathryn Rudie Harrigan, "Strategic Alliances and Partner Assymetries"; in *Cooperative Strategies in International Business*, edited by Farok J. Contractor and Peter Lorange; (Lexington, Mass.: Lexington Books, 1988).

8. "Cooperative Activities and Takeovers," Address at the Annual General Meeting of Philips N.V. shareholders, April 26, 1984.

Chapter 2

1. Peter F. Drucker, "Best R&D Is Business Driven," *Asian Wall Street Journal*, February 22, 1988.

2. Roy Rothwell and Walter Zegveld, *Innovation and the Small and Medium Sized Firm* (London: Francis Pinter, 1983).

3. Gifford Pinchot III, *Intrapreneuring* (Harper and Row, 1985).

Chapter 3

1. "On the Campus: Fat Endowments and Growing Clout," *Business Week*, July 11, 1988.

2. Robb Wilmot, "Change in Management and the Management of Change," *Long Range Planning*, 20, No. 6, 1987.

Chapter 4

1. David C. Mowery, *Alliance Politics and Economics—Multinational Joint Ventures in Commercial Aircraft* (Ballinger Publishing Company, 1987).

2. Keith Hayward, *International Collaboration in Civil Aerospace* (London: Francis Pinter, 1986).
3. International Collaboration in Aerospace—Problems, Progress and Prospects, Financial Times Conference, Paris, June 1987.
4. Richard N. Foster, *Innovation, the Attacker's Advantage* (MacMillan, 1986).
5. Daniel T. Jones, "Structural Adjustment in the Automobile Industry," *OECD STI Review*, 1988.
6. See, for example, D. T. Jones, "Maturity and Crisis in the European Car Industry: Structural Change and Public Policy," Sussex European Research Centre, 1981.
7. M.I.T.'s International Motor Vehicle Programme estimates North American automotive assembly overcapacity at 4 million units by 1990, roughly 37 percent of capacity.
8. William Abernathy, *The Productivity Dilemma: Roadblock to Innovation in the Automobile Industry* (Baltimore: Johns Hopkins University Press, 1978).
9. Gilbert-Francois Coty and Herbert Ungerer, "Les Télécommunications, Nouvelle Frontière de l'Europe," *Futuribles*, December 1984.
10. Carmela S. Haglisch, "Technical Alliances in the Semiconductor Industry," New York University, 1986.

Chapter 5

1. H. L. Bower and K. Furakawa, "The VLSI Technology Research Association," Harvard Case Study Note.

Chapter 6

1. Christopher Freeman, *The Economics of Industrial Innovation*, (London: Francis Pinter, 1982).
2. "When There Is No Such Thing as Too Many Cooks," *Financial Times*, July 30, 1987.
3. David Connell, "Bridging the Gap Between Academic Researchers and Industrial Corporations," in *Utilization of the Results of Public Research and Development*, H. Corsten and K.B. Junginger, eds. (Dittel: Commission of the European Communities, 1988).
4. For a good description of this process at work, see Gene Gregory, *The Canon Production System: Getting the Bottom Line Right* (Tokyo: Sophia University, 1988).
5. Thomas Peters and Robert H. Waterman, *In Search of Excellence* (New York: Bantam, 1982).
6. Gilfillan, Follet; *Inventing the Ship;* (Chicago: 1935).
7. Roy Rothwell and Walter Zegveld *Reindustrialization and Technology* (Chicago: Longman, 1985).

Chapter 7

1. *Electronics News*, June 15, 1981.
2. Herbert I. Fusefeld and Carmela S. Haglisch, "Cooperative R&D for Competitors" *Harvard Business Review*, November–December 1985.
3. "Strategic Alliances—The New Wave of Cooperative R&D Ventures," Office of Productivity, Technology and Innovation, U.S. Department of Commerce, Washington D.C., September 30, 1987. Also, "Cooperative R&D in Industrial Competitiveness," Office of

Productivity, Technology and Innovation, U.S. Department of Commerce, Washington, D.C., January 6, 1987.

4. Margaret Sharp and Claire Shearman, *European Technological Collaboration*, (Royal Institute of International Affairs, 1988).

5. House of Lords Select Committee on the European Communities, ESPRIT, Session 1984–85, 8th Report, London, HMSO.

6. *ESPRIT 1987 Annual Report—Commission of the European Communities*, 1988.

7. Ibid.

8. Jon Siguardson, "Industry and State Partnership in Japan—the Very Large Scale Integrated Circuits (VLSI) Project," Research Policy Institute, University of Lund, Sweden.

9. Ibid.

10. "The Micro-electronics and Computer Technology Corporation," Harvard Business School Case Study, 1982.

Chapter 8

1. See also, Yves L. Doz, "Technological Partnerships between Larger and Smaller Firms: Some Critical Issues," INSEAD, Fountainbleu.

2. *Venture Capital Journal*, April 1988.

3. *Japan's Small Hi-Tech Enterprises and Venture Capital;* Dominque V. Turpin, Tokyo: Sophia University, 1986.

4. *Corporate Venturing News*, March 25, 1987.

5. Hollister B. Sykes, "Exxon: Lessons from a New Ventures Program," *Harvard Business Review*, May–June 1986.

Chapter 9

1. Strategic Alliances and Partner Asymmetrics; Kathryn Rudie Harrigan; in Cooperative Strategies in International Business, eds. Farouk J. Contractor and Peter Lorange; Lexington Books, 1987.

Chapter 10

1. "Do Mergers Really Work?" *Business Week*, June 3, 1985.

2. *Acquisition in Europe, Cases of Corporate Success and Failure*, (Geneva: Business International, 1973).

3. Nicholas Vitrovich, Higher Productivity through Share Scale.

4. "Why Honeywell-Bull Is on a Turnaround Track," *Business Week*, February 22, 1988.

Chapter 12

1. *Fortune*, February 2, 1987.

2. "Joint Ventures May Damage Your Health," *Financial Times*, September 9, 1987.

3. Industrial Groupings in Japan 1986/87, Dodwell Marketing Consultants, Tokyo.

4. Reproduced with kind permission of Dodwell Marketing Consultants.

5. Direct Foreign Investment in Japan, The Challenge for Foreign Firms, America Chamber of Commerce in Japan and the Council of the European Business Community, Tokyo, September 1987.

6. Walter Ames and David N. Roberts, "Foreign Acquisitions in Japan—Hurdling the Ultimate Barrier," *The Journal of the American Chamber of Commerce in Japan*, January 1986.

7. "Tokyo's Stock Market—Stronger Than You Think," *Fortune*, April 11, 1988.

8. Azumi, Hull, and Wharton; *Productivity and Organization Design in Japanese versus American Factories;* Report to the United States Science Foundation, 1987.

9. Gary Hamel, Ives Doz, C.K. Prahalad, "Strategic Partnerships: Success or Surrender." *London Business School Working Paper No. 14.*

10. "Japan's Troubled Future," *Fortune*, March 30, 1987.

11. Department of Commerce, *Bureau of Economic Analysis Reports*.

12. "Can America Make It," *Financial Times*, May 20, 1987.

13. "Will the Auto Glut Choke Detroit?" *Business Week*, March 7, 1988.

EPILOGUE

PERESTROIKA*

Pity the poor American chief executive. Just as things seemed to be getting back to normal after a decade of domestic turmoil caused by everything from politics to buyouts, now along comes the economic unification of Europe, the dismantling of tariff barriers between the United States and Canada, the loosening of Japan's traditional insularity—all the themes of the body of this book.

And now there's even more. Suddenly the Soviet Union is moving toward free, or at least freer, enterprise; the U.S.S.R.'s erstwhile allies are opening up their economies even more rapidly and more completely; the reunification of the two Germanys has become inevitable, with implications that will profoundly affect not only the North American and Pacific Triad players but also the European Community.

Once again, the only constant for the executive is change.

Most of the extraordinary developments that are moving Eastern Europe and the Soviet Union toward "regulated market economies" took place after the research and analysis that led to this book were completed. Yet even a preliminary view indicates that the same principles and approaches will prevail as the developed world integrates those economies with their own.

Developing responses to *perestroika*, the economic restructuring occurring in the Soviet Union and Eastern Europe, will become a major issue, if it has not already, among senior strategists of many corporations. At stake for some is the competitive position their companies will hold in world markets as we move into the 21st century.

---

*This Epilogue is an adaptation and expansion of an article by our colleagues James Driscoll and Scott Fraser, both of Deloitte & Touche's strategy consulting division, Braxton Associates, that originally appeared in the periodical *Moscow International Business*. We are indebted both to the authors and to the journal.

327

The reconfiguration of Europe and the Soviet Union will shift the basis of competition in many industries. As economic and political barriers come down, the importance of scale in key activities—from R&D and manufacturing to sales and distribution—will become even more important.

In fact, most American CEOs realize by now that the emergence of a unified market in Europe will require shifts in their competitive strategies and operations. The companies that will enjoy the most emphatic success, however, will not be those that simply develop a new competitive approach in Europe, nor those that look at episodes such as 1992 or the Free Trade Agreement—but, rather, the companies that develop new global strategies for their businesses.

As the North American (or European, or Japanese) multinational begins to address new global realities, therefore, it should consider carefully the role that an operation based in the Soviet Union or in one of the Eastern bloc countries might play in its global competitive strategy. Although significant barriers must be overcome in order to do business in these countries, enterprising businesspeople on both sides of the equation, in the Triad and in Eastern Europe, can find innovative ways to remove these obstacles—thus expanding trade, investment, and profitability.

NEW OPPORTUNITIES, OLD PROBLEMS

Although North American companies have operated in the Triad economies for many years, and in the less-developed countries of the Third World for almost as long, few have had the opportunity, until now, to consider expanding into the relatively uncharted trading waters of the Soviet Union and its allies.

With the advent of *perestroika,* the Soviet Union has finally come up on the radar screen of the CEO scanning for global opportunities—and with the third-largest gross national product in the world, the Soviet economy creates a fairly large image on that screen.

Despite its size, however, the Soviet economy is only semi-developed. When coupled with its historical economic isolation from the West, this discrepancy between size and development creates unusual challenges to Triad companies searching for profit opportunities amid perestroika.

Although a number of companies have done business in the U.S.S.R.

for years, *perestroika* creates a distinctly new climate for expanded U.S.-Soviet commercial relations. As early as 1986, American business began taking an unprecedented interest in Soviet business opportunities, trying to sell everything from suntan lotion to cotton sweaters. Interest swelled after the U.S.S.R. began allowing 49-percent foreign-owned joint ventures in 1987. Armed with business plans complete with titles neatly translated into Russian, the Western entrepreneur sat down with Soviet government ministers, economists, and enterprise directors to make a deal. For their part, the Soviets have been no less eager: *Fortune* reports that half a dozen Russian entrepreneurs show up at the U.S. Embassy every day in search of partners.

Yet despite the tidal wave of interest, only a trickle of sales and investments have resulted. H. Michael Mears, the former U.S. Commerce Department representative in Moscow, estimates that in 1987, 1,000 American businesses called his office for help in cracking the Soviet market. Of these, only 10 were successful in consummating deals; the rest either gave up or failed.

The reason is that the barriers to doing business in the Soviet Union pose problems that few U.S. businesses have ever faced before.

THE NATURE OF EASTERN-BLOC BARRIERS

While *perestroika* may have done much to reduce the psychological aversion many U.S. businesses have had to doing business in the Soviet Union, it has yet to remove the major barrier to foreign investment—how to handle the money. Cash is the lifeblood of business, and the Soviet ruble does not circulate within the Western financial blood-stream.

Because the ruble is not readily convertible into hard Western currency, payment for sales and profit patriation top the list of concerns of foreign companies seeking to enter Soviet markets.

To overcome this currency barrier, Western companies have devised a number of clever solutions. Some enterprises target Soviet consumer markets, which are composed of both ruble and hard-currency customers. McDonalds' first Moscow restaurant on Pushkin Square accepts rubles, for example, but the chain also plans to open a hard-currency-only restaurant on fashionable Gorky Street, catering mainly to tourists, diplomats, and foreign business visitors. The rubles pay salaries and buy locally available goods, while the hard-currency revenue streams buy supplies abroad and patriate the Western partner's share of profits.

An even simpler solution is to require payment from all customers in Western currency. This technique is being used by companies such as PRIS, a joint venture set up to sell process-control systems to Soviet oil refineries with payment to be made in hard currency. Because it is able to export crude oil and refined products abroad, the Soviet petroleum industry earns a great deal of hard currency. But such cash-rich Soviet enterprises are scarce, and Soviet authorities appropriate much of the hard cash brought in by these enterprises to purchase grain and other necessities of the Soviet economy. Consequently, there is little hard currency available to buy products not at the top of national procurement priorities. Companies using this hard-cash-only approach thus restrict their own opportunity to narrow market niches.

Harking back to a different time in economic history, a third solution, perhaps the most popular today, is the simple bartering of one good for another. The best-known example of this practice, called countertrade, has made Russians part of the Pepsi generation. Under its canny chairman Donald M. Kendall, who saw an immense and largely untapped soft-drink market in the Soviet Union, PepsiCo entered a licensing arrangement with a Soviet partner in the early 1970s. In exchange for cola syrup and management expertise, Pepsi received an exclusive contract to market Stolichnaya vodka in the West.

In 1990, the scope of the agreement was greatly enlarged. In the largest deal ever struck by an American company in the U.S.S.R., PepsiCo agreed to double its bottling capacity there. In exchange, not only will PepsiCo receive more Stoli; the Soviets are giving title to 10 freighters and tankers as well. PepsiCo will use some of the revenue generated by the ships to establish Pizza Hut, which it owns, in Moscow.

Unfortunately, there are few Soviet products that are as marketable in the West as Stolichnaya. Most countertrade agreements have involved trading Western goods for Soviet raw materials that are often completely unrelated to the business of the company making the sale. To gain hard currency, PepsiCo's arch-rival, Coca-Cola, exports the Soviet car Lada into Great Britain. RJR Nabisco's Reynolds Tobacco unit has been known to accept payment in Czechoslovakian shovels. Romania struck a $1-billion deal with Candu, the Canadian atomic-energy company, to build a reactor; in something of an irony, Candu will be paid in coal and railway cars.

These barter arrangements, whether used to pay Western exporters, to make royalty or license payments, or to patriate profits to Western investors, almost always require the brokering of the goods received. While the costs of the resale can often be included in the price charged the Soviet customer, the disposal of extraneous barter goods is a nuisance and risk that most companies would like to avoid. ("It's tough to run a business," John Georgas, president of Coke's international soft-drink operations, told Reuters, "when you don't get paid until all the goods you received from Poland get sold in Chicago.")

A fourth strategy is perhaps the most innovative. It seeks to cope with the currency barrier by forming a consortium to share hard-currency cash flow among the members. Members whose ventures can earn foreign currency assist other members by participating in special currency auctions and barter sessions. In effect, the consortium becomes a small, hard-currency capital market.

A who's who in American business makes up the first of such consortiums. Among the current members are Chevron, Johnson & Johnson, Eastman Kodak, and RJR Nabisco. These members have announced their intention to invest $5 billion to $10 billion in the Soviet Union over the next 15 years. Although the consortium begins to address the sorely felt need for a hard-currency capital market, how successful it will be remains to be seen.

A strategic weakness in what otherwise appears to be an imaginative approach may be the dependency of each enterprise on the success of others in the consortium. To the extent that they rely exclusively on a collective solution to the currency problem, consortium members are putting their own success or the future return on their investments at additional risk. The old saying "a chain is only as strong as its weakest link" is pertinent.

THE SECOND GENERATION
OF U.S.-SOVIET INVESTMENT

As we have seen, each of the strategies to overcoming the currency barrier has its weaknesses. Because the first two approaches depend on hard-currency revenue streams within the Soviet Union itself, the size of the potential market is limited. Countertrade's need to liquidate the medium of payment creates hardship or inefficiency (either the Western seller bears additional costs or the Soviet buyer pays a higher price—in neither case adding any value to the product or transaction). In the currency consortium approach, the potential strategic "weak link" may diminish the attractiveness of an investment opportunity.

Before incorporating one of these four approaches into their market entry strategy, the smart Triad company will explore a different tack.

That company will begin by exploring how a Soviet venture might be used to create competitive advantage not only in Soviet markets, but in other world markets as well. Companies considering investment in the Soviet Union should ask themselves these questions:

- Are there elements of our product's value chain that we can procure, provide, or produce at less cost in the Soviet Union?
- Are there markets in the world that we can serve better from a Soviet platform than from one based elsewhere?
- Are there ways we can leverage a position in Soviet markets to create competitive advantage in markets outside the Soviet Union?

In short, the creative Triad company should examine the potential for using an operating base in the Soviet Union as a key component in a global competitive strategy for their business.

To illustrate how a joint-venture investment in the Soviet Union might fit into a U.S. corporation's global competitive strategy, consider the strategic dilemma faced several years ago by a company we will call Chemco, and contemplate how a Soviet joint venture might have been used to solve the problem.

Chemco was a multinational, billion-dollar manufacturer of pesticides and herbicides. The key to the company's success was a strong R&D operation that enabled it to bring to the market a steady stream of new proprietary products. Chemco also spent heavily on marketing, distribution, and customer support. Its strategy was to charge relatively high prices for high real and perceived value, and although it operated with a fairly high cost structure, it was consistently profitable.

In the past, volume from sales of Chemco's new products had been sufficient to offset lost volume when old products lost their patent protection. Now, however, it was becoming tougher and more expensive to keep up the pace of new-product development, and Chemco's rate of return began to decline. Long-term financial performance seemed at risk.

Chemco's traditional markets were in the developed countries. It had never sought very hard to penetrate the newly developing nations of India, South America, Africa, and Southeast Asia. Its patented products were too expensive for these markets, and its off-patent products enjoyed wide market acceptance in the form of generic substitutes sold by Chemco's competitors.

Thus if Chemco wanted to prevent the near-total loss of a product's revenue stream once it went off-patent, the company would have to compete on a cost basis with generic producers. And that meant that Chemco would need to build a new world-scale production facility to bring production costs in line with the costs of its competitors. And that meant that Chemco had to have additional sales volume to fill the new plant. But the lack of a strong market position in the developing world presented a seemingly intractable obstacle.

Consequently, Chemco's management decided that to maintain a satisfactory rate of return, the company would have to invest not only in a new plant, but also in building market position and distribution channels in Second- and Third-World countries. Analysis showed that the costs and risks would be enormous. In addition to the financial risks, Chemco was concerned about its ability to run both a high-cost, proprietary-product business and a low-cost, generic-product business at once.

When the real Chemco faced this dilemma several years ago, a joint venture with a Soviet partner was not in the cards. Today, however, it would not be at all surprising to find a Chemco establishing a joint venture in the U.S.S.R. to address issues of global competitive strategy.

Let's briefly explore how a Soviet joint venture might have provided the solution to Chemco's global strategic dilemma.

Because Chemco's competitive strategy, corporate culture, and cost structure had all been geared toward the high end of the agricultural chemical market, creating a new, separate operating entity seems to make sense. But why a joint venture, and why with a Soviet partner?

Chemco might have done it to gain access of two kinds: To a large, relatively underserved market, and to potentially low-cost production and raw materials.

Being a low-cost producer in the chemical business usually means operating large-scale facilities at high rates of capacity utilization. If Chemco's Soviet partner could bring to the venture a significant share of the Soviet market, the joint venture could have built a world-scale plant knowing that much of its output could be absorbed locally. If the raw material happened to be compounds that are readily and inexpensively available in the Soviet Union, the joint venture derives further cost advantages.

Under this scenario, Chemco would not only syndicate the cost of building the plant, but would also avoid the need to build market share and channels of distribution in several developing countries simultaneously. In fact, Chemco would be in the attractive position of being able to build market share from a low-cost position, rather than attempting to create a low-cost position by building share.

The hard currency earned by exports would repay hard-currency loans assumed by the joint venture to build the production facilities, as well as to pay Chemco its license fees, royalties, and share of the profits.

As the end of patent protection neared, Chemco would continue to transfer product technology to the joint venture. Thus the joint venture would have continuous competitive advantage over other generic producers.

What would Chemco offer a Soviet partner? Exactly the same benefits sought by all the other strategic-partnership participants discussed in this book: high-technology products, proprietary production methods, experience in operations management, and not least, market access, both domestic and export.

THE U.S.S.R.: A PIECE IN THE
GLOBAL STRATEGY PUZZLE

Our hypothetical Chemco-Soviet joint venture is a win-win proposition. Chemco's strategic problem is solved and the Soviet Union gains access to Western product and process technology, exposure to Chemco's management systems, and benefits from the hard currency the venture earns.

As with any of the other kinds of strategic partnerships examined in this book, making a U.S.-Soviet joint venture actually succeed would be no small challenge. The problems associated with deal development, negotiation, and execution are easily underestimated, as are the time, money, and executive attention the enterprise would demand.

In the future, strategic thinkers in American industry will be increasingly challenged to include developing countries in their global strategic plans. Perhaps the most important point is that it will be possible—indeed, it will be necessary—to integrate the global competitive strategy of the U.S. multinational company with *perestroika*.

CASE E-1
The McDonald's Approach

From the day he took a group of Soviet officials who were attending the 1976 Montréal Olympics on a McDonald's tour, George Cohon, the exuberant president and chief executive of the burger chain's Canadian operations, wanted to open a restaurant in the Soviet Union. He realized that goal 14 years later, when an estimated 30,000 Muscovites in one day streamed through the largest McDonald's in the world, smack on Pushkin Square, not far from the Kremlin, to spend a third of the average worker's daily pay on a Bolshoi Mac.

How Cohon achieved his vision provides a near-textbook study in structuring a strategic alliance.

Cohon's Canadian unit owns 49 percent of the U.S.S.R. operation; the Moscow City Council owns 51 percent. Its approach, however, is 100-percent McDonald's.

Never mind that the potato is practically the Soviet Union's emblem. Cohon brought in seedling Russet Burbanks, because they're the McDonald's french-fry standard, and he brought in 20 agricultural experts to teach Soviet farmers how they should really grow them. When they were through, the potato harvest per acre had doubled.

The venture buys as much as it can inside the U.S.S.R.: cheese, flour, yeast, sugar, shortening. Pickles are made from special cucumbers, grown from imported seeds. Under Cohon's system, apples come from Bulgaria, McDonald's sends mustard from Canada, and the Soviets import tomato paste from Portugal.

Fourteen countries, from Taiwan to Turkey, Austria to Yugoslavia, supplied equipment for the Finnish-built processing plant and distribution center outside Moscow. (As a sort of side business, the plant will sell its surplus apple-pie capacity to other countries.)

Perhaps Cohon's biggest challenge was importing the relentlessly cheerful, efficient culture of McDonald's to Moscow, where surliness and lethargy are an art form. Yet in the end, the Pushkin Square flagship outlet's 600 employees (chosen from 27,000 applicants) learned, some for the first time, to smile and say "thank you." (Encountering such unaccustomed friendliness at first distressed one customer, who thought the counter workers were mocking him.)

A key to entrenching the McDonald's smile was putting local managers in charge. The four top Pushkin Square managers are Russians, although they were educated at McDonald's Hamburger

University at its worldwide headquarters in Illinois and took post-graduate training in Toronto.

Profit patriation isn't a problem yet; for now, profits are being re-invested in building up the U.S.S.R. chain, and Cohon says that he and his partners intend eventually to open 19 more Soviet Mc-Donald's stores. Later, as the U.S.S.R. economy becomes less and less insular, hard currency may be more generally available and the problem may diminish; or the multi-location venture, with a mix of currency sources, could simply institute its own internal currency-conversion market.

The jury is still out on the question of whether the venture will ultimately succeed. Yes, the lines are short, quality is a sure bet, ser-vice is first-rate, and they're never out of anything—but the fact is, the prices are awfully high. There are clouds, plenty of them dark, all across the Soviet economic horizon. And will the concept of Russian fast food, in the end, turn out to be an oxymoron?

This much, however, is certain: In creating a model strategic alli-ance that would have been unimaginable before *perestroika,* Cohon has launched an experiment that—succeed in the long run or fail—will yield important lessons for every expansion-minded multina-tional company.

CASE E–2
Capitalist Ferment at Czech Brewer*

PILSEN, Czechoslovakia—With its ancient copper mash vats, ponderous oak barrels and age-old beer-making techniques, this city's famed Pilsner Urquell brewery long took a back seat to other enterprises as Communist central planners invested massively in favored industries like machinery and steel.

But now that Czechoslovakia has thrown off Communist rule, workers and managers here are eager to transform their 158-year-old brewery into a dynamic, modern operation.

For the 2,000 managers and workers here at the nation's largest brewery, 55 miles southwest of Prague, the dawn of capitalism means a series of needed reforms, led by a vigorous international marketing campaign. Indeed, company officials believe that Pilsner Urquell, perhaps more so than any other operation in Czechoslovakia, can be turned into an export powerhouse—and a large producer of hard currency.

The ambitious goal is mainly an effort to exploit the Pilsner Urquell brand, renowned among the beer-quaffing cognoscenti. Pilsner Urquell, which is German for "Original Pilsner," was a 19th-century pioneer, creating a new beer category that was then widely imitated. Today, the "pilsner" name is attached to beers throughout the world, meaning a pale gold-colored beer with a strong hops taste. The end of Communism has produced a whirl of talk at Pilsner Urquell about the need to do business differently: establishing its own marketing arm, finding a foreign partner, modernizing its equipment, increasing exports, and setting up an employee ownership plan.

"We realize that we're sitting on a gold mine—the old government failed to appreciate that," said Jaroslav Pesler, production manager at the brewery, a 130-acre jumble of dark, sprawling structures. "The government looked at us as an interesting oddity that happened to produce hard currency."

· · ·

For a century after the Pilsen brewery was founded, Pilsner Urquell was hailed as one of the world's great beers. Its popularity stumbled after World War II, however, partly because of heavy bomb damage during the war and partly because of the Communists' half-hearted efforts to export it.

Soon after the peaceful revolution of December 1989, pushed out the Communist government and created the prospect of economic changes, the brewery's managers set up their own exporting arm to put an end to the indifferent marketing. For decades, the brewery had to rely on Koospol, the state food- and beverage-export monopoly.

A third of the brewery's annual production of 40 million gallons is exported. Brewery managers say that with some sophisticated marketing they can almost double exports so they represent 60 percent of production.

When a journalist visited one recent week, the brewery's general manager, Vaclav Spalek, was traveling in West Germany to meet with officials from a half dozen beer companies that have offered to buy a stake in Pilsner Urquell, while several British and Australian companies have also made offers to acquire a stake.

For the most part, brewery managers and employees want to remain independent, saying it would be better for a foreign partner to buy just a small stake.

"We wouldn't like a foreign partner to obtain a majority," Mr. Pesler, the production manager, said. "We'd like it to buy maybe a 25 percent stake."

There is widespread agreement that an injection of foreign capital could be used to help finance a more modern, less labor-intensive pumping system to transfer the beer between mash vats, barrels, and bottling plants.

"We are profitable enough to pay for it out of our own earnings, but we can do it much faster with foreign help," Mr. Pesler said.

Many employees are frustrated that the slow pace of legislating economic reforms on foreign investment and in other areas is keeping the company from selecting a partner and making other key decisions. "We're eagerly waiting for the new laws to see what all the changes mean for us," said Jaroslav Hodan, the brewery's chief microbiologist.

At the moment, the brewery's management is talking far more about finding a foreign company to cooperate with than about privatizing the company. There is some discussion about changing Pilsner Urquell's legal structure into that of a shareholding company, which would remain majority state-owned, at least for now. Many managers say the employees should be allowed to buy 10 or 20 percent of the shares to create more incentives for the workers.

INDEX